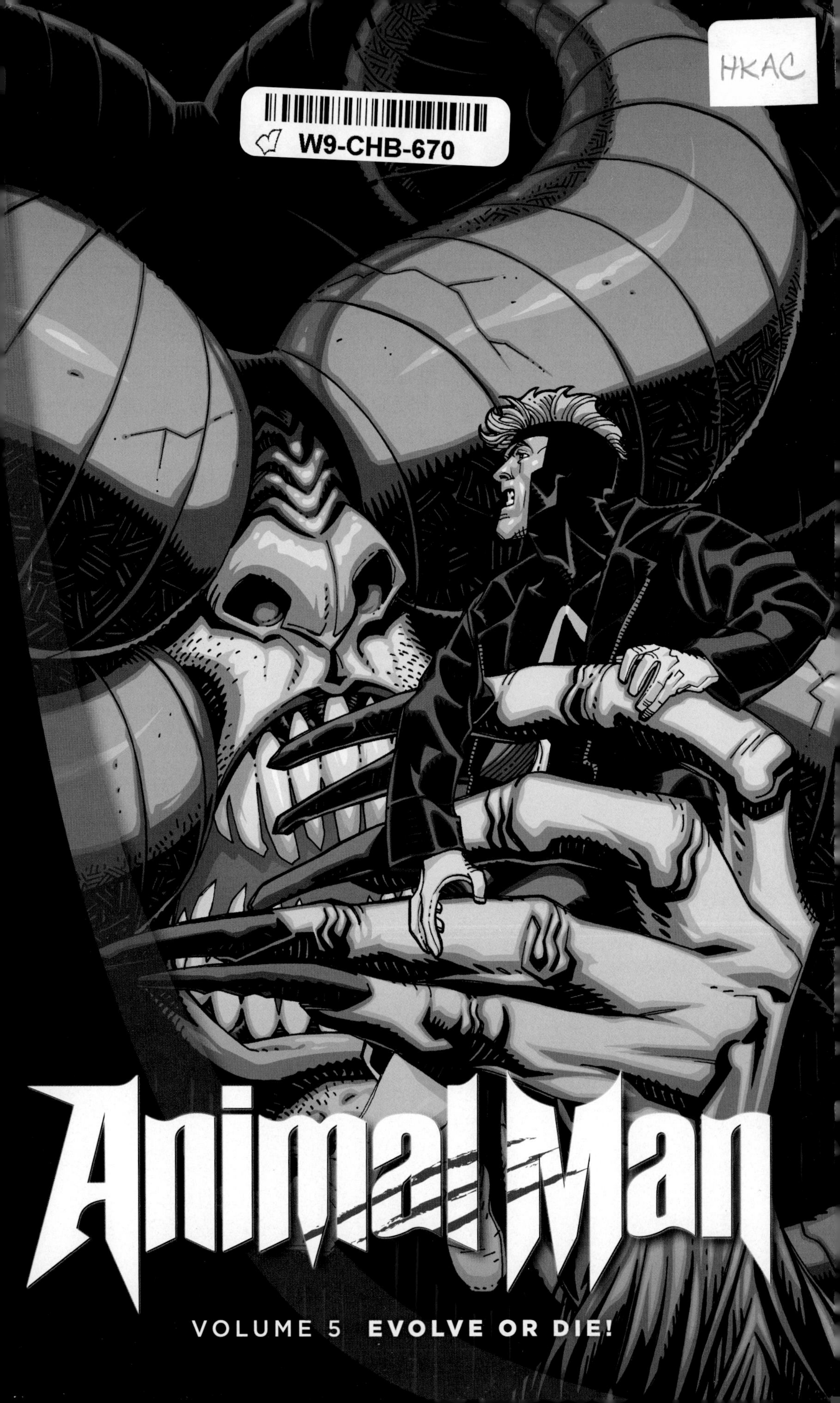

Animal Man

VOLUME 5 **EVOLVE OR DIE!**

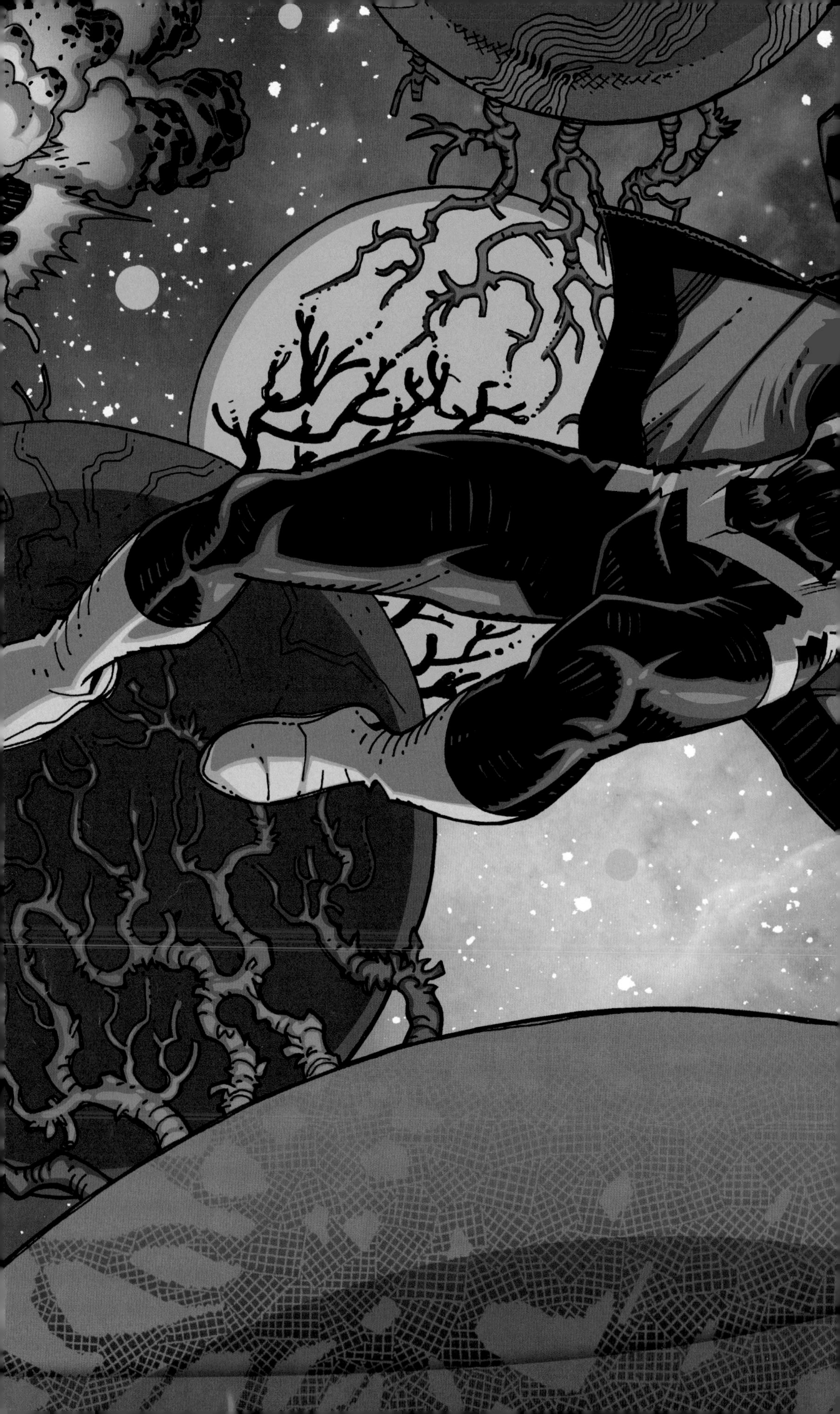

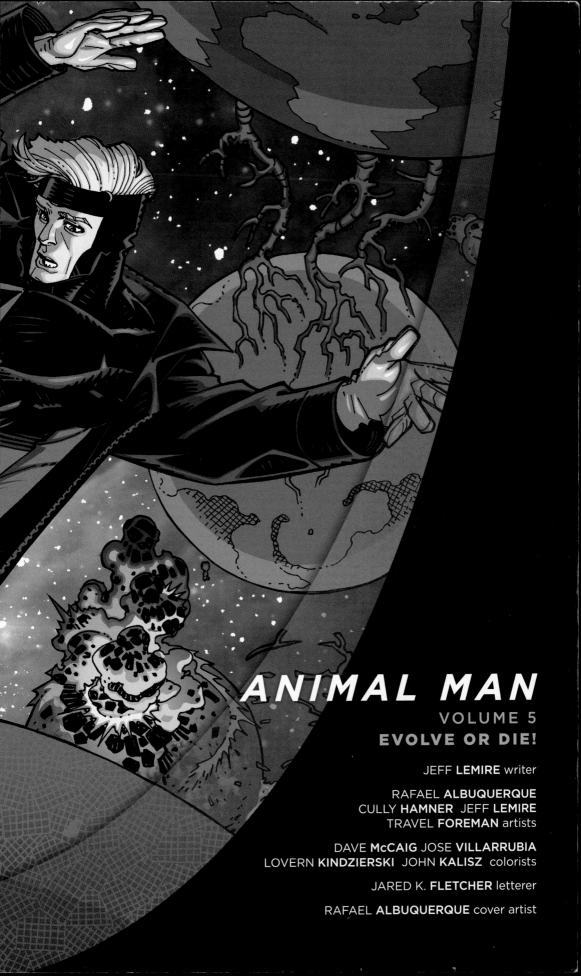

ANIMAL MAN

VOLUME 5
EVOLVE OR DIE!

JEFF **LEMIRE** writer

RAFAEL **ALBUQUERQUE**
CULLY **HAMNER** JEFF **LEMIRE**
TRAVEL **FOREMAN** artists

DAVE **McCAIG** JOSE **VILLARRUBIA**
LOVERN **KINDZIERSKI** JOHN **KALISZ** colorists

JARED K. **FLETCHER** letterer

RAFAEL **ALBUQUERQUE** cover artist

JOEY CAVALIERI Editor – Original Series KYLE ANDRUKIEWICZ Assistant Editor – Original Series
LIZ ERICKSON Editor ROBBIN BROSTERMAN Design Director – Books ROBBIE BIEDERMAN Publication Design

BOB HARRAS Senior VP – Editor-in-Chief, DC Comics

DIANE NELSON President DAN DIDIO and JIM LEE Co-Publishers GEOFF JOHNS Chief Creative Officer
AMIT DESAI Senior VP – Marketing & Franchise Management AMY GENKINS Senior VP – Business & Legal Affairs
NAIRI GARDINER Senior VP – Finance JEFF BOISON VP – Publishing Planning MARK CHIARELLO VP – Art Direction & Design
JOHN CUNNINGHAM VP – Marketing TERRI CUNNINGHAM VP – Editorial Administration LARRY GANEM VP – Talent Relations & Services
ALISON GILL Senior VP – Manufacturing & Operations HANK KANALZ Senior VP – Vertigo & Integrated Publishing
JAY KOGAN VP – Business & Legal Affairs, Publishing JACK MAHAN VP – Business Affairs, Talent
NICK NAPOLITANO VP – Manufacturing Administration SUE POHJA VP – Book Sales FRED RUIZ VP – Manufacturing Operations
COURTNEY SIMMONS Senior VP – Publicity BOB WAYNE SENIOR VP – SALES

ANIMAL MAN VOLUME 5: EVOLVE OR DIE!

Published by DC Comics. Cover and compilation Copyright © 2014 DC Comics. All Rights Reserved.

Originally published in single magazine form in ANIMAL MAN 24-29. Copyright © 2013, 2014 DC Comics. All Rights Reserved.
All characters, their distinctive likenesses and related elements featured in this publication are trademarks of DC Comics.
The stories, characters and incidents featured in this publication are entirely fictional. DC Comics does not read or
accept unsolicited ideas, stories or artwork.

DC Comics, 1700 Broadway, New York, NY 10019
A Warner Bros. Entertainment Company.
Printed by RR Donnelley, Salem, VA, USA. 10/3/14. First Printing.
ISBN: 978-1-4012-4994-6

SUSTAINABLE FORESTRY INITIATIVE Certified Chain of Custody
20% Certified Forest Content,
80% Certified Sourcing
www.sfiprogram.org
SFI-01042
APPLIES TO TEXT STOCK ONLY

Library of Congress Cataloging-in-Publication Data

Lemire, Jeff, author.
Animal Man. Volume 5, Evolve or die! / Jeff Lemire, writer ; Rafael Alburquerque, Travel Foreman, artists.
pages cm. — (The New 52!)
ISBN 978-1-4012-4994-6 (paperback)
1. Graphic novels. I. Albuquerque, Rafael, 1981- illustrator. II. Foreman, Travel, illustrator. III. Title. IV. Title: Evolve or die!

PN6728.A58L53 2014
741.5'973—dc23

2014027345

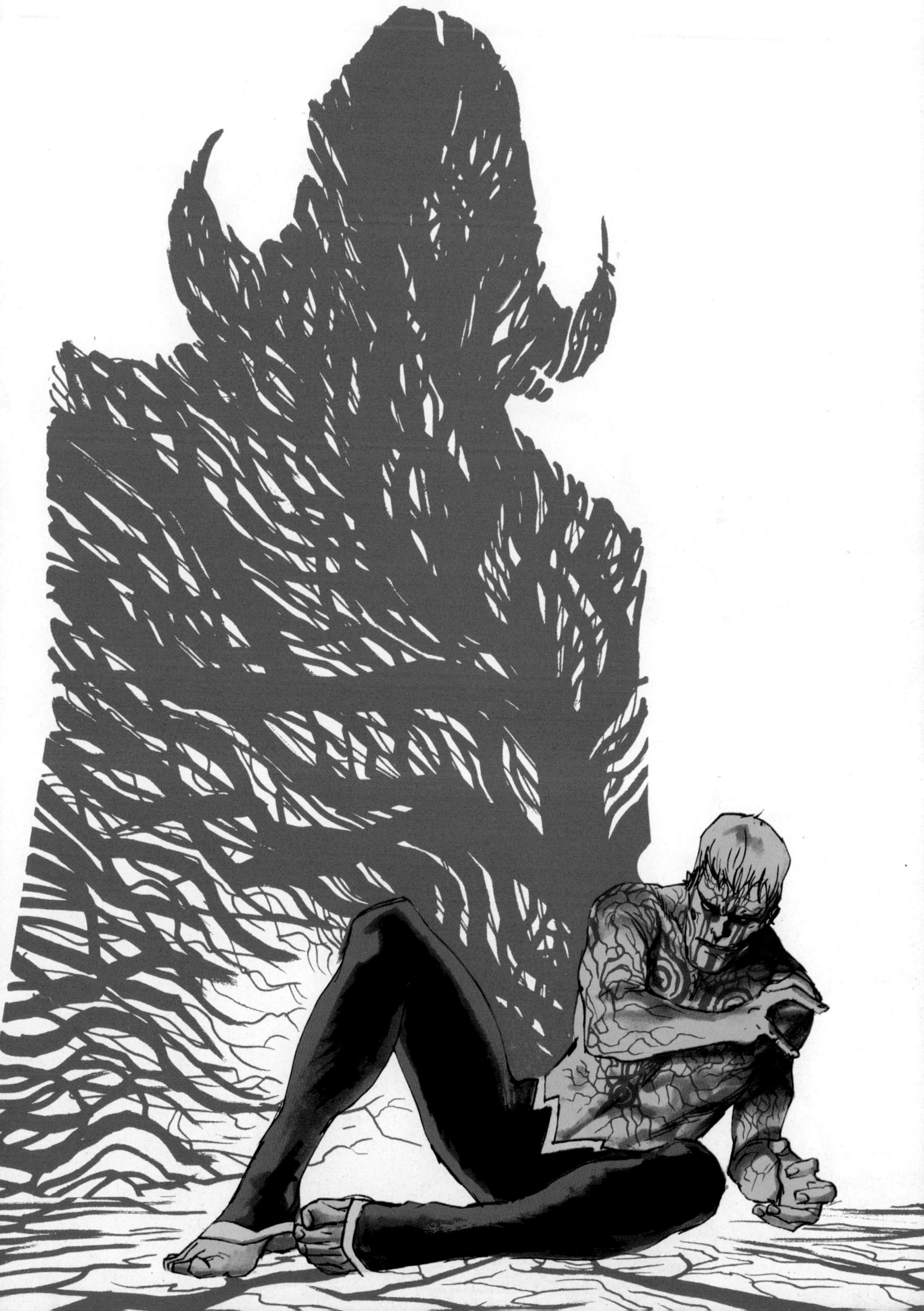

HOLLYWOOD BABYLON PART 1 OF 2
JEFF LEMIRE writer **RAFAEL ALBUQUERQUE** artist, interior and cover
DAVE McCAIG colorist **JARED K. FLETCHER** letterer

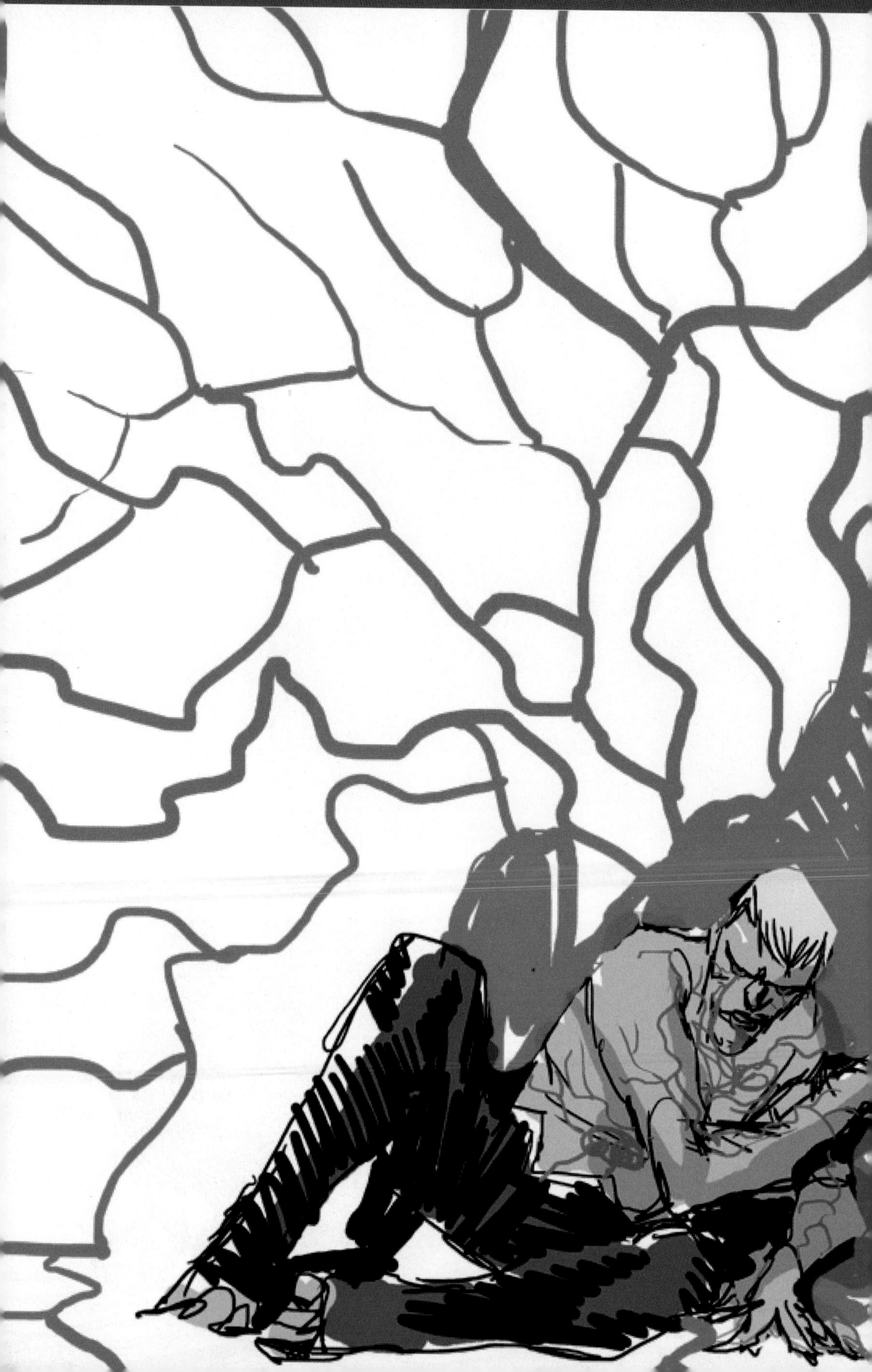

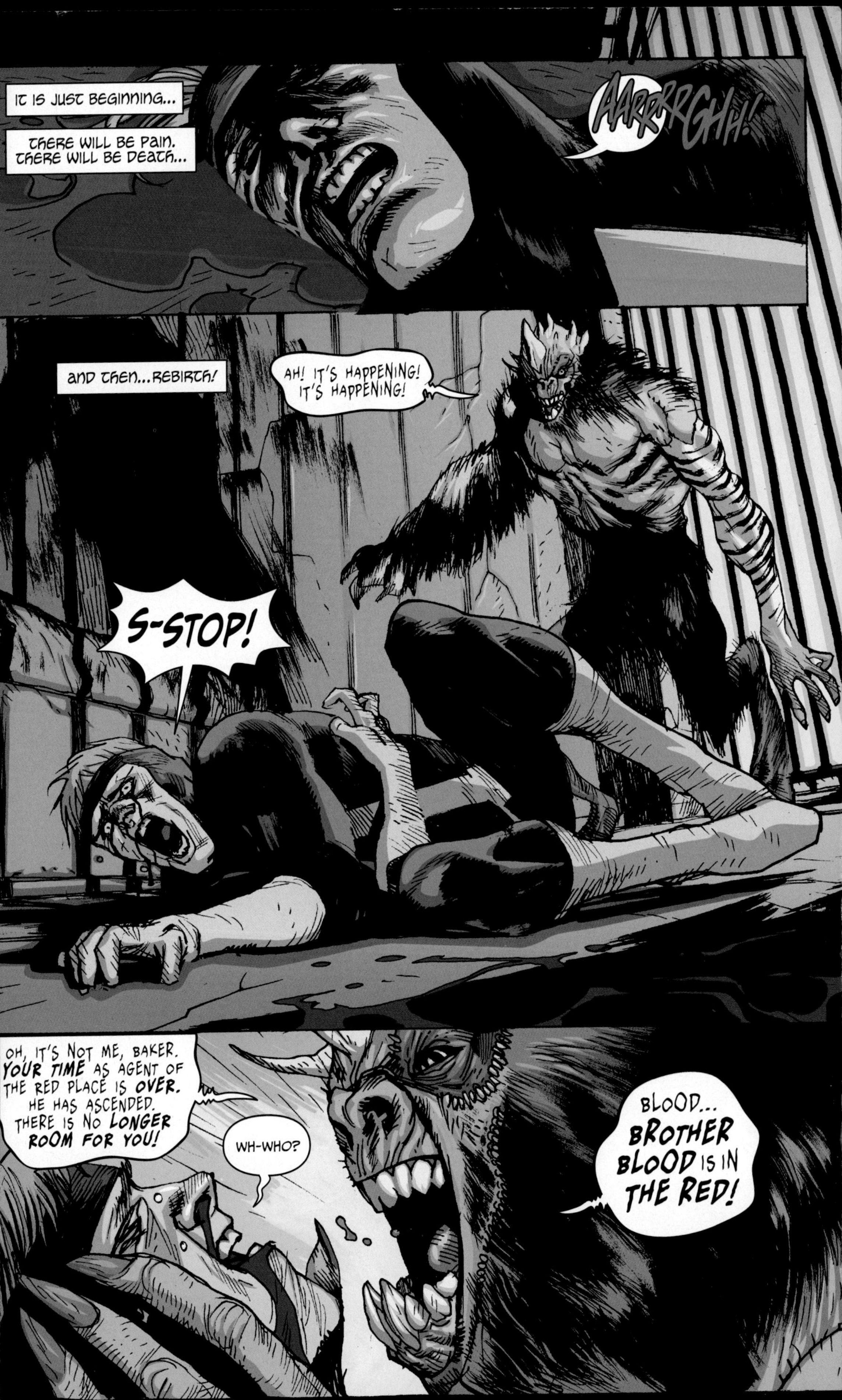
IT IS JUST BEGINNING...
THERE WILL BE PAIN. THERE WILL BE DEATH...
AARRRRGHH!
AND THEN...REBIRTH!
AH! IT'S HAPPENING! IT'S HAPPENING!
S-STOP!
OH, IT'S NOT ME, BAKER. YOUR TIME AS AGENT OF THE RED PLACE IS OVER. HE HAS ASCENDED. THERE IS NO LONGER ROOM FOR YOU!
WH-WHO?
BLOOD... BROTHER BLOOD IS IN THE RED!

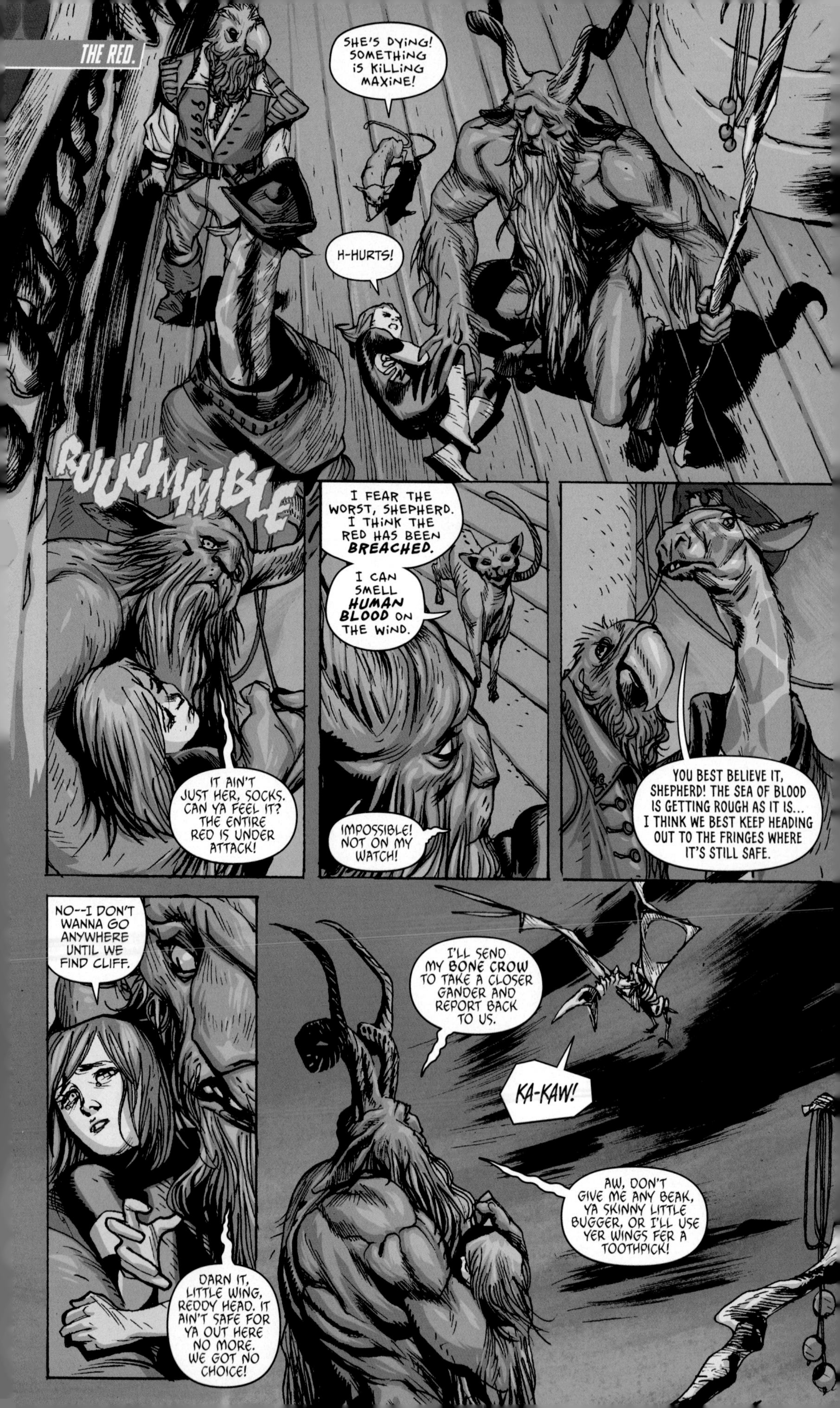
THE RED.
SHE'S DYING! SOMETHING IS KILLING MAXINE!
H-HURTS!
RUUMMBLE
I FEAR THE WORST, SHEPHERD. I THINK THE RED HAS BEEN BREACHED.
I CAN SMELL HUMAN BLOOD ON THE WIND.
IT AIN'T JUST HER, SOCKS. CAN YA FEEL IT? THE ENTIRE RED IS UNDER ATTACK!
IMPOSSIBLE! NOT ON MY WATCH!
YOU BEST BELIEVE IT, SHEPHERD! THE SEA OF BLOOD IS GETTING ROUGH AS IT IS... I THINK WE BEST KEEP HEADING OUT TO THE FRINGES WHERE IT'S STILL SAFE.
NO--I DON'T WANNA GO ANYWHERE UNTIL WE FIND CLIFF.
I'LL SEND MY BONE CROW TO TAKE A CLOSER GANDER AND REPORT BACK TO US.
KA-KAW!
AW, DON'T GIVE ME ANY BEAK, YA SKINNY LITTLE BUGGER, OR I'LL USE YER WINGS FER A TOOTHPICK!
DARN IT, LITTLE WING, REDDY HEAD. IT AIN'T SAFE FOR YA OUT HERE NO MORE. WE GOT NO CHOICE!

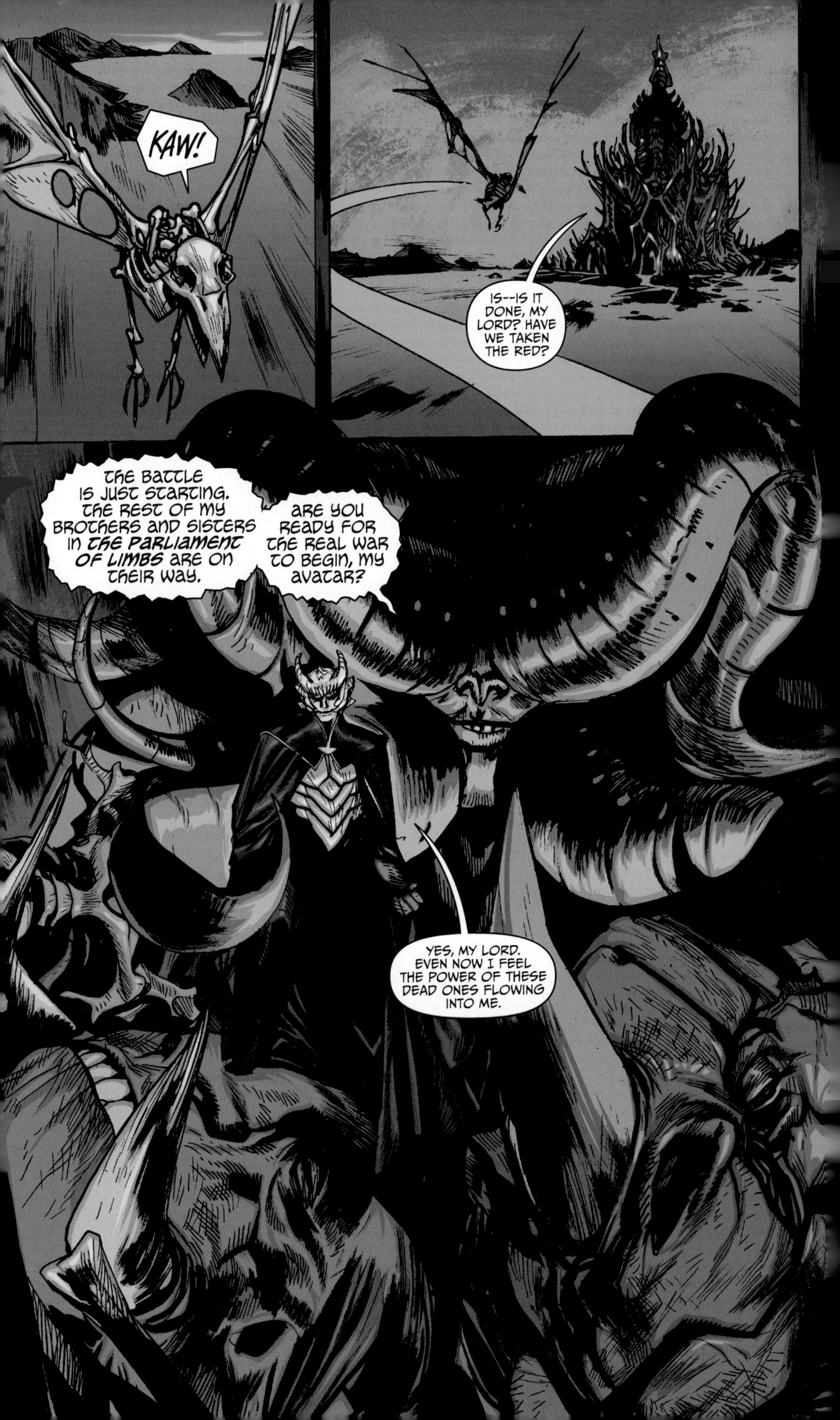
KAW!
IS--IS IT DONE, MY LORD? HAVE WE TAKEN THE RED?
THE BATTLE IS JUST STARTING. THE REST OF MY BROTHERS AND SISTERS IN *THE PARLIAMENT OF LIMBS* ARE ON THEIR WAY.
ARE YOU READY FOR THE REAL WAR TO BEGIN, MY AVATAR?
YES, MY LORD. EVEN NOW I FEEL THE POWER OF THESE DEAD ONES FLOWING INTO ME.

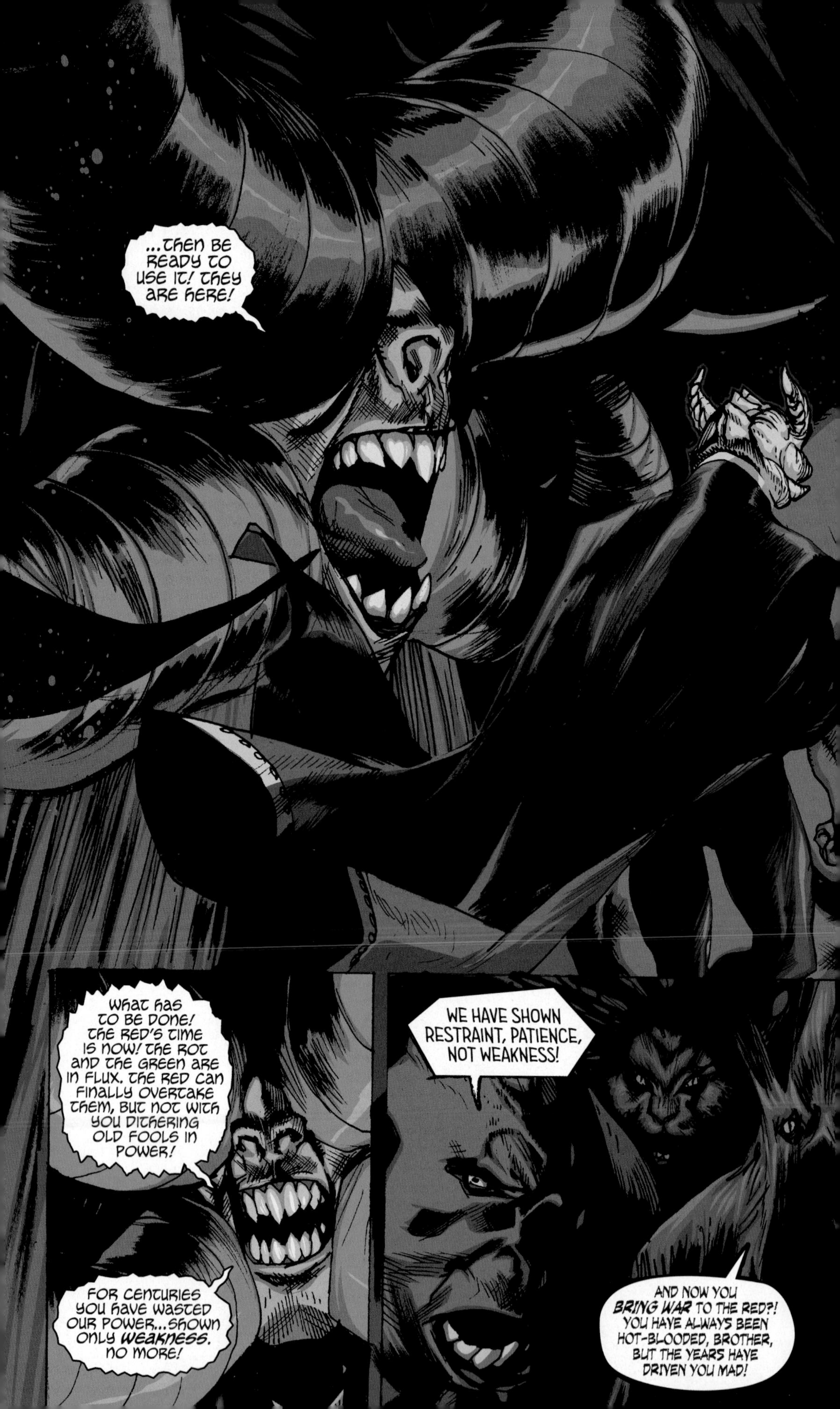

...THEN BE READY TO USE IT! THEY ARE HERE!
WHAT HAS TO BE DONE! THE RED'S TIME IS NOW! THE ROT AND THE GREEN ARE IN FLUX. THE RED CAN FINALLY OVERTAKE THEM, BUT NOT WITH YOU DITHERING OLD FOOLS IN POWER!
FOR CENTURIES YOU HAVE WASTED OUR POWER...SHOWN ONLY WEAKNESS. NO MORE!
WE HAVE SHOWN RESTRAINT, PATIENCE, NOT WEAKNESS!
AND NOW YOU BRING WAR TO THE RED?! YOU HAVE ALWAYS BEEN HOT-BLOODED, BROTHER, BUT THE YEARS HAVE DRIVEN YOU MAD!

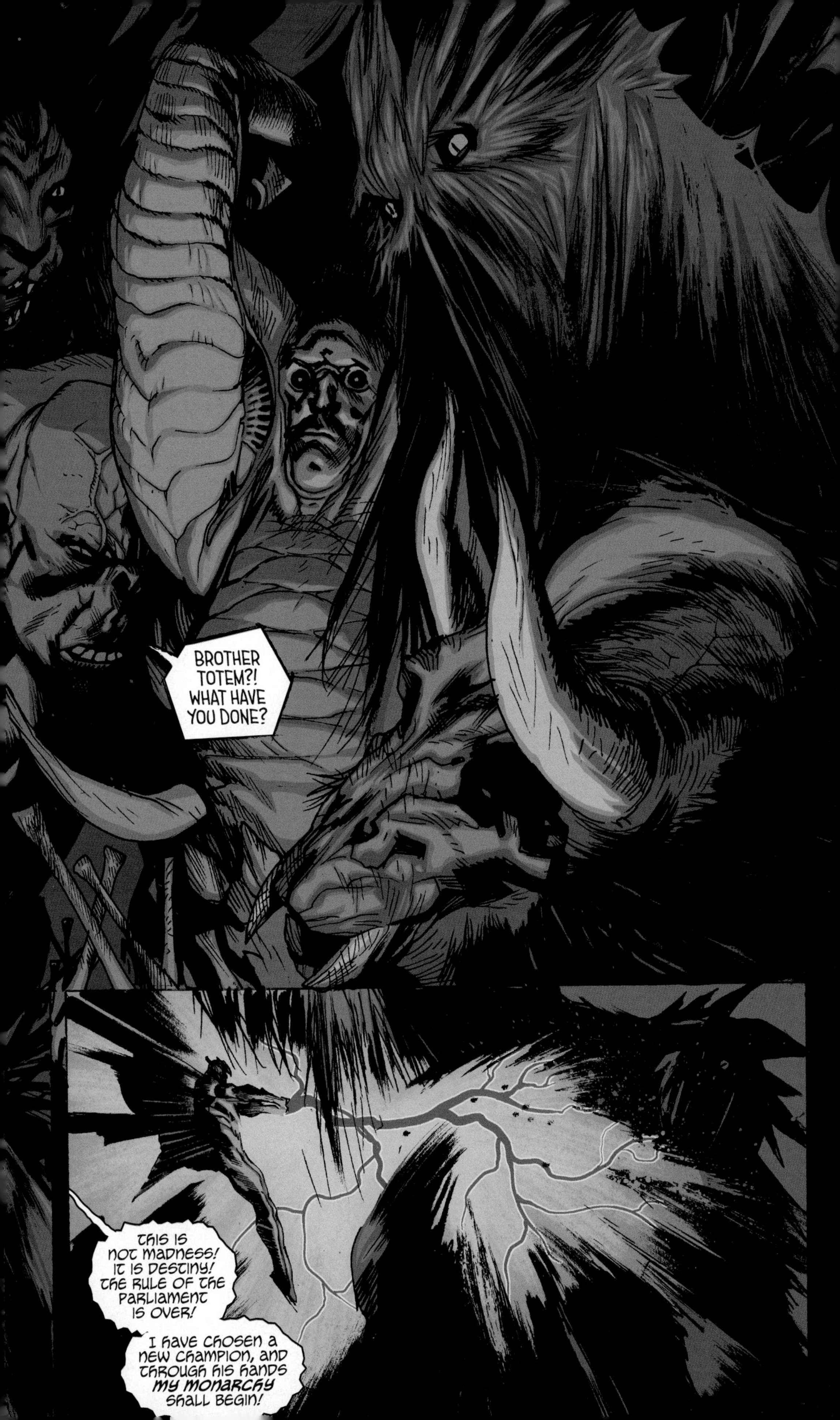
BROTHER TOTEM?! WHAT HAVE YOU DONE?
THIS IS NOT MADNESS! IT IS DESTINY! THE RULE OF THE PARLIAMENT IS OVER!
I HAVE CHOSEN A NEW CHAMPION, AND THROUGH HIS HANDS *MY MONARCHY* SHALL BEGIN!

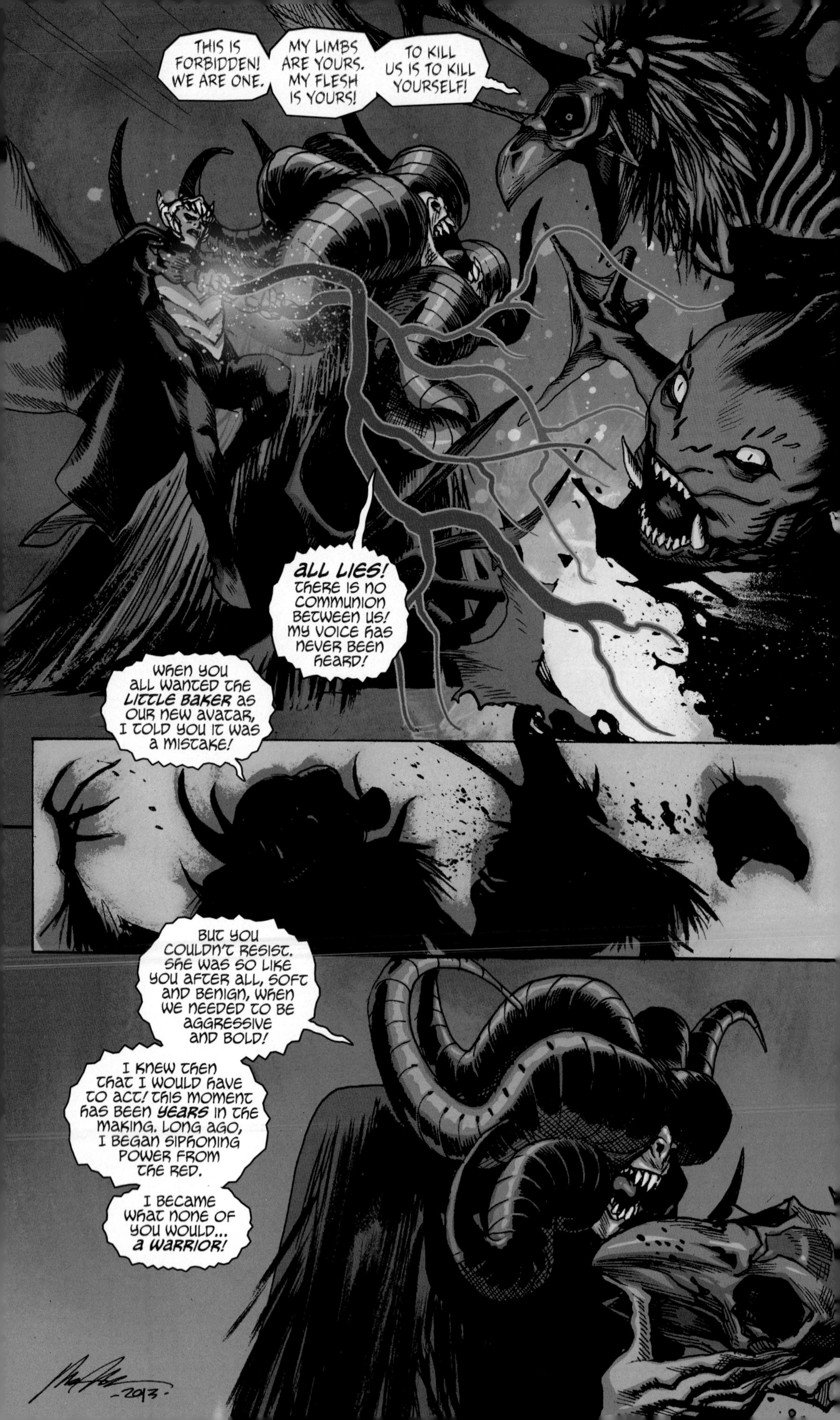
THIS IS FORBIDDEN! WE ARE ONE.
MY LIMBS ARE YOURS. MY FLESH IS YOURS!
TO KILL US IS TO KILL YOURSELF!
ALL LIES! THERE IS NO COMMUNION BETWEEN US! MY VOICE HAS NEVER BEEN HEARD!
WHEN YOU ALL WANTED THE LITTLE BAKER AS OUR NEW AVATAR, I TOLD YOU IT WAS A MISTAKE!
BUT YOU COULDN'T RESIST. SHE WAS SO LIKE YOU AFTER ALL, SOFT AND BENIGN, WHEN WE NEEDED TO BE AGGRESSIVE AND BOLD!
I KNEW THEN THAT I WOULD HAVE TO ACT! THIS MOMENT HAS BEEN YEARS IN THE MAKING. LONG AGO, I BEGAN SIPHONING POWER FROM THE RED.
I BECAME WHAT NONE OF YOU WOULD... A WARRIOR!
-2013-

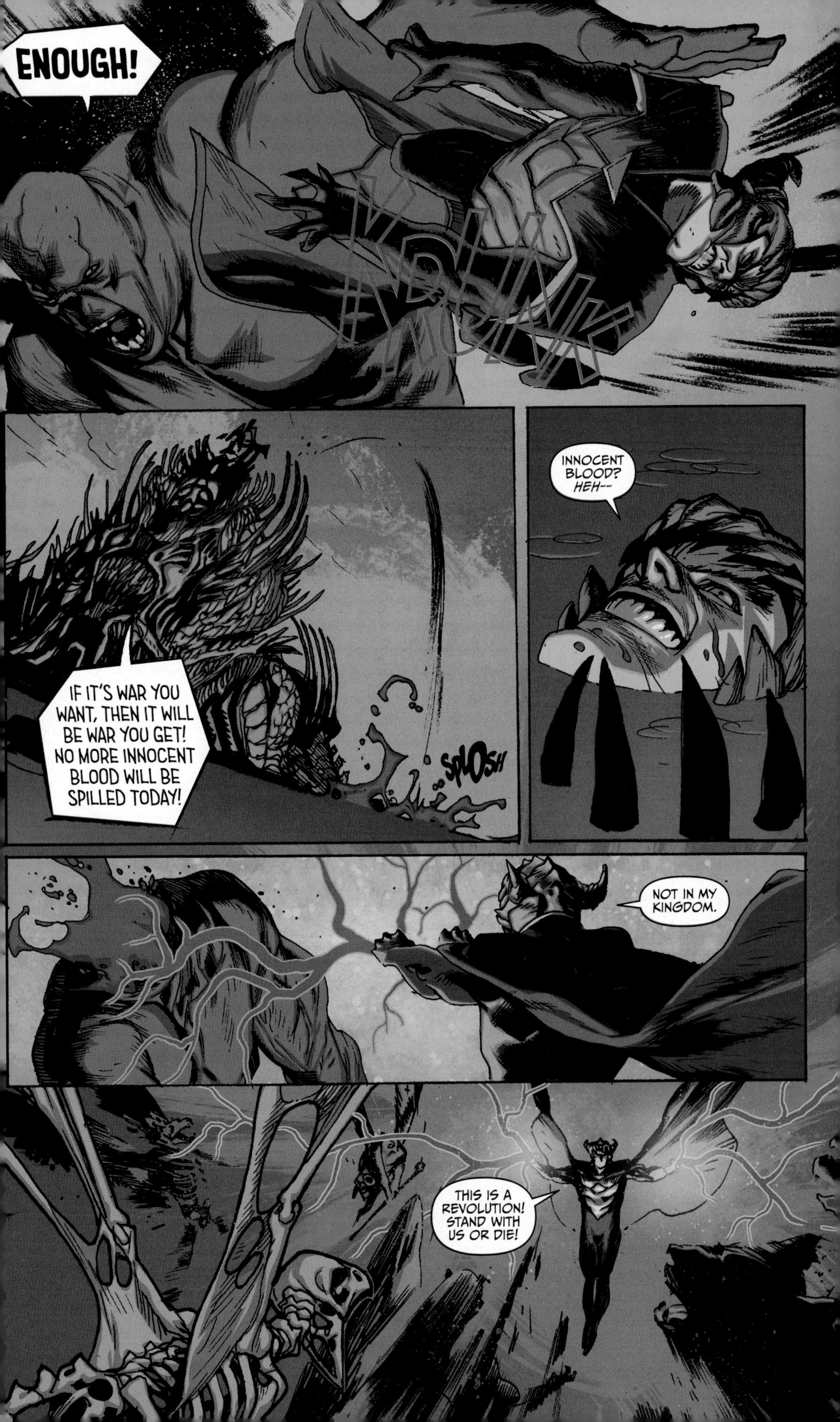
ENOUGH!
KDUNK
IF IT'S WAR YOU WANT, THEN IT WILL BE WAR YOU GET! NO MORE INNOCENT BLOOD WILL BE SPILLED TODAY!
SPLOSH
INNOCENT BLOOD? HEH--
NOT IN MY KINGDOM.
THIS IS A REVOLUTION! STAND WITH US OR DIE!

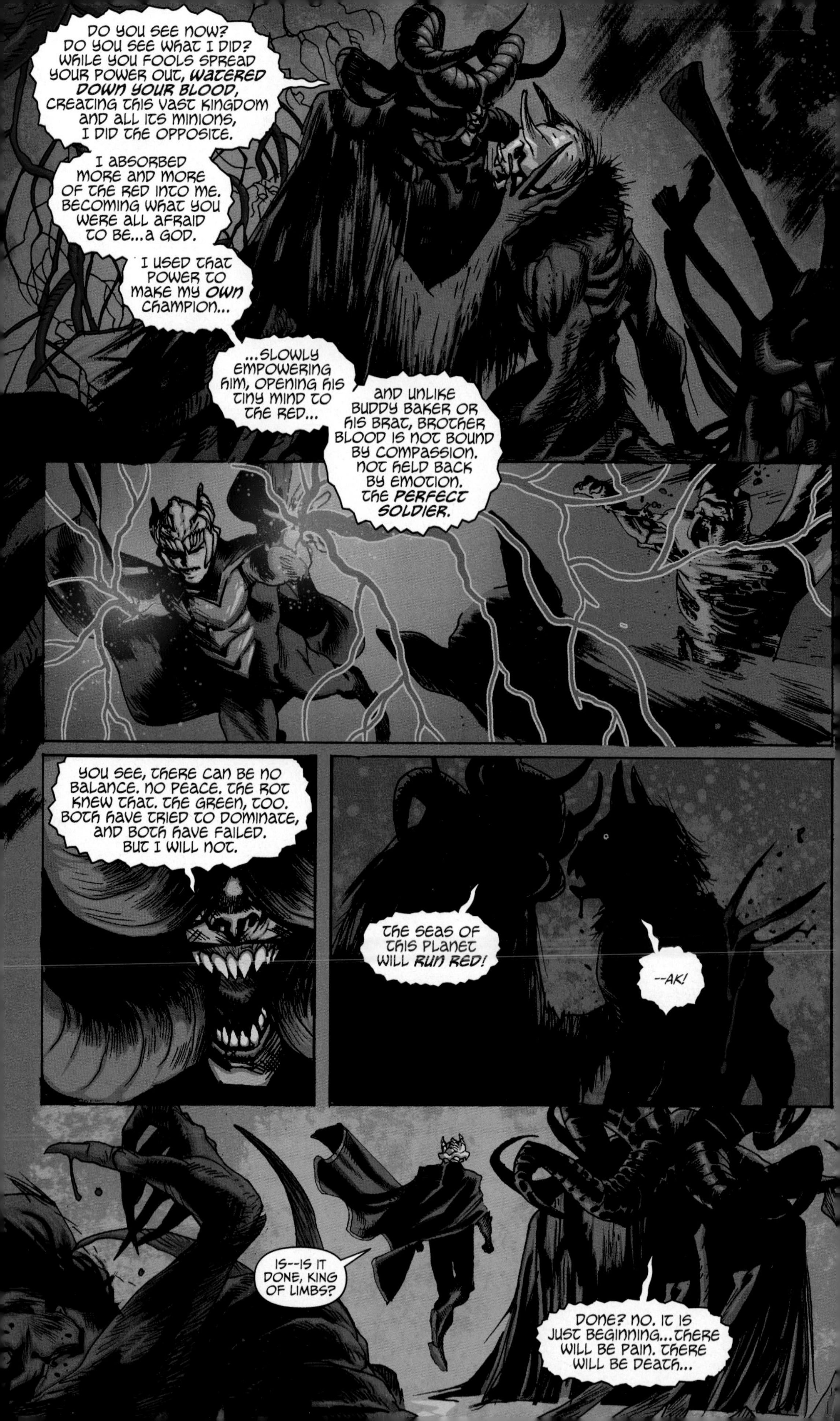
DO YOU SEE NOW? DO YOU SEE WHAT I DID? WHILE YOU FOOLS SPREAD YOUR POWER OUT, WATERED DOWN YOUR BLOOD, CREATING THIS VAST KINGDOM AND ALL ITS MINIONS, I DID THE OPPOSITE.
I ABSORBED MORE AND MORE OF THE RED INTO ME. BECOMING WHAT YOU WERE ALL AFRAID TO BE...A GOD.
I USED THAT POWER TO MAKE MY OWN CHAMPION...
...SLOWLY EMPOWERING HIM, OPENING HIS TINY MIND TO THE RED...
AND UNLIKE BUDDY BAKER OR HIS BRAT, BROTHER BLOOD IS NOT BOUND BY COMPASSION. NOT HELD BACK BY EMOTION. THE PERFECT SOLDIER.
YOU SEE, THERE CAN BE NO BALANCE. NO PEACE. THE ROT KNEW THAT. THE GREEN, TOO. BOTH HAVE TRIED TO DOMINATE, AND BOTH HAVE FAILED. BUT I WILL NOT.
THE SEAS OF THIS PLANET WILL RUN RED!
--AK!
IS--IS IT DONE, KING OF LIMBS?
DONE? NO. IT IS JUST BEGINNING...THERE WILL BE PAIN. THERE WILL BE DEATH...

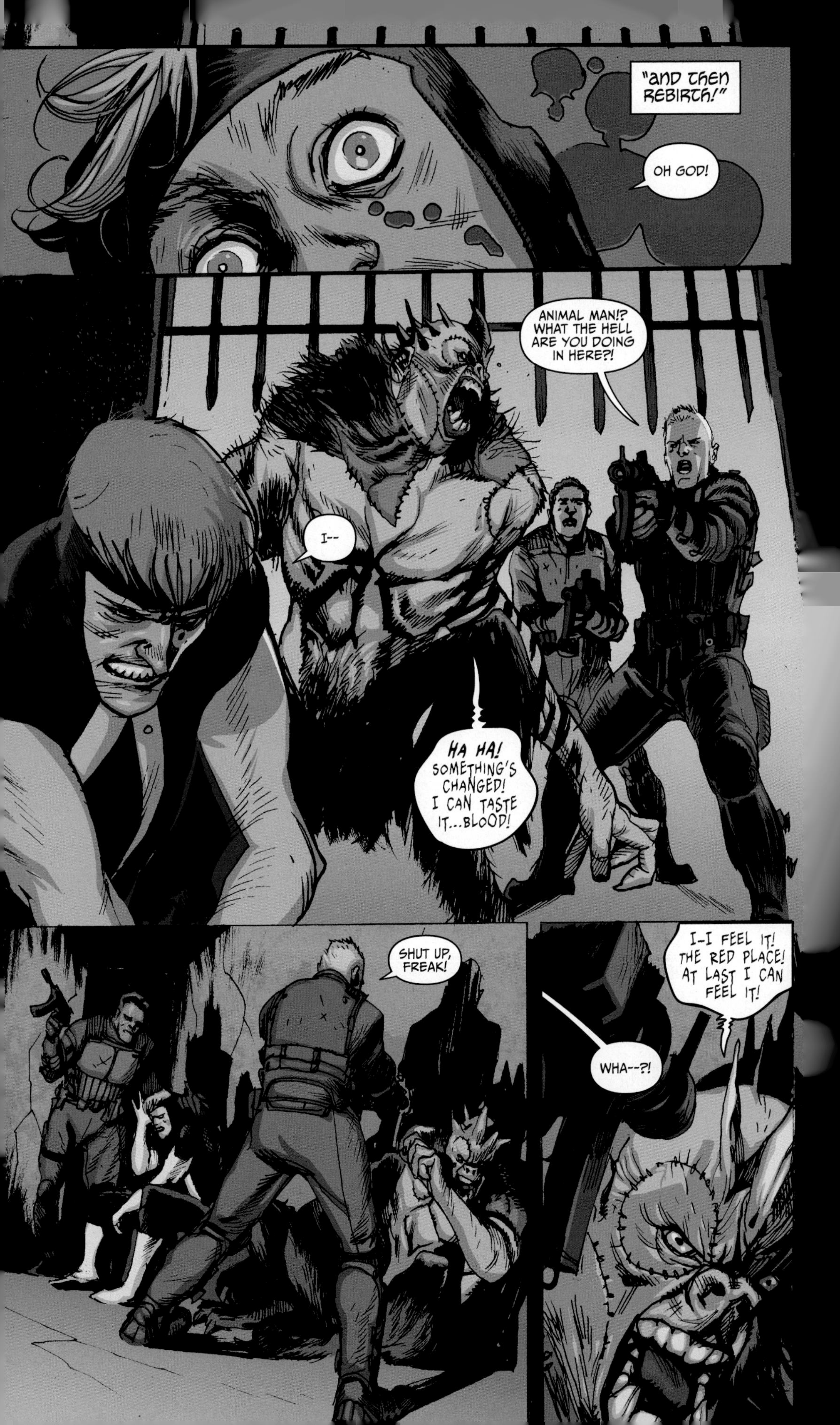
"AND THEN REBIRTH!"
OH GOD!
ANIMAL MAN!? WHAT THE HELL ARE YOU DOING IN HERE?!
I--
HA HA! SOMETHING'S CHANGED! I CAN TASTE IT...BLOOD!
SHUT UP, FREAK!
I-I FEEL IT! THE RED PLACE! AT LAST I CAN FEEL IT!
WHA--?!

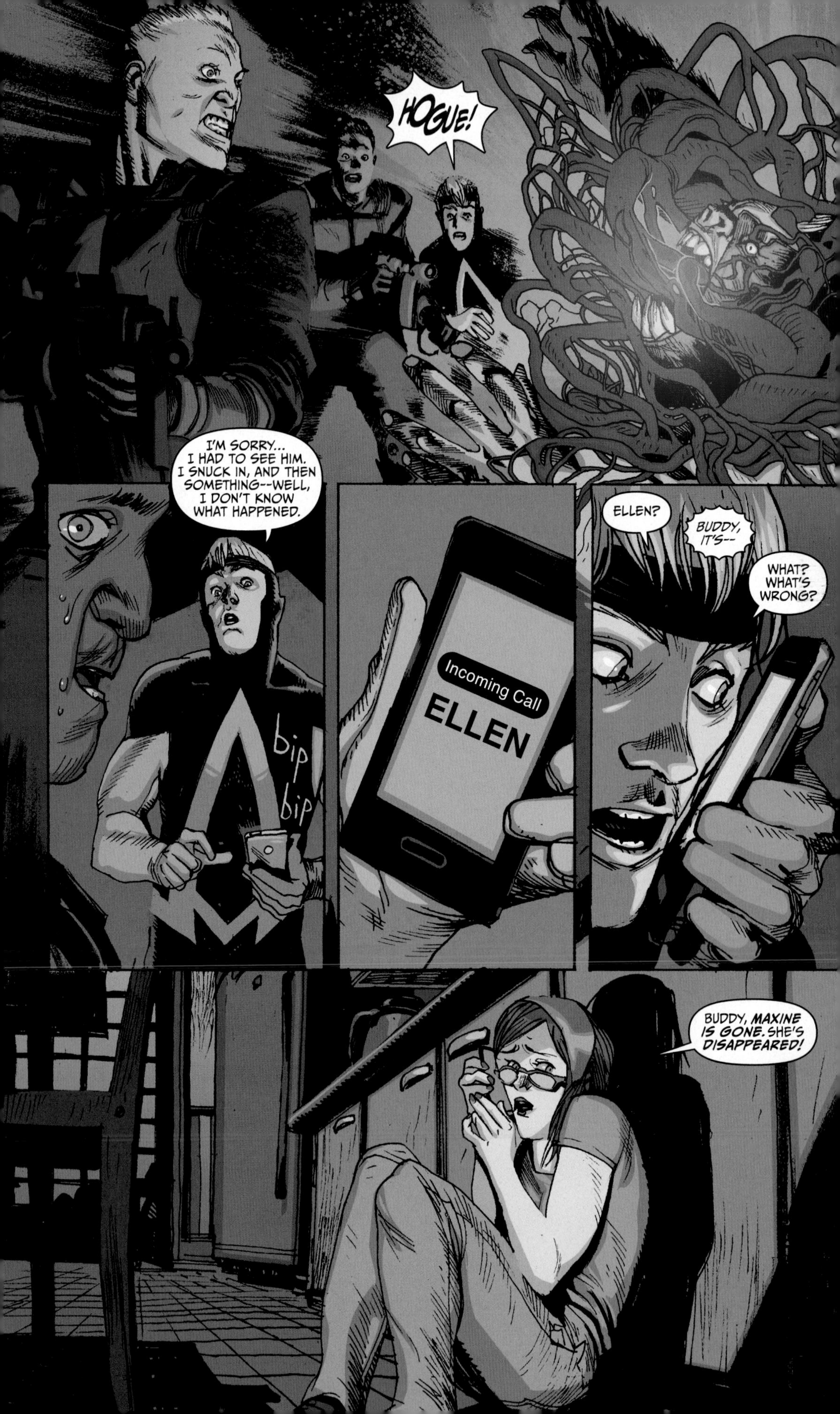
HOGUE!
I'M SORRY... I HAD TO SEE HIM. I SNUCK IN, AND THEN SOMETHING--WELL, I DON'T KNOW WHAT HAPPENED.
bip bip
Incoming Call
ELLEN
ELLEN?
BUDDY, IT'S--
WHAT? WHAT'S WRONG?
BUDDY, MAXINE IS GONE. SHE'S DISAPPEARED!

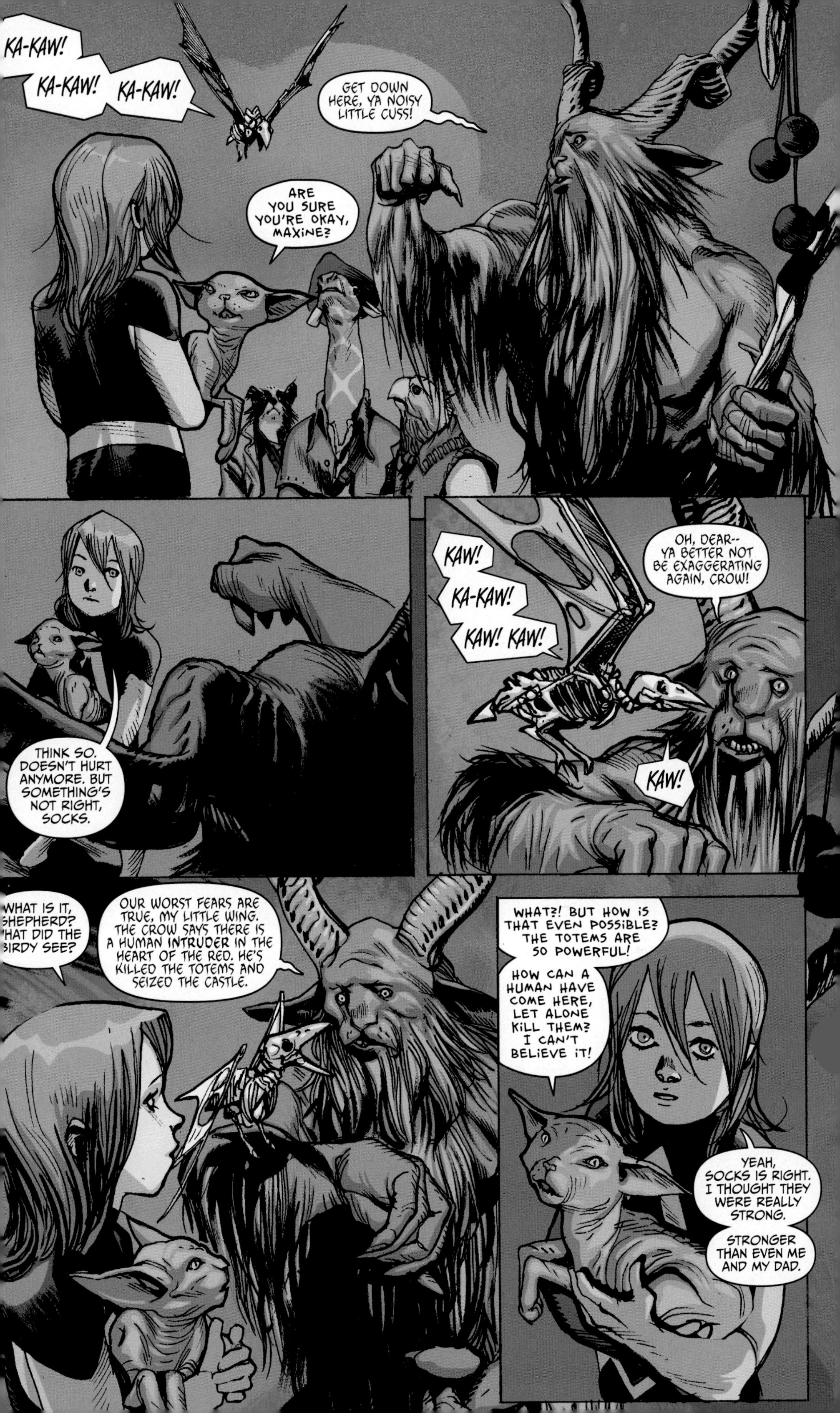
KA-KAW!
KA-KAW!
KA-KAW!
GET DOWN HERE, YA NOISY LITTLE CUSS!
ARE YOU SURE YOU'RE OKAY, MAXINE?
THINK SO. DOESN'T HURT ANYMORE. BUT SOMETHING'S NOT RIGHT, SOCKS.
KAW!
KA-KAW!
KAW! KAW!
OH, DEAR-- YA BETTER NOT BE EXAGGERATING AGAIN, CROW!
KAW!
WHAT IS IT, SHEPHERD? WHAT DID THE BIRDY SEE?
OUR WORST FEARS ARE TRUE, MY LITTLE WING. THE CROW SAYS THERE IS A HUMAN INTRUDER IN THE HEART OF THE RED. HE'S KILLED THE TOTEMS AND SEIZED THE CASTLE.
WHAT?! BUT HOW IS THAT EVEN POSSIBLE? THE TOTEMS ARE SO POWERFUL!
HOW CAN A HUMAN HAVE COME HERE, LET ALONE KILL THEM? I CAN'T BELIEVE IT!
YEAH, SOCKS IS RIGHT. I THOUGHT THEY WERE REALLY STRONG.
STRONGER THAN EVEN ME AND MY DAD.

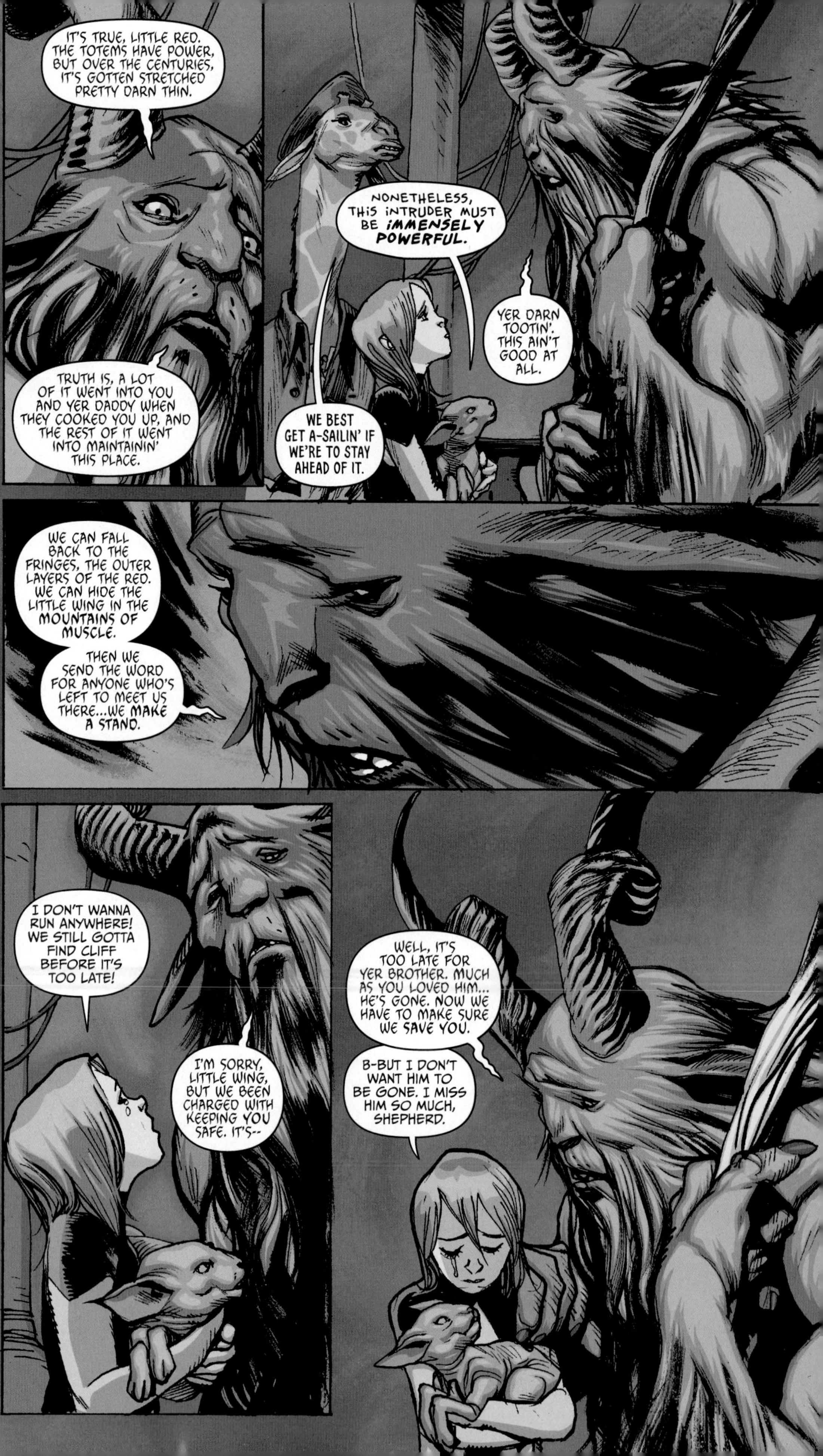
IT'S TRUE, LITTLE RED. THE TOTEMS HAVE POWER, BUT OVER THE CENTURIES, IT'S GOTTEN STRETCHED PRETTY DARN THIN.
TRUTH IS, A LOT OF IT WENT INTO YOU AND YER DADDY WHEN THEY COOKED YOU UP, AND THE REST OF IT WENT INTO MAINTAININ' THIS PLACE.
NONETHELESS, THIS INTRUDER MUST BE IMMENSELY POWERFUL.
WE BEST GET A-SAILIN' IF WE'RE TO STAY AHEAD OF IT.
YER DARN TOOTIN'. THIS AIN'T GOOD AT ALL.
WE CAN FALL BACK TO THE FRINGES, THE OUTER LAYERS OF THE RED. WE CAN HIDE THE LITTLE WING IN THE MOUNTAINS OF MUSCLE.
THEN WE SEND THE WORD FOR ANYONE WHO'S LEFT TO MEET US THERE...WE MAKE A STAND.
I DON'T WANNA RUN ANYWHERE! WE STILL GOTTA FIND CLIFF BEFORE IT'S TOO LATE!
I'M SORRY, LITTLE WING, BUT WE BEEN CHARGED WITH KEEPING YOU SAFE. IT'S--
WELL, IT'S TOO LATE FOR YER BROTHER. MUCH AS YOU LOVED HIM... HE'S GONE. NOW WE HAVE TO MAKE SURE WE SAVE YOU.
B-BUT I DON'T WANT HIM TO BE GONE. I MISS HIM SO MUCH, SHEPHERD.

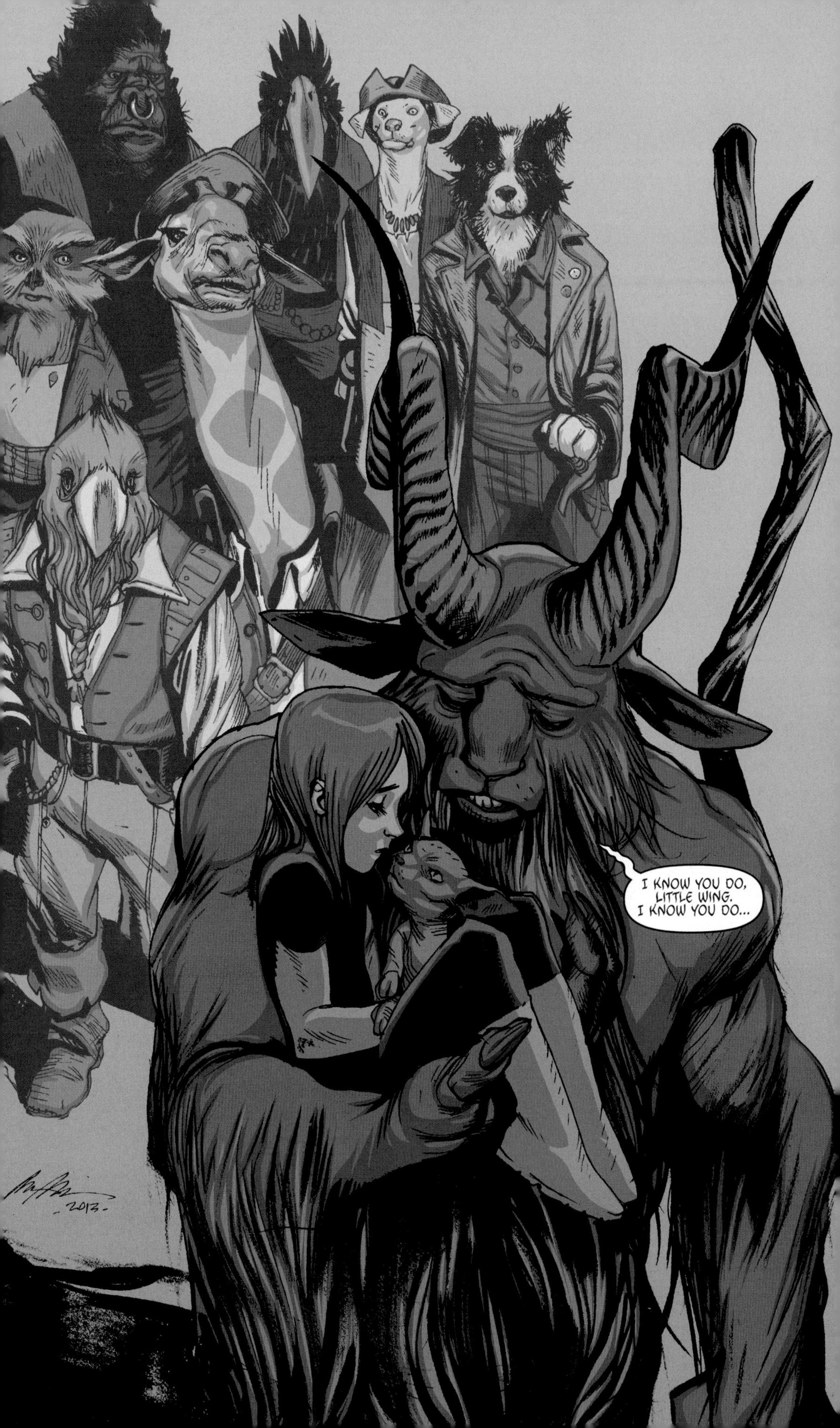
I KNOW YOU DO, LITTLE WING. I KNOW YOU DO...
2013

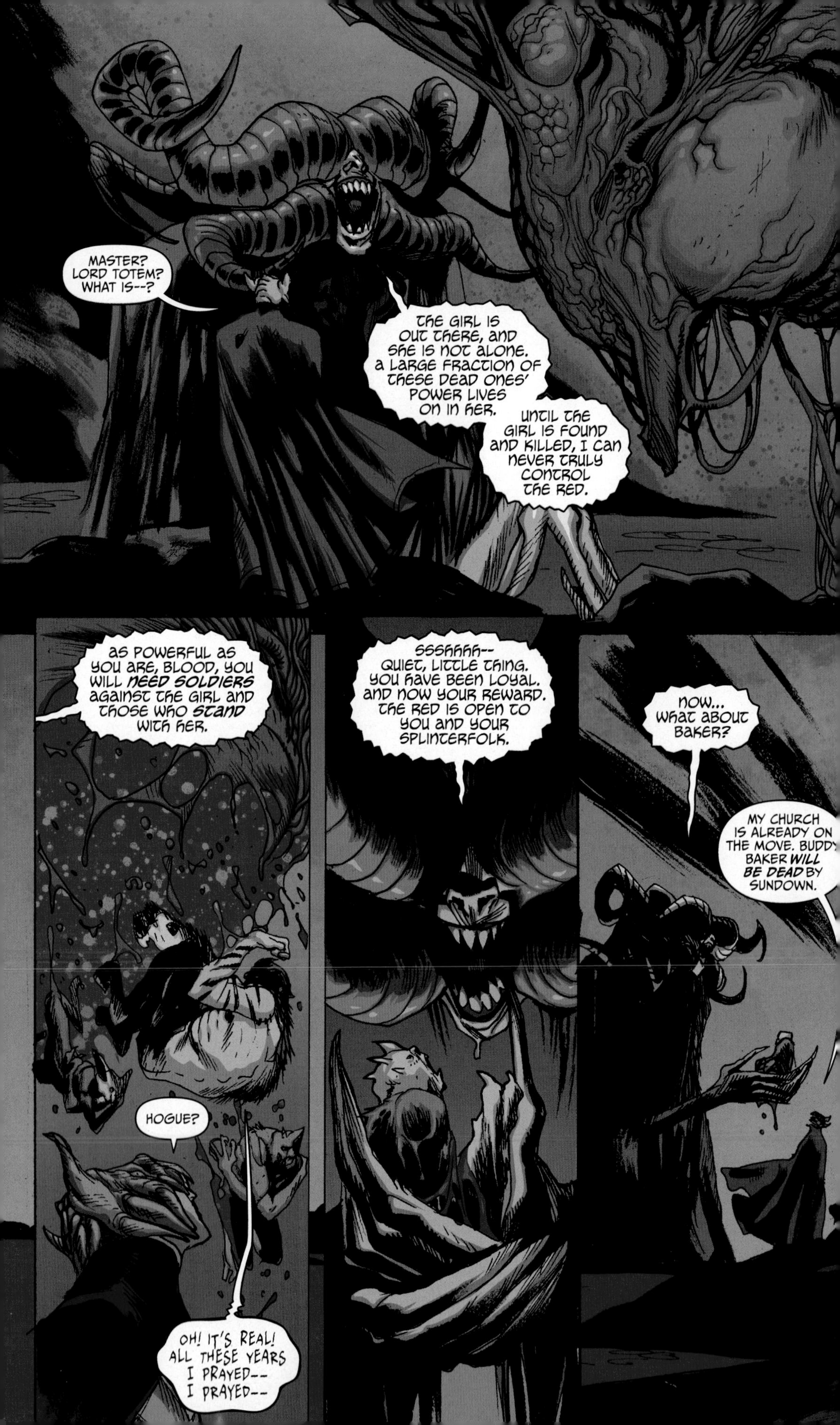
MASTER? LORD TOTEM? WHAT IS--?
THE GIRL IS OUT THERE, AND SHE IS NOT ALONE. A LARGE FRACTION OF THESE DEAD ONES' POWER LIVES ON IN HER.
UNTIL THE GIRL IS FOUND AND KILLED, I CAN NEVER TRULY CONTROL THE RED.
AS POWERFUL AS YOU ARE, BLOOD, YOU WILL NEED SOLDIERS AGAINST THE GIRL AND THOSE WHO STAND WITH HER.
HOGUE?
OH! IT'S REAL! ALL THESE YEARS I PRAYED-- I PRAYED--
SSSHHHH-- QUIET, LITTLE THING. YOU HAVE BEEN LOYAL. AND NOW YOUR REWARD. THE RED IS OPEN TO YOU AND YOUR SPLINTERFOLK.
NOW... WHAT ABOUT BAKER?
MY CHURCH IS ALREADY ON THE MOVE. BUDDY BAKER WILL BE DEAD BY SUNDOWN.

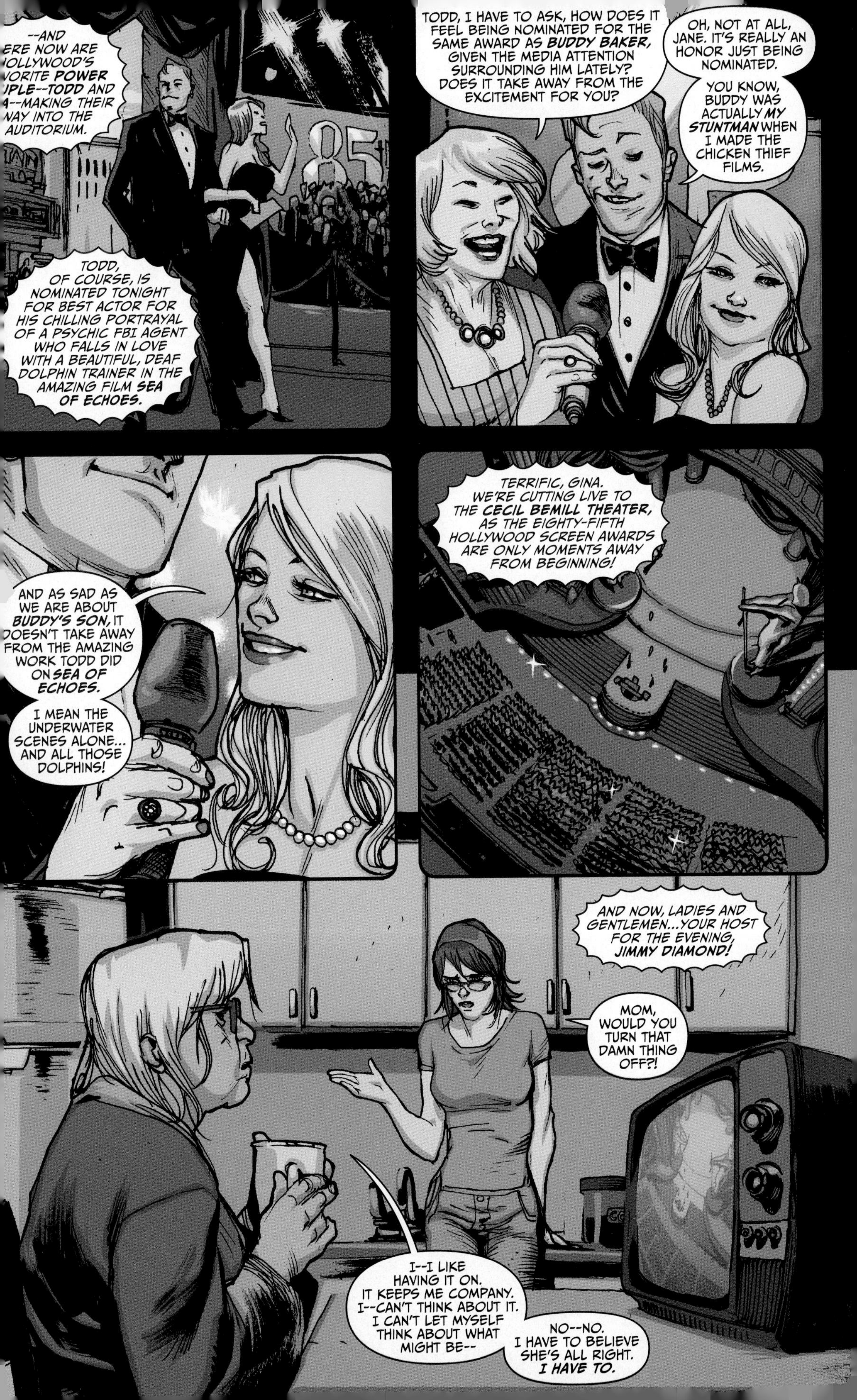
--AND
ERE NOW ARE
OLLYWOOD'S
VORITE POWER
UPLE--TODD AND
A--MAKING THEIR
WAY INTO THE
AUDITORIUM.
TODD, OF COURSE, IS NOMINATED TONIGHT FOR BEST ACTOR FOR HIS CHILLING PORTRAYAL OF A PSYCHIC FBI AGENT WHO FALLS IN LOVE WITH A BEAUTIFUL, DEAF DOLPHIN TRAINER IN THE AMAZING FILM SEA OF ECHOES.
TODD, I HAVE TO ASK, HOW DOES IT FEEL BEING NOMINATED FOR THE SAME AWARD AS BUDDY BAKER, GIVEN THE MEDIA ATTENTION SURROUNDING HIM LATELY? DOES IT TAKE AWAY FROM THE EXCITEMENT FOR YOU?
OH, NOT AT ALL, JANE. IT'S REALLY AN HONOR JUST BEING NOMINATED.
YOU KNOW, BUDDY WAS ACTUALLY MY STUNTMAN WHEN I MADE THE CHICKEN THIEF FILMS.
AND AS SAD AS WE ARE ABOUT BUDDY'S SON, IT DOESN'T TAKE AWAY FROM THE AMAZING WORK TODD DID ON SEA OF ECHOES.
I MEAN THE UNDERWATER SCENES ALONE... AND ALL THOSE DOLPHINS!
TERRIFIC, GINA. WE'RE CUTTING LIVE TO THE CECIL BEMILL THEATER, AS THE EIGHTY-FIFTH HOLLYWOOD SCREEN AWARDS ARE ONLY MOMENTS AWAY FROM BEGINNING!
AND NOW, LADIES AND GENTLEMEN...YOUR HOST FOR THE EVENING, JIMMY DIAMOND!
MOM, WOULD YOU TURN THAT DAMN THING OFF?!
I--I LIKE HAVING IT ON. IT KEEPS ME COMPANY. I--CAN'T THINK ABOUT IT. I CAN'T LET MYSELF THINK ABOUT WHAT MIGHT BE--
NO--NO. I HAVE TO BELIEVE SHE'S ALL RIGHT. I HAVE TO.

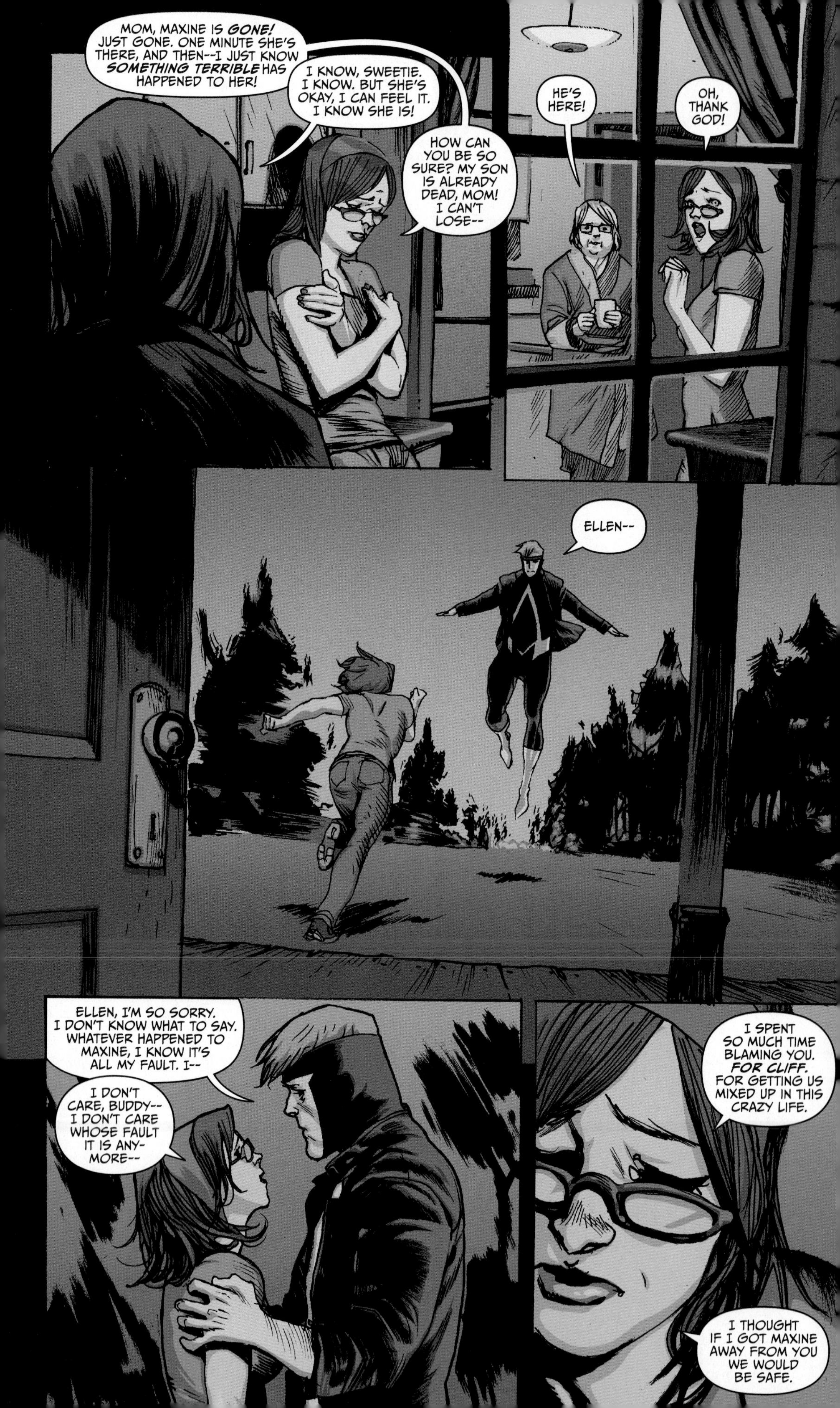

MOM, MAXINE IS GONE! JUST GONE. ONE MINUTE SHE'S THERE, AND THEN--I JUST KNOW SOMETHING TERRIBLE HAS HAPPENED TO HER!
I KNOW, SWEETIE. I KNOW. BUT SHE'S OKAY, I CAN FEEL IT. I KNOW SHE IS!
HOW CAN YOU BE SO SURE? MY SON IS ALREADY DEAD, MOM! I CAN'T LOSE--
HE'S HERE!
OH, THANK GOD!
ELLEN--
ELLEN, I'M SO SORRY. I DON'T KNOW WHAT TO SAY. WHATEVER HAPPENED TO MAXINE, I KNOW IT'S ALL MY FAULT. I--
I DON'T CARE, BUDDY-- I DON'T CARE WHOSE FAULT IT IS ANY-MORE--
I SPENT SO MUCH TIME BLAMING YOU. FOR CLIFF. FOR GETTING US MIXED UP IN THIS CRAZY LIFE.
I THOUGHT IF I GOT MAXINE AWAY FROM YOU WE WOULD BE SAFE.

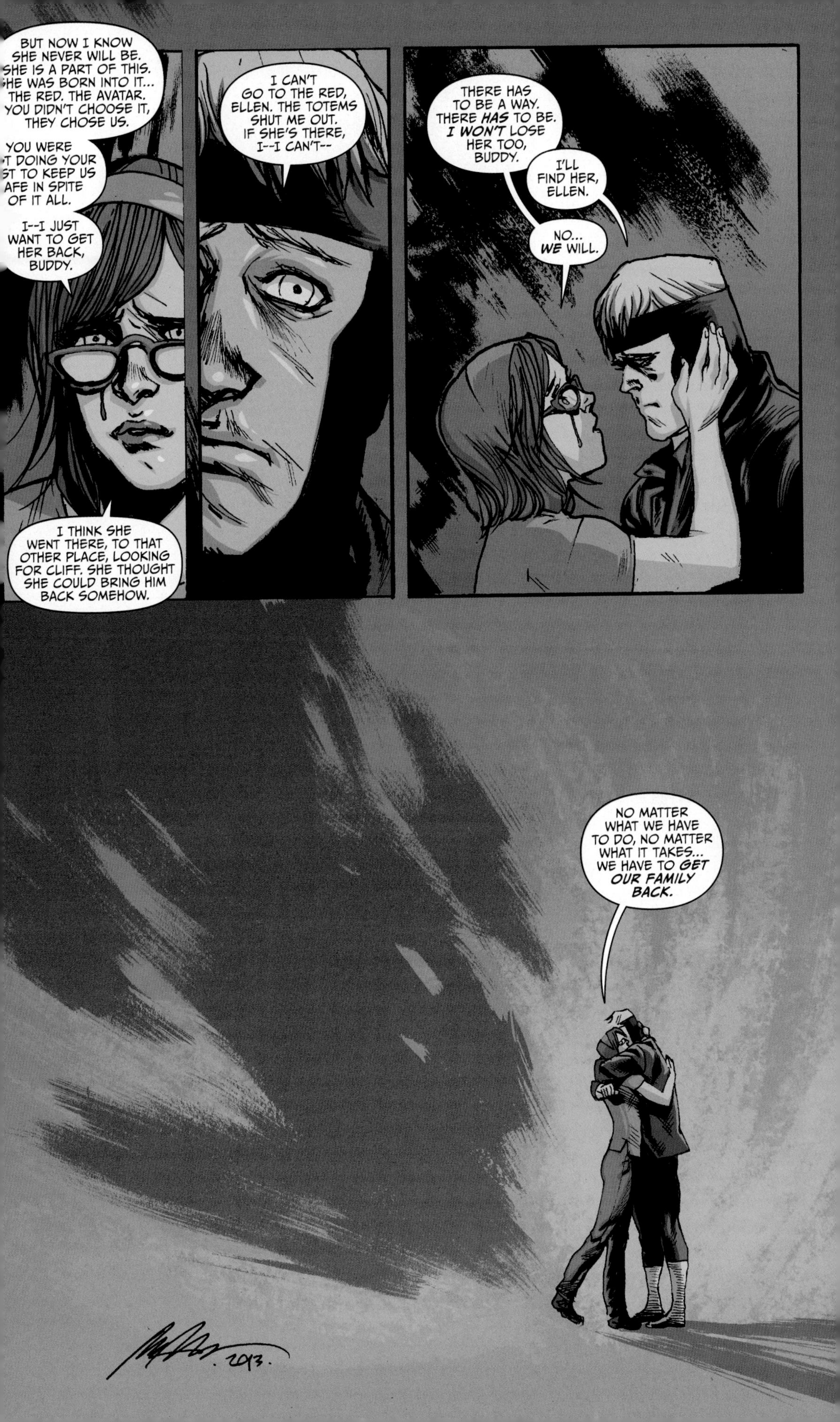
BUT NOW I KNOW SHE NEVER WILL BE. HE IS A PART OF THIS. HE WAS BORN INTO IT... THE RED. THE AVATAR. OU DIDN'T CHOOSE IT, THEY CHOSE US.
YOU WERE T DOING YOUR T TO KEEP US AFE IN SPITE OF IT ALL.
I--I JUST WANT TO GET HER BACK, BUDDY.
I THINK SHE WENT THERE, TO THAT OTHER PLACE, LOOKING FOR CLIFF. SHE THOUGHT SHE COULD BRING HIM BACK SOMEHOW.
I CAN'T GO TO THE RED, ELLEN. THE TOTEMS SHUT ME OUT. IF SHE'S THERE, I--I CAN'T--
THERE HAS TO BE A WAY. THERE *HAS* TO BE. *I WON'T* LOSE HER TOO, BUDDY.
I'LL FIND HER, ELLEN.
NO... *WE* WILL.
NO MATTER WHAT WE HAVE TO DO, NO MATTER WHAT IT TAKES... WE HAVE TO *GET OUR FAMILY BACK.*

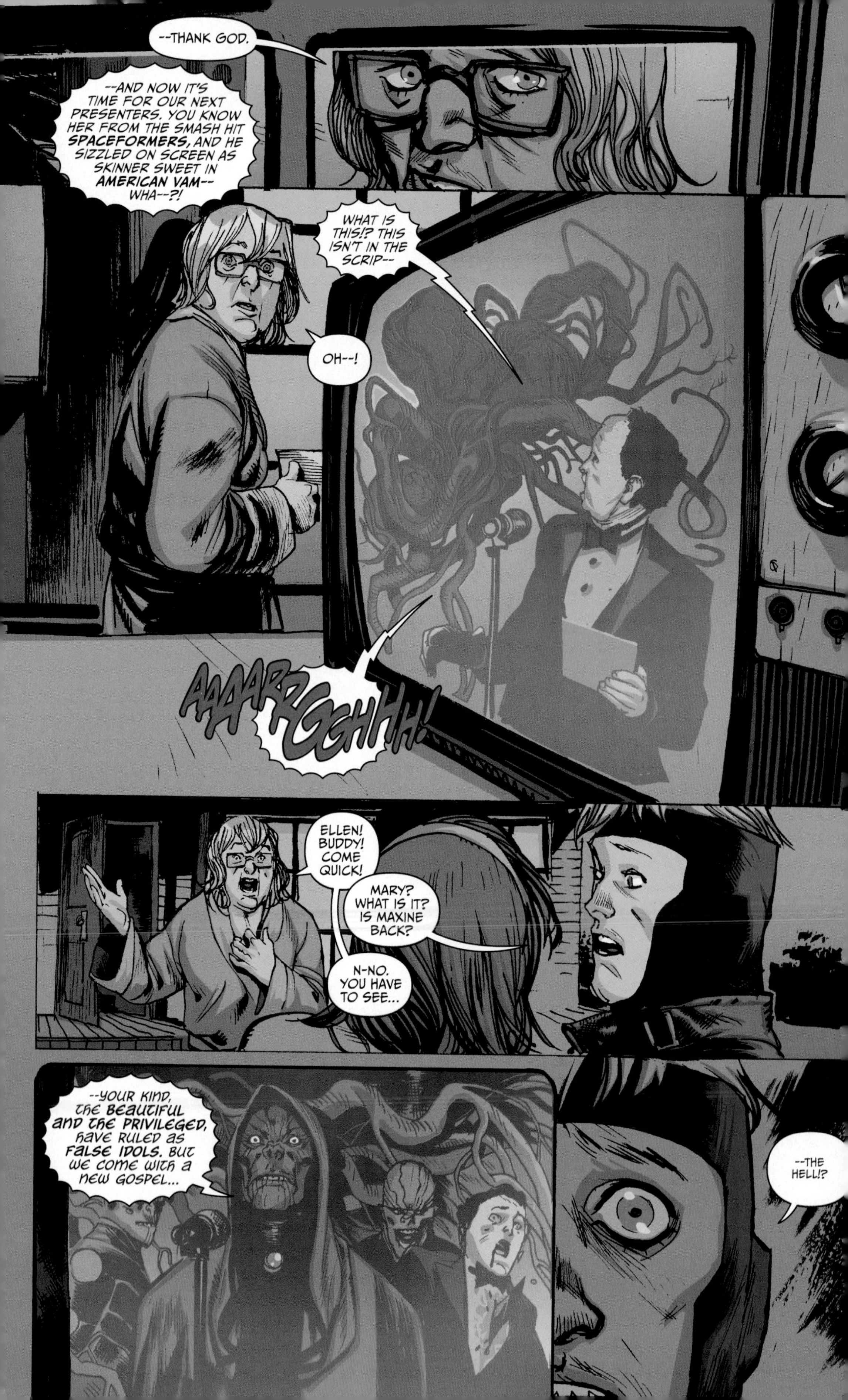
--THANK GOD.
--AND NOW IT'S TIME FOR OUR NEXT PRESENTERS. YOU KNOW HER FROM THE SMASH HIT SPACEFORMERS, AND HE SIZZLED ON SCREEN AS SKINNER SWEET IN AMERICAN VAM-- WHA--?!
WHAT IS THIS!? THIS ISN'T IN THE SCRIP--
OH--!
AAAARRGGHHH!
ELLEN! BUDDY! COME QUICK!
MARY? WHAT IS IT? IS MAXINE BACK?
N-NO. YOU HAVE TO SEE...
--YOUR KIND, THE BEAUTIFUL AND THE PRIVILEGED, HAVE RULED AS FALSE IDOLS. BUT WE COME WITH A NEW GOSPEL...
--THE HELL!?

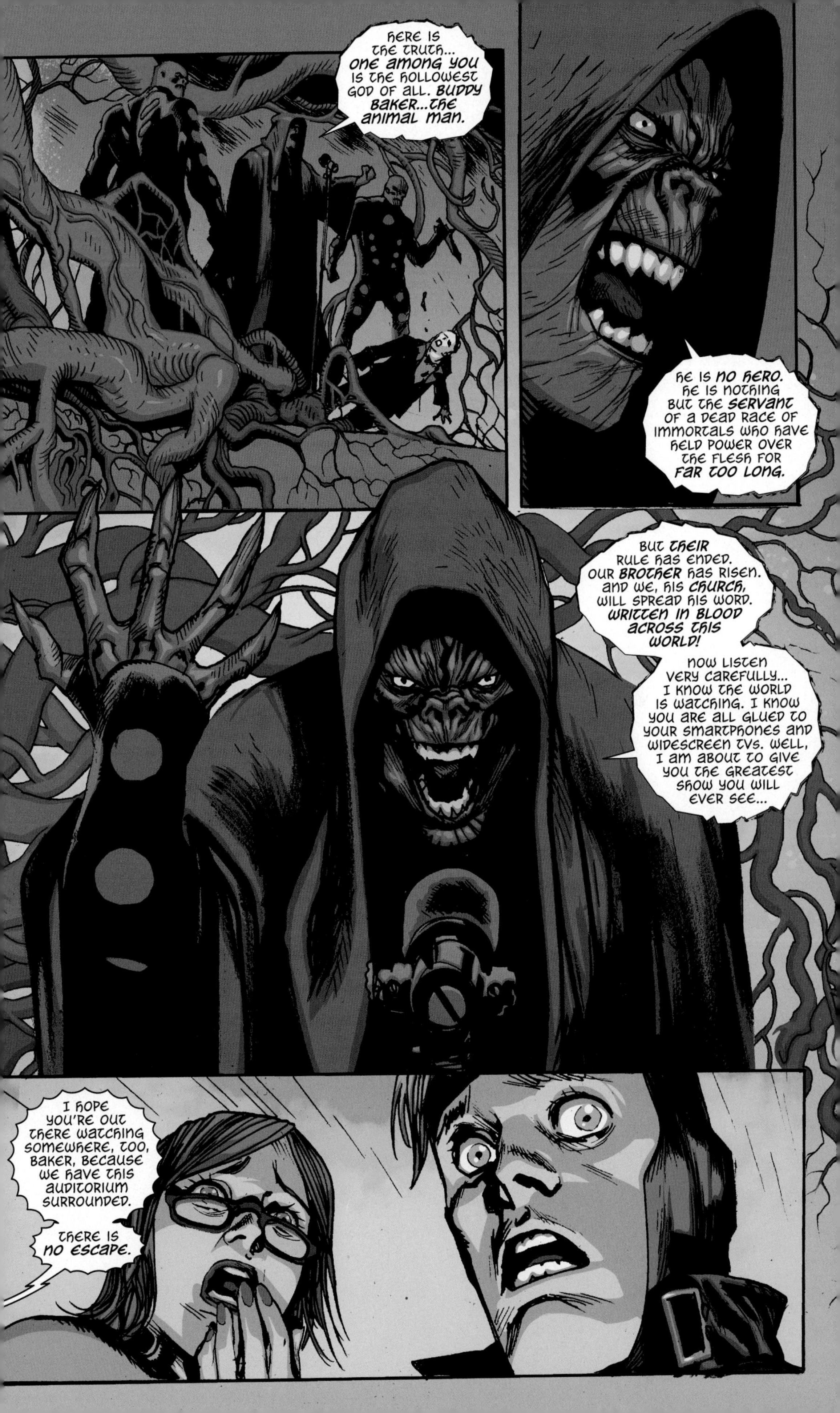

HERE IS THE TRUTH... ONE AMONG YOU IS THE HOLLOWEST GOD OF ALL. BUDDY BAKER...THE ANIMAL MAN.
HE IS NO HERO. HE IS NOTHING BUT THE SERVANT OF A DEAD RACE OF IMMORTALS WHO HAVE HELD POWER OVER THE FLESH FOR FAR TOO LONG.
BUT THEIR RULE HAS ENDED. OUR BROTHER HAS RISEN. AND WE, HIS CHURCH, WILL SPREAD HIS WORD. WRITTEN IN BLOOD ACROSS THIS WORLD!
NOW LISTEN VERY CAREFULLY... I KNOW THE WORLD IS WATCHING. I KNOW YOU ARE ALL GLUED TO YOUR SMARTPHONES AND WIDESCREEN TVS. WELL, I AM ABOUT TO GIVE YOU THE GREATEST SHOW YOU WILL EVER SEE...
I HOPE YOU'RE OUT THERE WATCHING SOMEWHERE, TOO, BAKER, BECAUSE WE HAVE THIS AUDITORIUM SURROUNDED.
THERE IS NO ESCAPE.

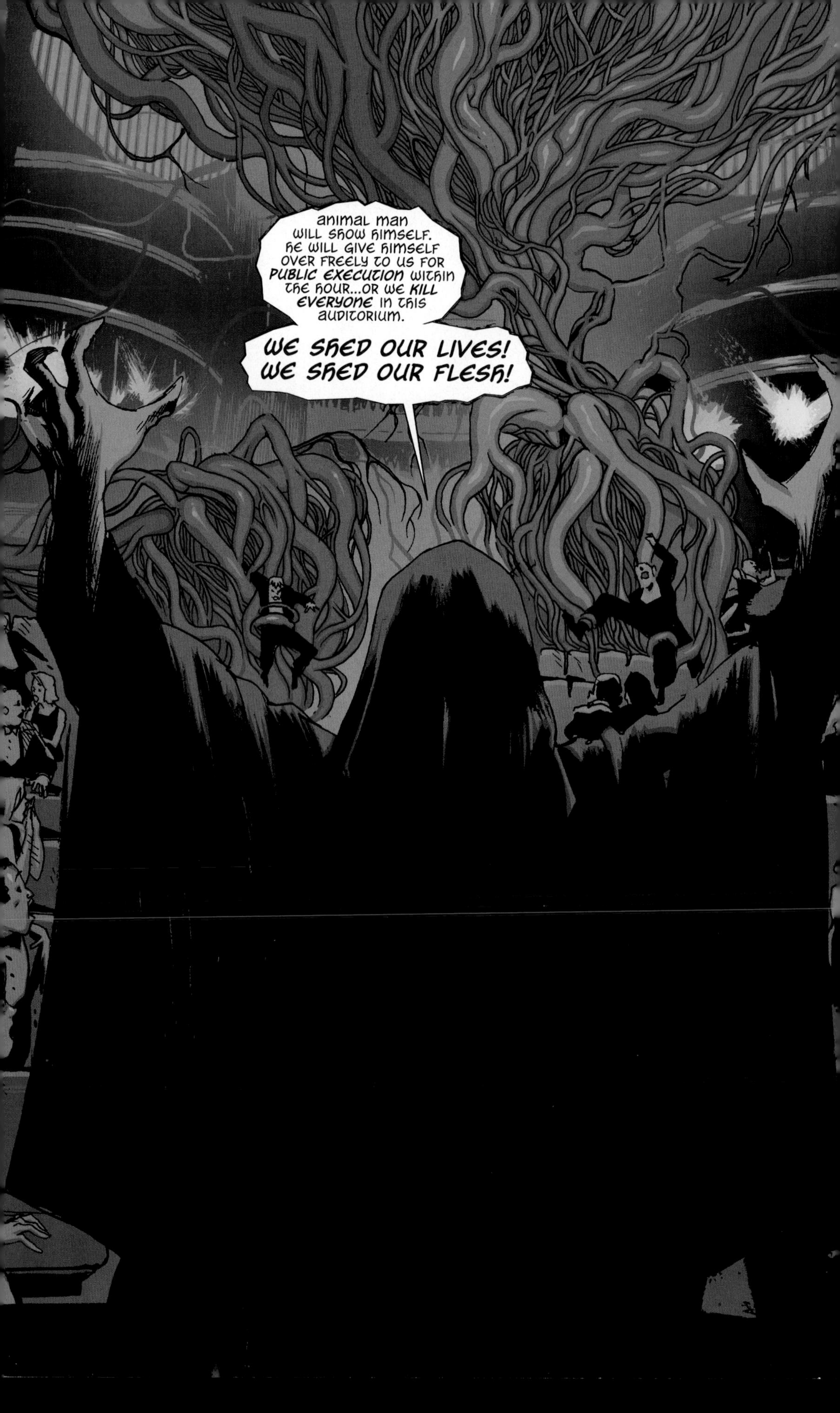
ANIMAL MAN WILL SHOW HIMSELF. HE WILL GIVE HIMSELF OVER FREELY TO US FOR PUBLIC EXECUTION WITHIN THE HOUR...OR WE KILL EVERYONE IN THIS AUDITORIUM.
WE SHED OUR LIVES! WE SHED OUR FLESH!

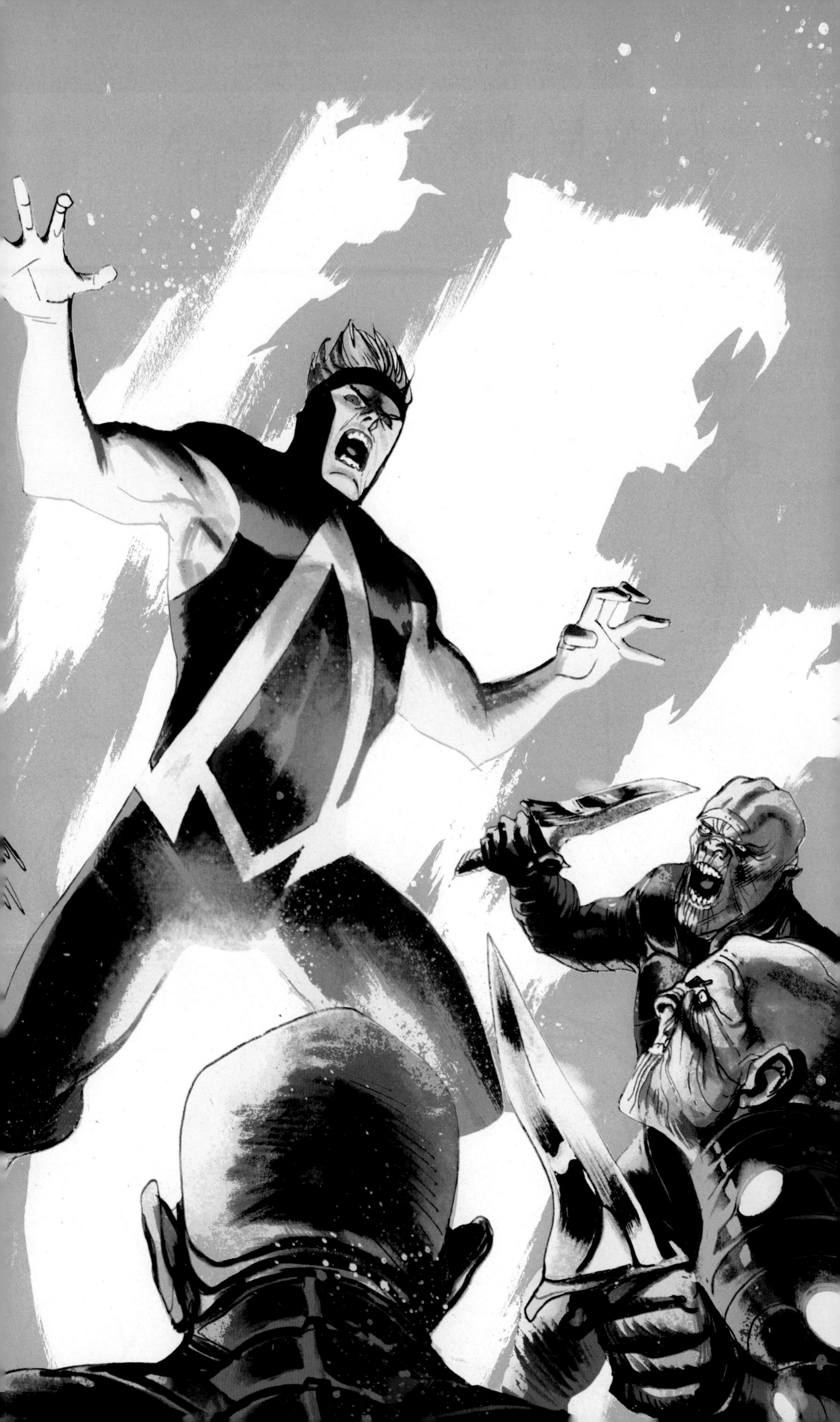

HOLLYWOOD BABYLON PART 2 OF 2
JEFF LEMIRE writer **RAFAEL ALBUQUERQUE** artist, interior and cover
DAVE McCAIG colorist **JARED K. FLETCHER** letterer

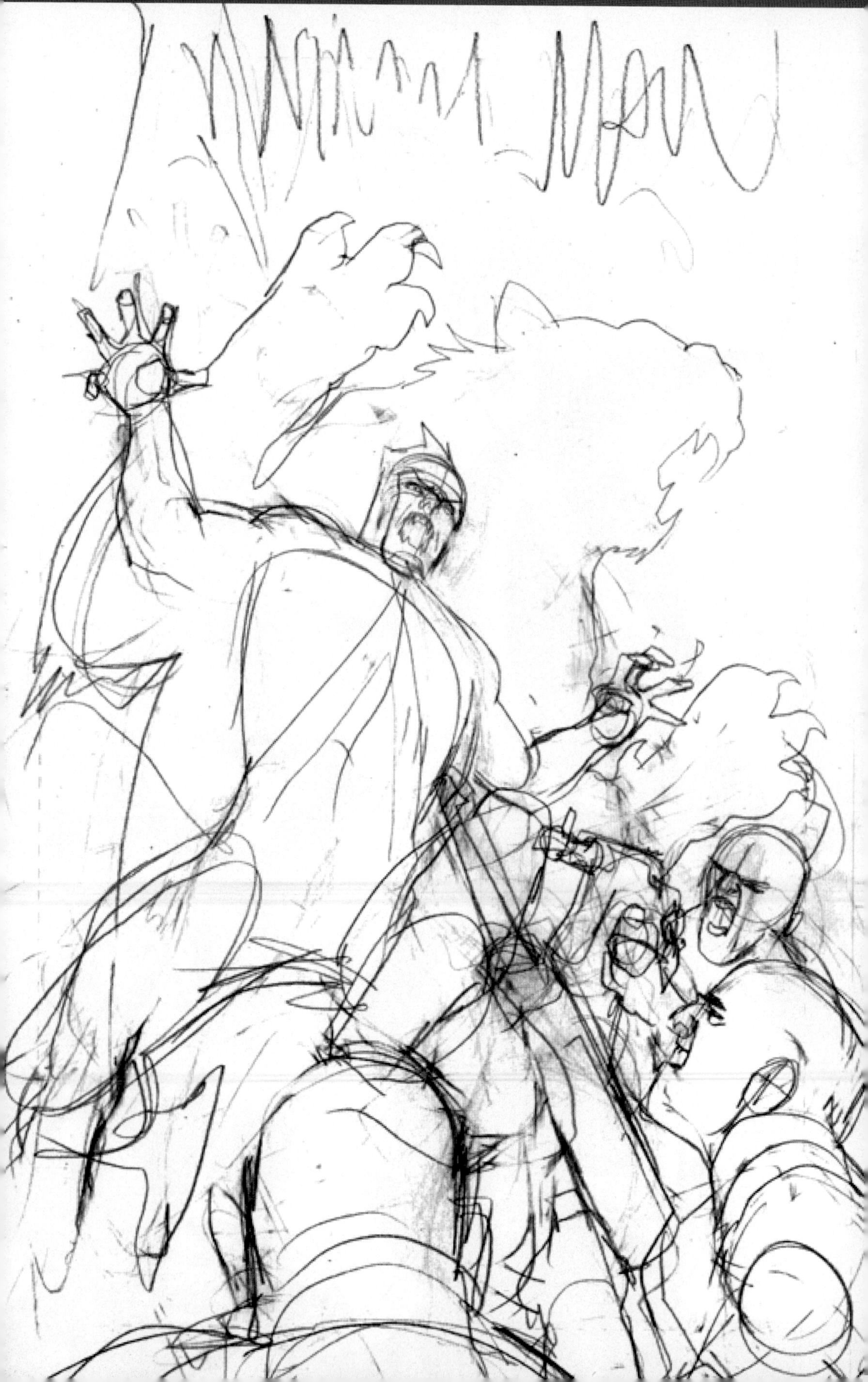

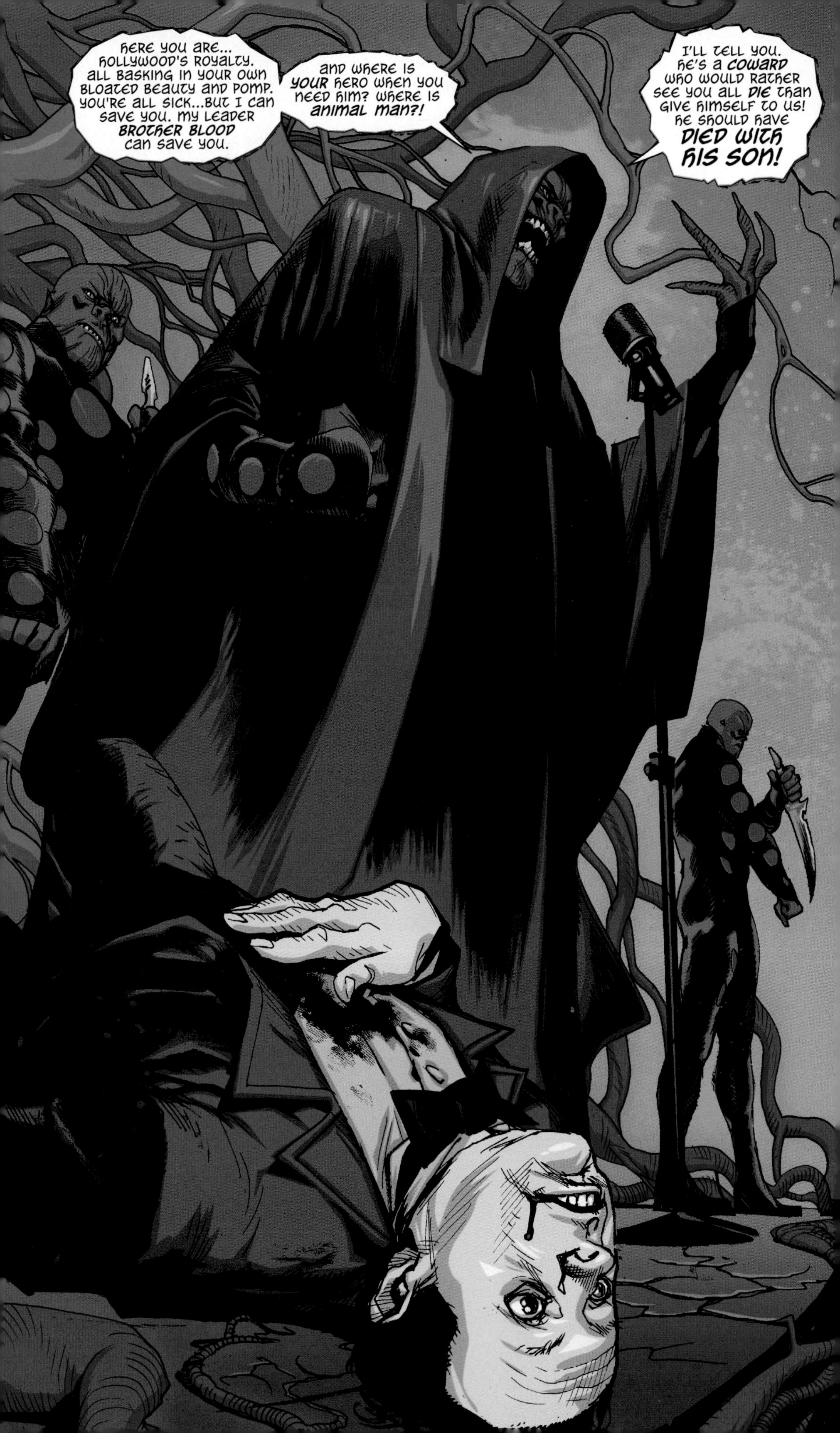
HERE YOU ARE... HOLLYWOOD'S ROYALTY. ALL BASKING IN YOUR OWN BLOATED BEAUTY AND POMP. YOU'RE ALL SICK...BUT I CAN SAVE YOU. MY LEADER BROTHER BLOOD CAN SAVE YOU.
AND WHERE IS YOUR HERO WHEN YOU NEED HIM? WHERE IS ANIMAL MAN?!
I'LL TELL YOU. HE'S A COWARD WHO WOULD RATHER SEE YOU ALL DIE THAN GIVE HIMSELF TO US! HE SHOULD HAVE DIED WITH HIS SON!

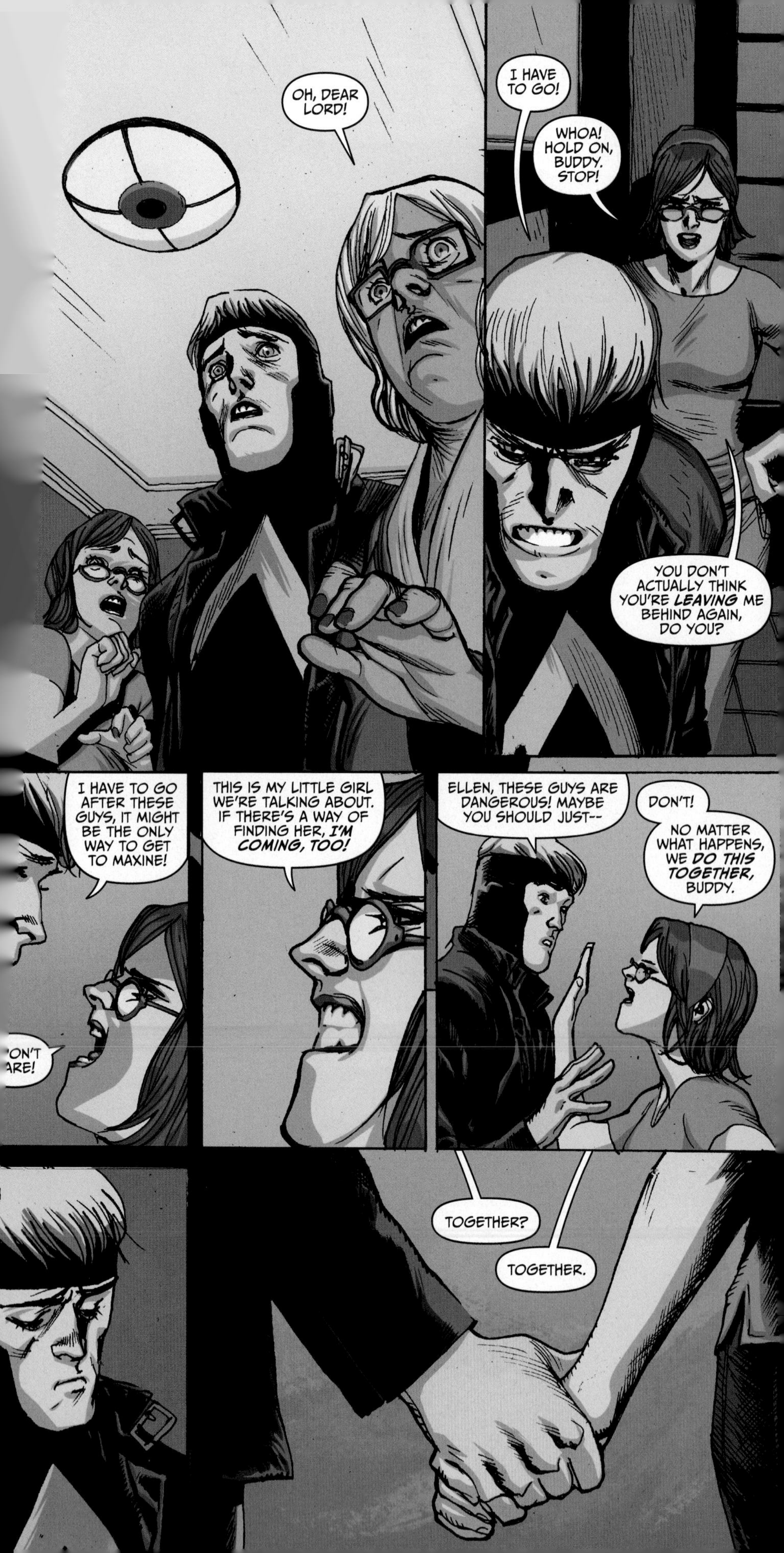
OH, DEAR LORD!
I HAVE TO GO!
WHOA! HOLD ON, BUDDY. STOP!
YOU DON'T ACTUALLY THINK YOU'RE *LEAVING* ME BEHIND AGAIN, DO YOU?
I HAVE TO GO AFTER THESE GUYS, IT MIGHT BE THE ONLY WAY TO GET TO MAXINE!
THIS IS MY LITTLE GIRL WE'RE TALKING ABOUT. IF THERE'S A WAY OF FINDING HER, *I'M COMING, TOO!*
ELLEN, THESE GUYS ARE DANGEROUS! MAYBE YOU SHOULD JUST--
DON'T!
NO MATTER WHAT HAPPENS, WE *DO THIS TOGETHER,* BUDDY.
TOGETHER?
TOGETHER.

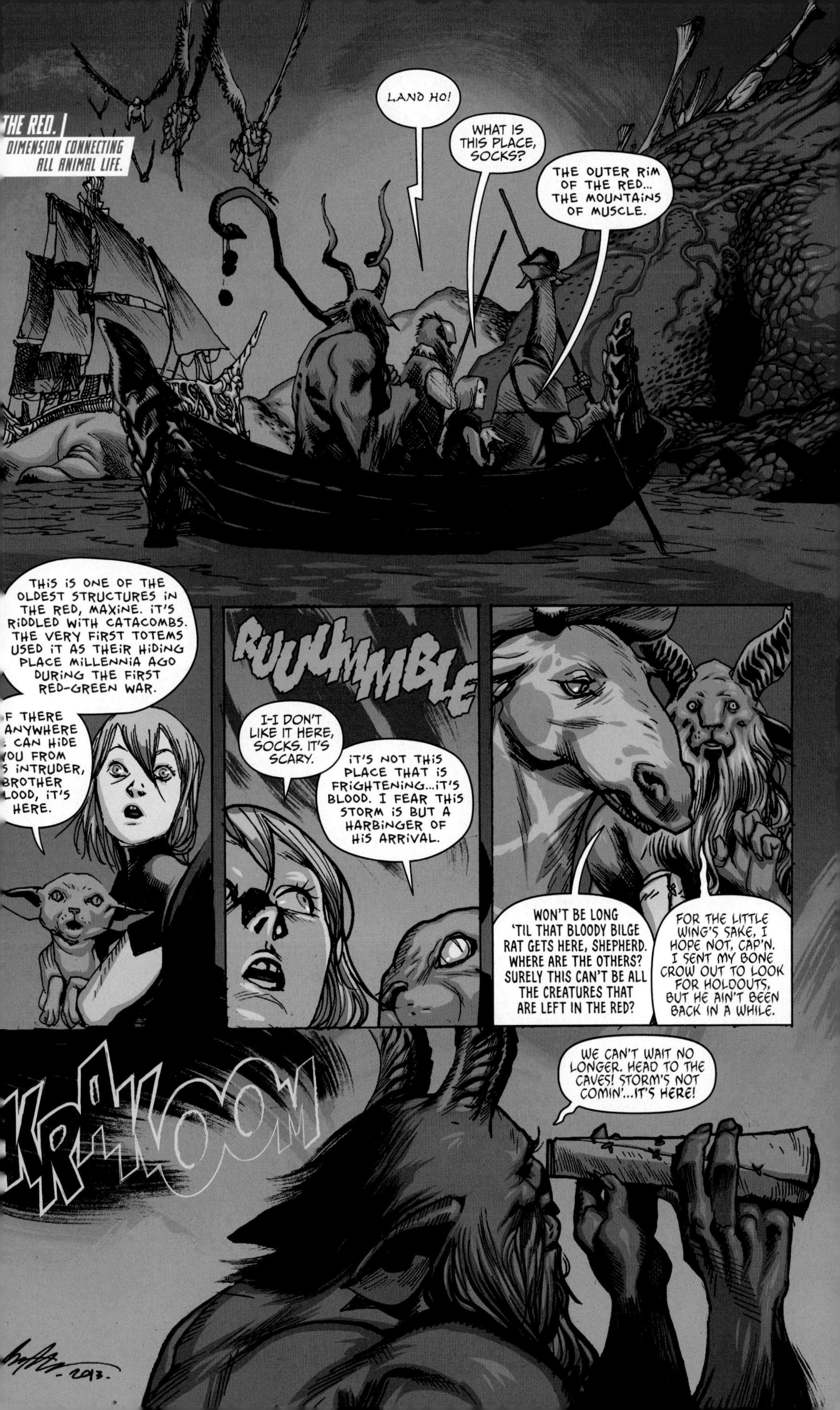
THE RED.
DIMENSION CONNECTING ALL ANIMAL LIFE.
LAND HO!
WHAT IS THIS PLACE, SOCKS?
THE OUTER RIM OF THE RED... THE MOUNTAINS OF MUSCLE.
THIS IS ONE OF THE OLDEST STRUCTURES IN THE RED, MAXINE. IT'S RIDDLED WITH CATACOMBS. THE VERY FIRST TOTEMS USED IT AS THEIR HIDING PLACE MILLENNIA AGO DURING THE FIRST RED-GREEN WAR.
F THERE ANYWHERE CAN HIDE YOU FROM S INTRUDER, BROTHER LOOD, IT'S HERE.
RUUUMMBLE
I-I DON'T LIKE IT HERE, SOCKS. IT'S SCARY.
IT'S NOT THIS PLACE THAT IS FRIGHTENING...IT'S BLOOD. I FEAR THIS STORM IS BUT A HARBINGER OF HIS ARRIVAL.
WON'T BE LONG 'TIL THAT BLOODY BILGE RAT GETS HERE, SHEPHERD. WHERE ARE THE OTHERS? SURELY THIS CAN'T BE ALL THE CREATURES THAT ARE LEFT IN THE RED?
FOR THE LITTLE WING'S SAKE, I HOPE NOT, CAP'N. I SENT MY BONE CROW OUT TO LOOK FOR HOLDOUTS, BUT HE AIN'T BEEN BACK IN A WHILE.
KRAKOOM
WE CAN'T WAIT NO LONGER. HEAD TO THE CAVES! STORM'S NOT COMIN'...IT'S HERE!
-2013-

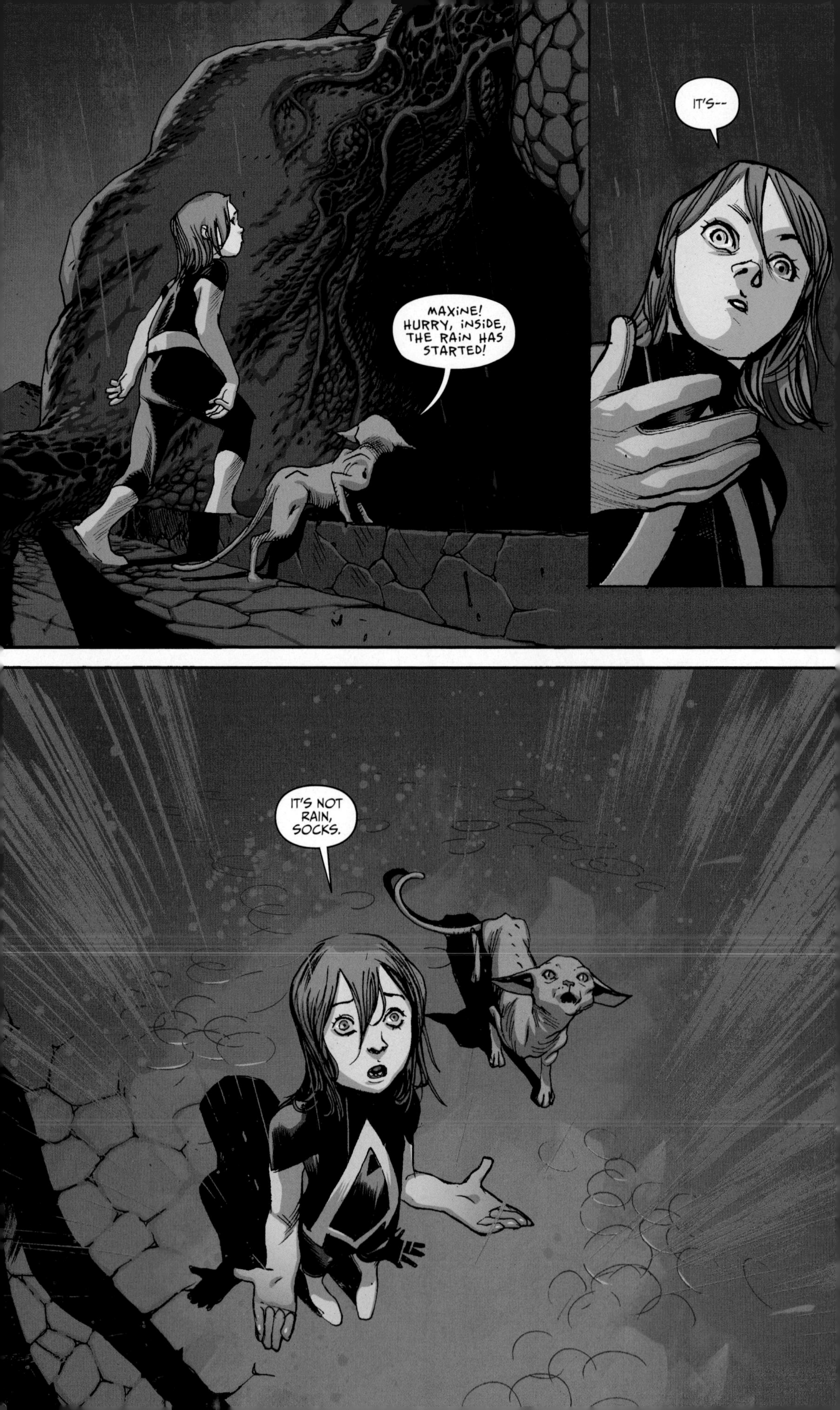
MAXINE! HURRY, INSIDE, THE RAIN HAS STARTED!
IT'S--
IT'S NOT RAIN, SOCKS.

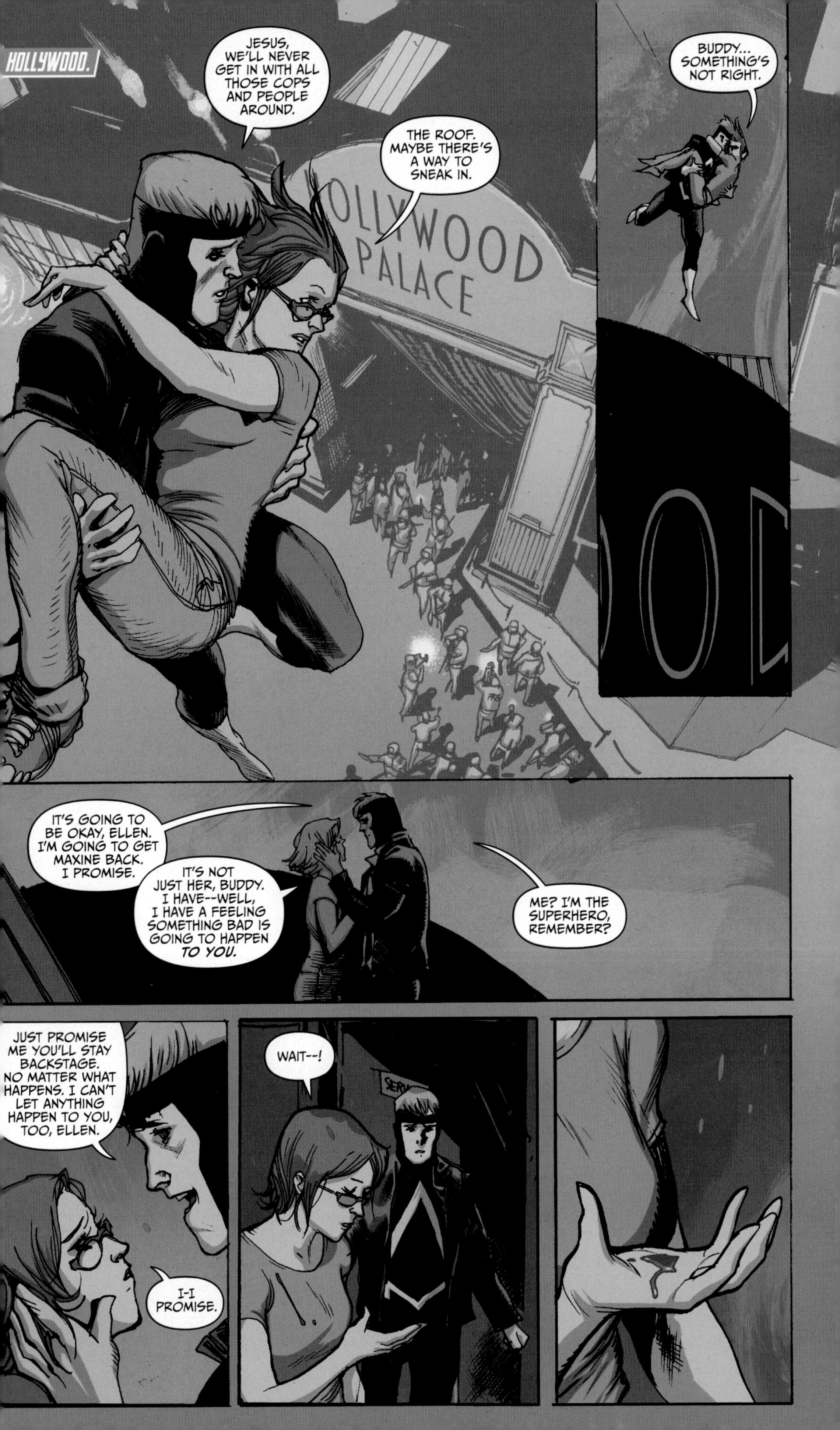
HOLLYWOOD.
JESUS, WE'LL NEVER GET IN WITH ALL THOSE COPS AND PEOPLE AROUND.
THE ROOF. MAYBE THERE'S A WAY TO SNEAK IN.
HOLLYWOOD PALACE
BUDDY... SOMETHING'S NOT RIGHT.
IT'S GOING TO BE OKAY, ELLEN. I'M GOING TO GET MAXINE BACK. I PROMISE.
IT'S NOT JUST HER, BUDDY. I HAVE--WELL, I HAVE A FEELING SOMETHING BAD IS GOING TO HAPPEN *TO YOU.*
ME? I'M THE SUPERHERO, REMEMBER?
JUST PROMISE ME YOU'LL STAY BACKSTAGE. NO MATTER WHAT HAPPENS. I CAN'T LET ANYTHING HAPPEN TO YOU, TOO, ELLEN.
I-I PROMISE.
WAIT--!

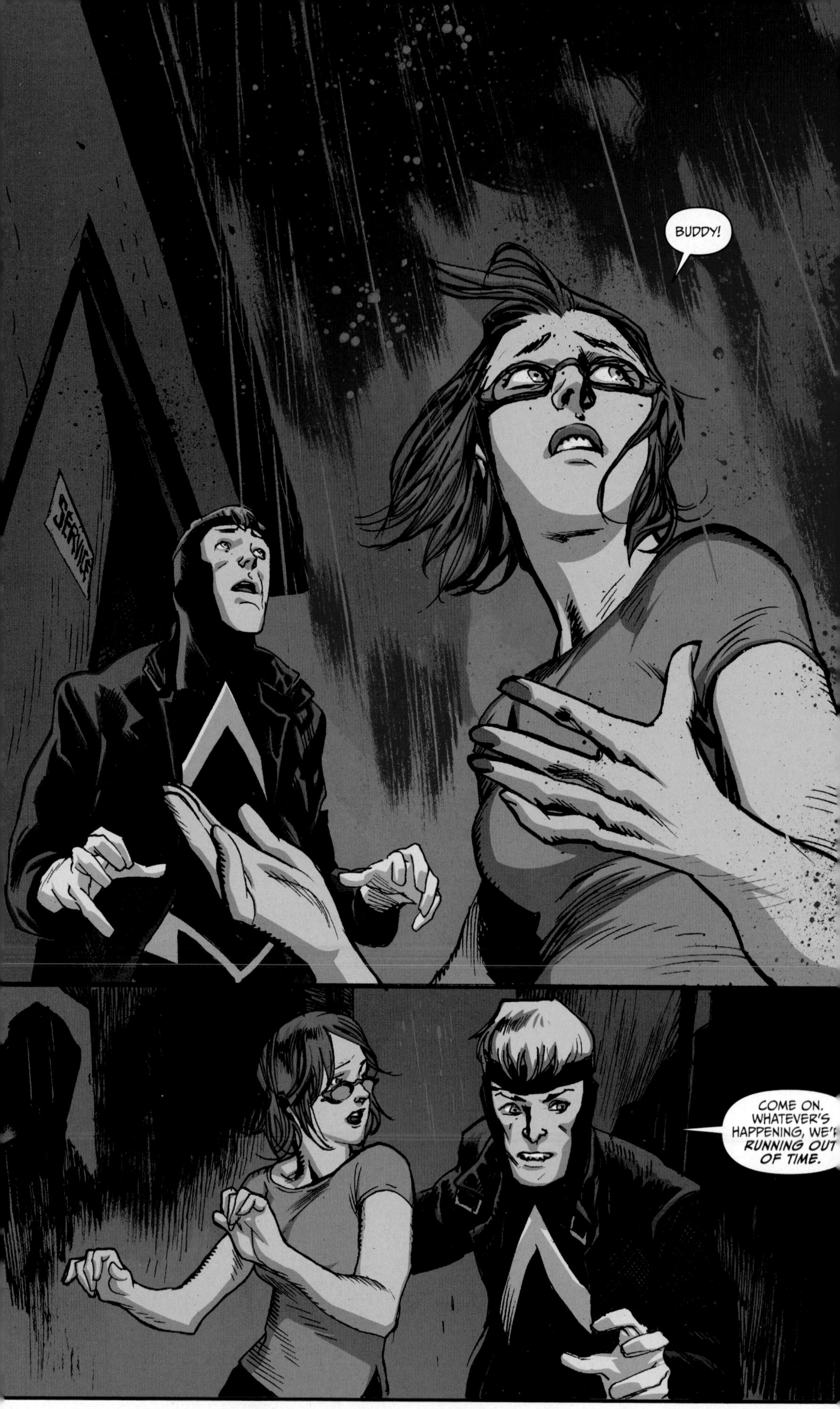
SERVICE
BUDDY!
COME ON. WHATEVER'S HAPPENING, WE' RUNNING OUT OF TIME.

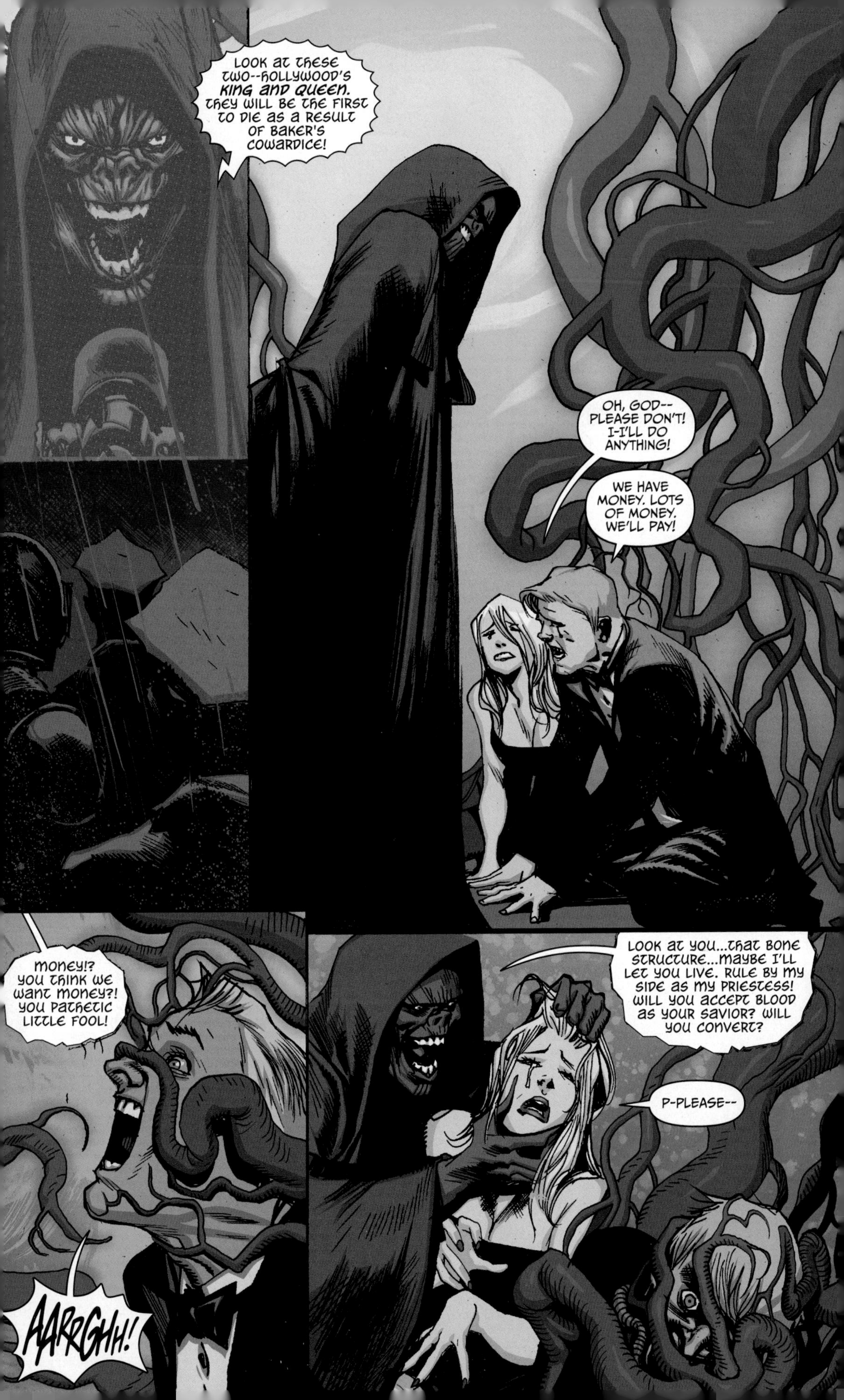
LOOK AT THESE TWO--HOLLYWOOD'S KING AND QUEEN. THEY WILL BE THE FIRST TO DIE AS A RESULT OF BAKER'S COWARDICE!
OH, GOD-- PLEASE DON'T! I-I'LL DO ANYTHING!
WE HAVE MONEY. LOTS OF MONEY. WE'LL PAY!
MONEY!? YOU THINK WE WANT MONEY?! YOU PATHETIC LITTLE FOOL!
AARRGHH!
LOOK AT YOU...THAT BONE STRUCTURE...MAYBE I'LL LET YOU LIVE. RULE BY MY SIDE AS MY PRIESTESS! WILL YOU ACCEPT BLOOD AS YOUR SAVIOR? WILL YOU CONVERT?
P-PLEASE--

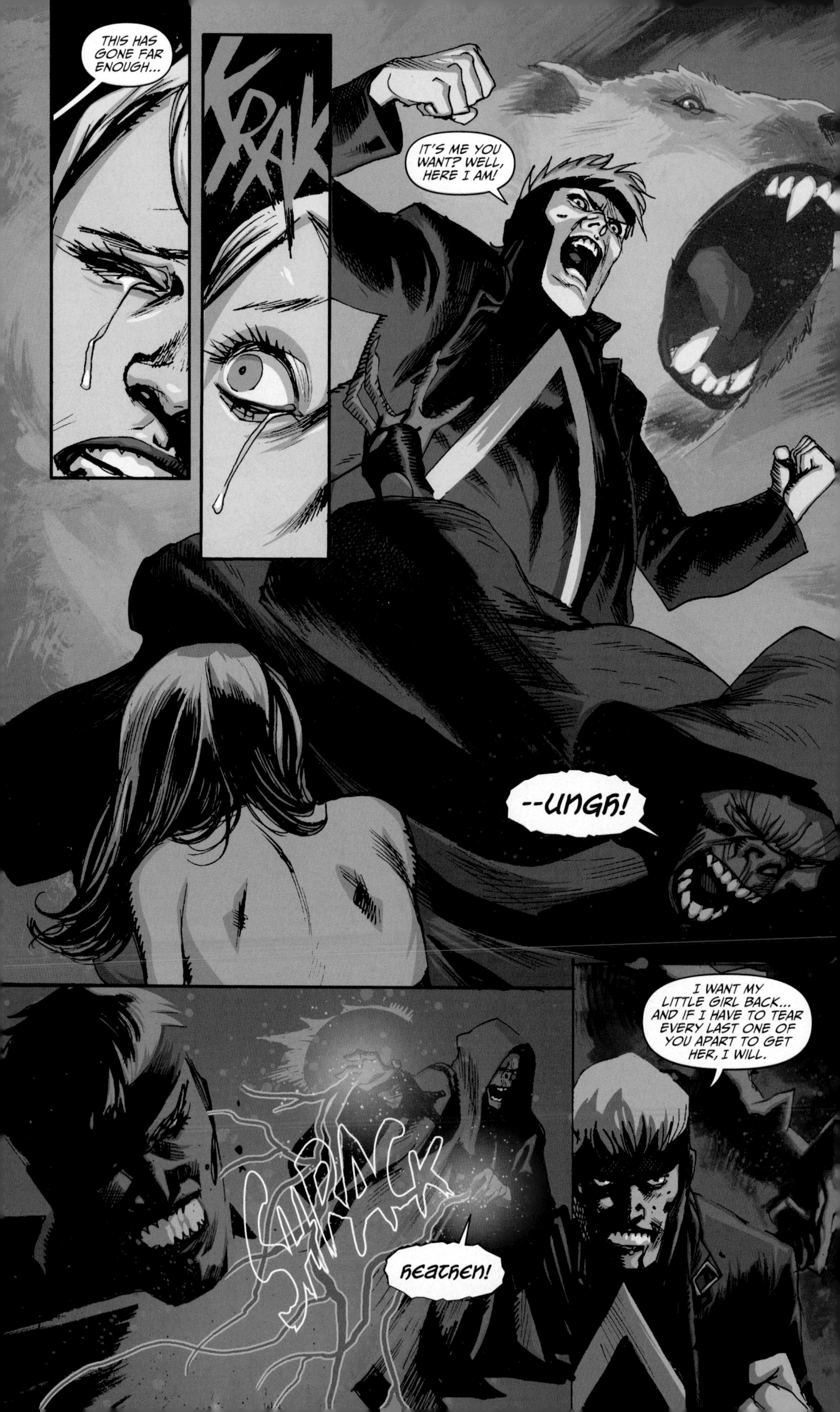
THIS HAS GONE FAR ENOUGH...
KRAK
IT'S ME YOU WANT? WELL, HERE I AM!
--UNGH!
SHRACK
HEATHEN!
I WANT MY LITTLE GIRL BACK... AND IF I HAVE TO TEAR EVERY LAST ONE OF YOU APART TO GET HER, I WILL.

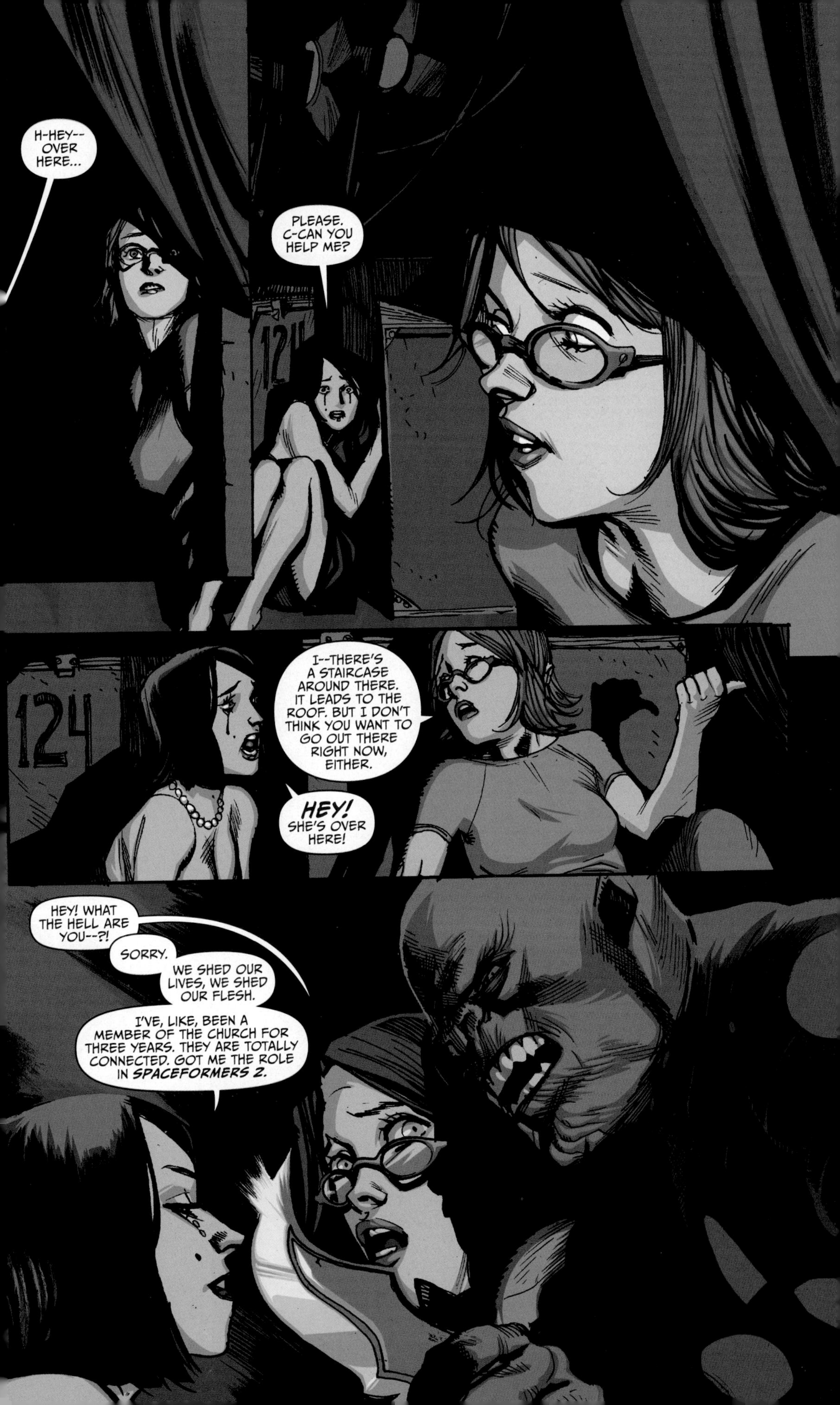

H-HEY-- OVER HERE...
PLEASE. C-CAN YOU HELP ME?
124
I--THERE'S A STAIRCASE AROUND THERE. IT LEADS TO THE ROOF. BUT I DON'T THINK YOU WANT TO GO OUT THERE RIGHT NOW, EITHER.
HEY! SHE'S OVER HERE!
HEY! WHAT THE HELL ARE YOU--?!
SORRY.
WE SHED OUR LIVES, WE SHED OUR FLESH.
I'VE, LIKE, BEEN A MEMBER OF THE CHURCH FOR THREE YEARS. THEY ARE TOTALLY CONNECTED. GOT ME THE ROLE IN SPACEFORMERS 2.

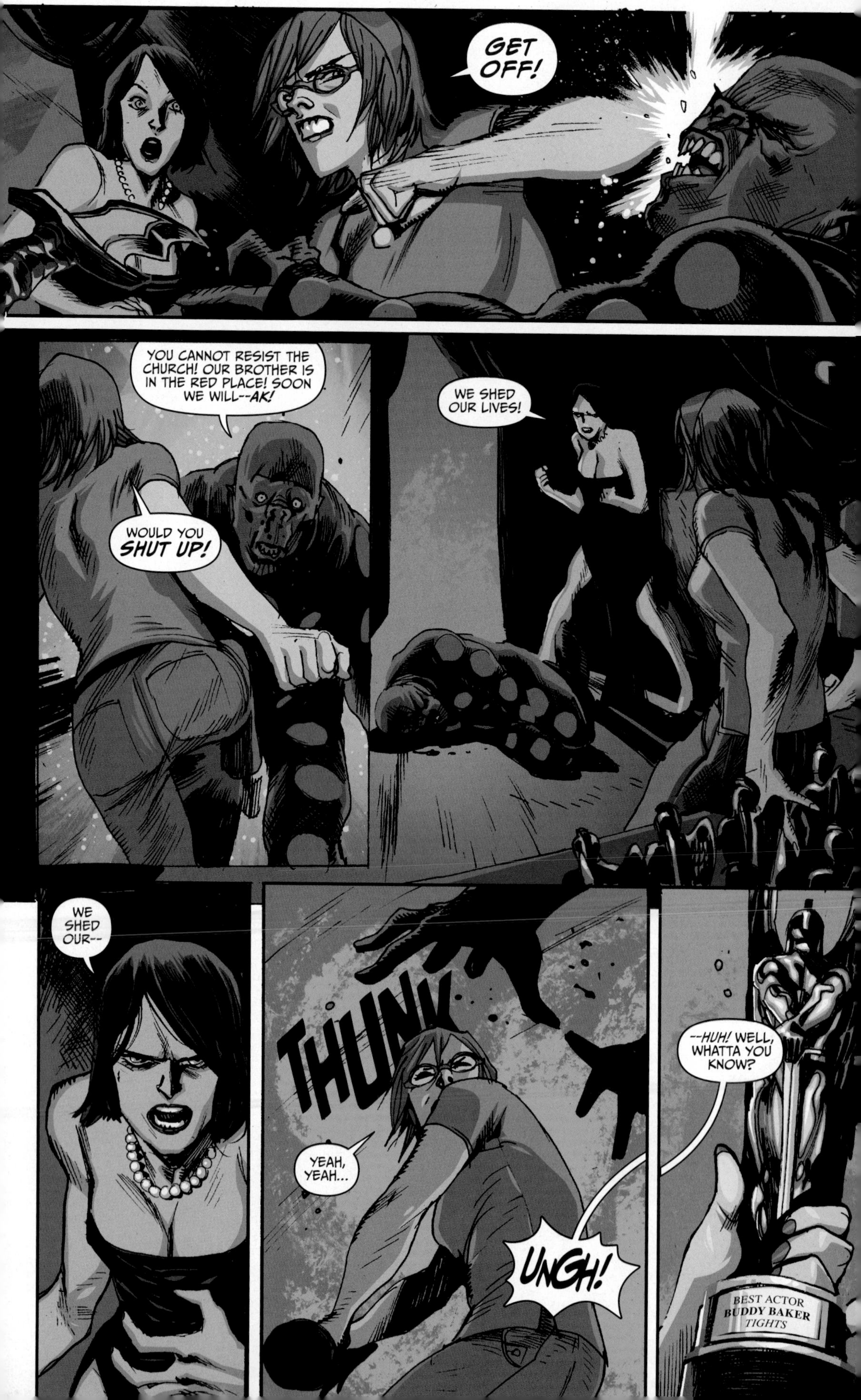
GET OFF!
YOU CANNOT RESIST THE CHURCH! OUR BROTHER IS IN THE RED PLACE! SOON WE WILL--AK!
WOULD YOU SHUT UP!
WE SHED OUR LIVES!
WE SHED OUR--
THUNK
YEAH, YEAH...
UNGH!
--HUH! WELL, WHATTA YOU KNOW?
BEST ACTOR
BUDDY BAKER
TIGHTS

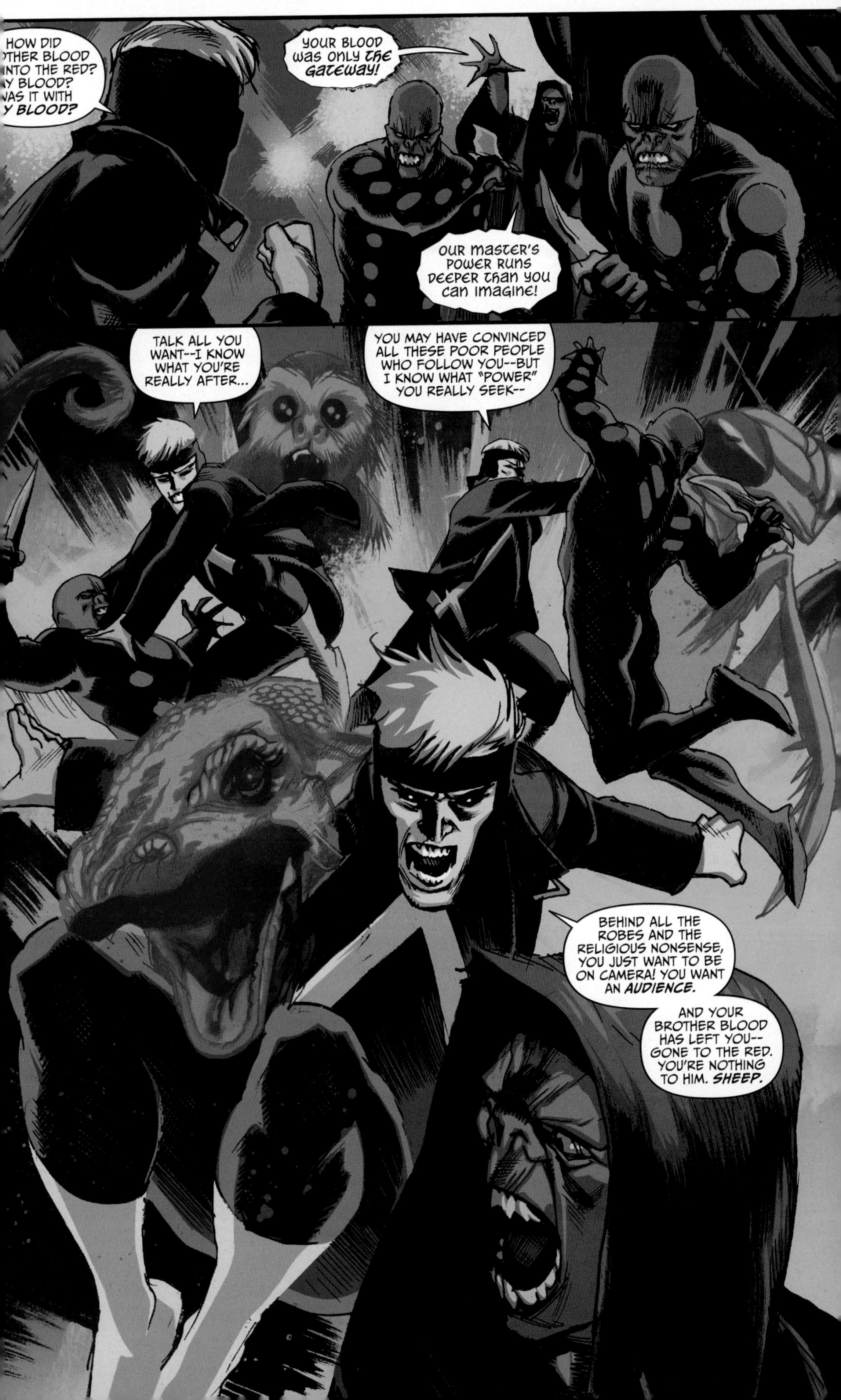

HOW DID
THER BLOOD
INTO THE RED?
Y BLOOD?
VAS IT WITH
Y BLOOD?
YOUR BLOOD WAS ONLY THE GATEWAY!
OUR MASTER'S POWER RUNS DEEPER THAN YOU CAN IMAGINE!
TALK ALL YOU WANT--I KNOW WHAT YOU'RE REALLY AFTER...
YOU MAY HAVE CONVINCED ALL THESE POOR PEOPLE WHO FOLLOW YOU--BUT I KNOW WHAT "POWER" YOU REALLY SEEK--
BEHIND ALL THE ROBES AND THE RELIGIOUS NONSENSE, YOU JUST WANT TO BE ON CAMERA! YOU WANT AN AUDIENCE.
AND YOUR BROTHER BLOOD HAS LEFT YOU--GONE TO THE RED. YOU'RE NOTHING TO HIM. SHEEP.

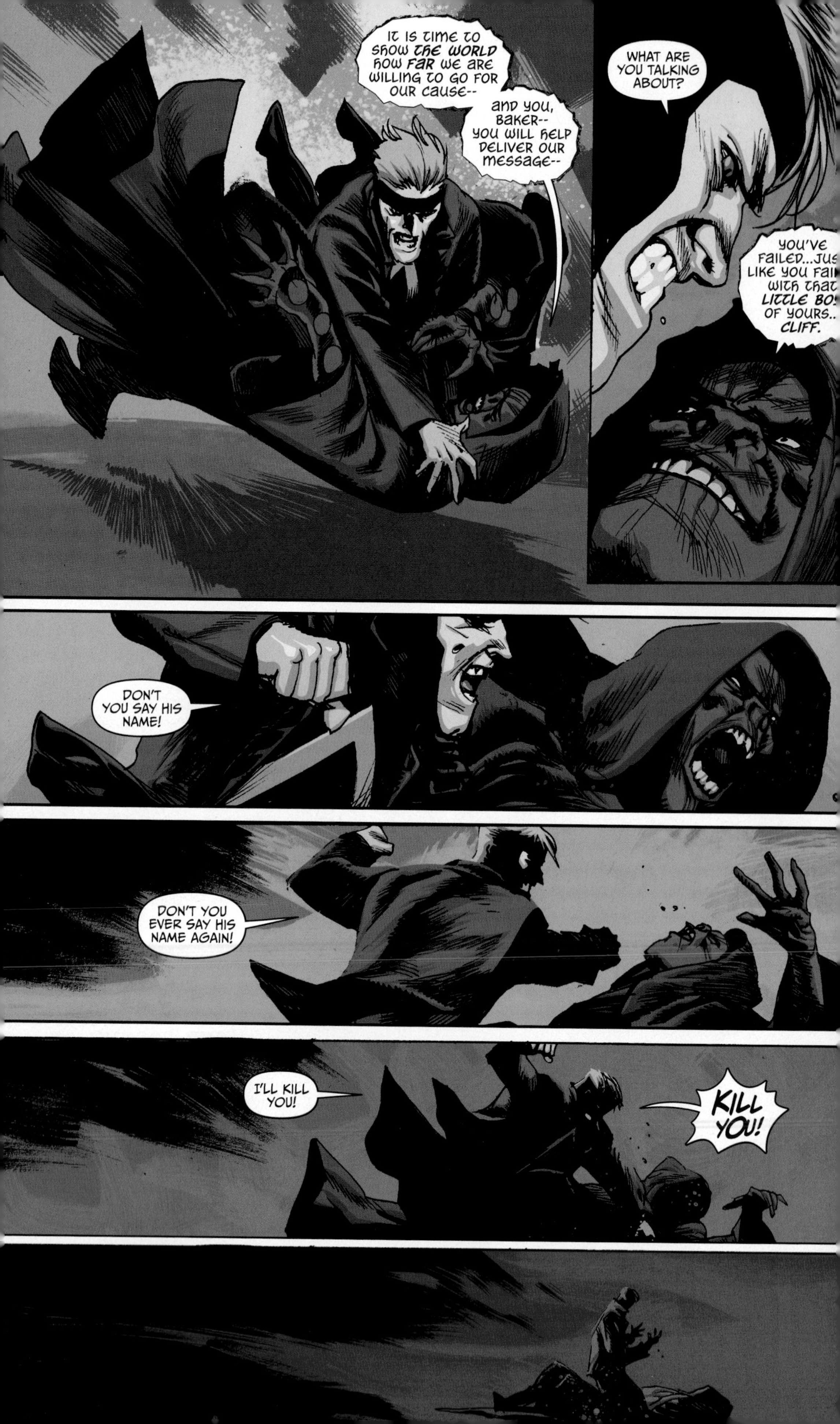
IT IS TIME TO SHOW THE WORLD HOW FAR WE ARE WILLING TO GO FOR OUR CAUSE--
AND YOU, BAKER-- YOU WILL HELP DELIVER OUR MESSAGE--
WHAT ARE YOU TALKING ABOUT?
YOU'VE FAILED...JUS LIKE YOU FAI WITH THAT LITTLE BO OF YOURS.. CLIFF.
DON'T YOU SAY HIS NAME!
DON'T YOU EVER SAY HIS NAME AGAIN!
I'LL KILL YOU!
KILL YOU!

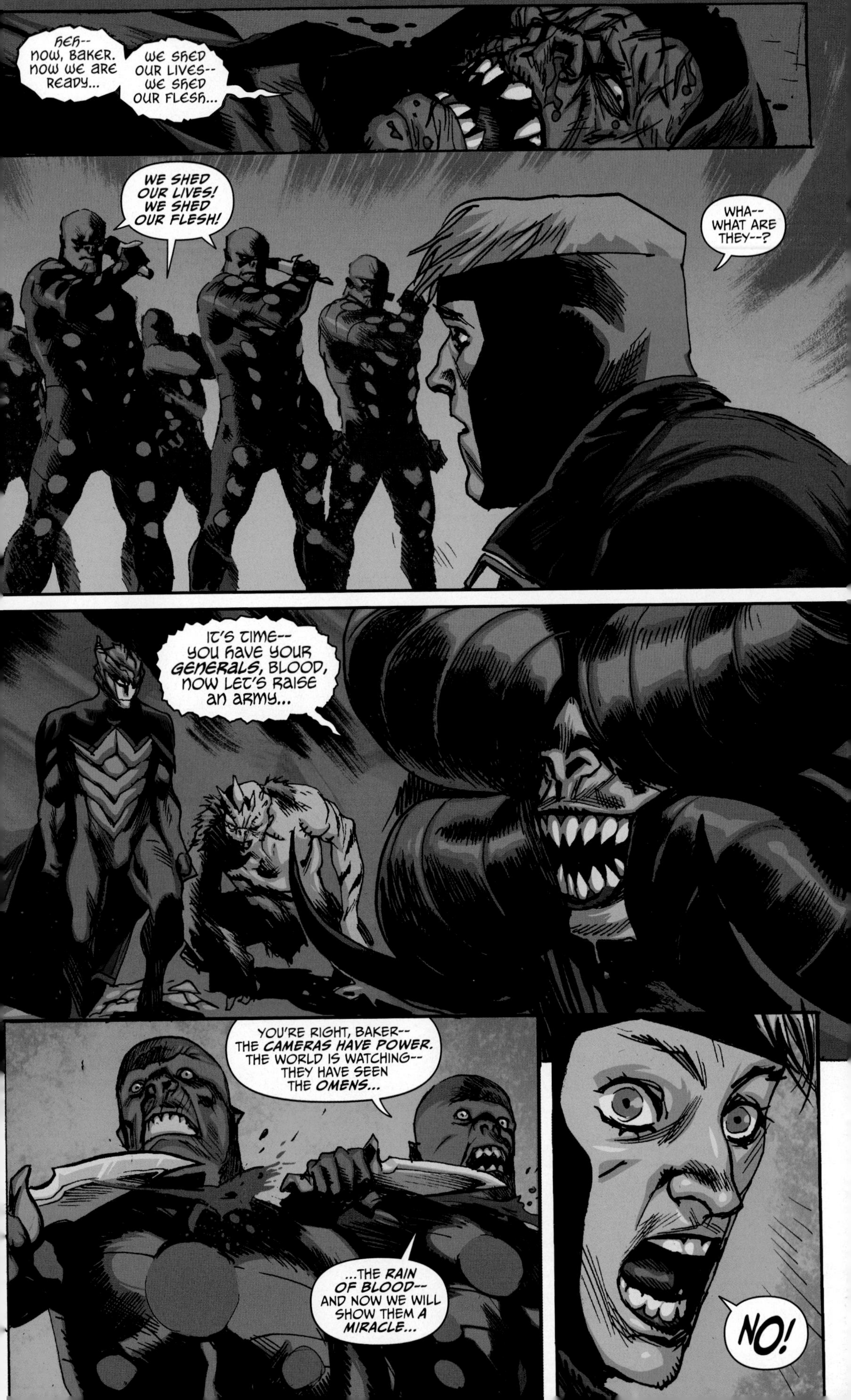
HEH--
NOW, BAKER.
NOW WE ARE
READY...
WE SHED
OUR LIVES--
WE SHED
OUR FLESH...
WE SHED
OUR LIVES!
WE SHED
OUR FLESH!
WHA--
WHAT ARE
THEY--?
IT'S TIME--
YOU HAVE YOUR
GENERALS, BLOOD,
NOW LET'S RAISE
AN ARMY...
YOU'RE RIGHT, BAKER--
THE CAMERAS HAVE POWER.
THE WORLD IS WATCHING--
THEY HAVE SEEN
THE OMENS...
...THE RAIN
OF BLOOD--
AND NOW WE WILL
SHOW THEM A
MIRACLE...
NO!

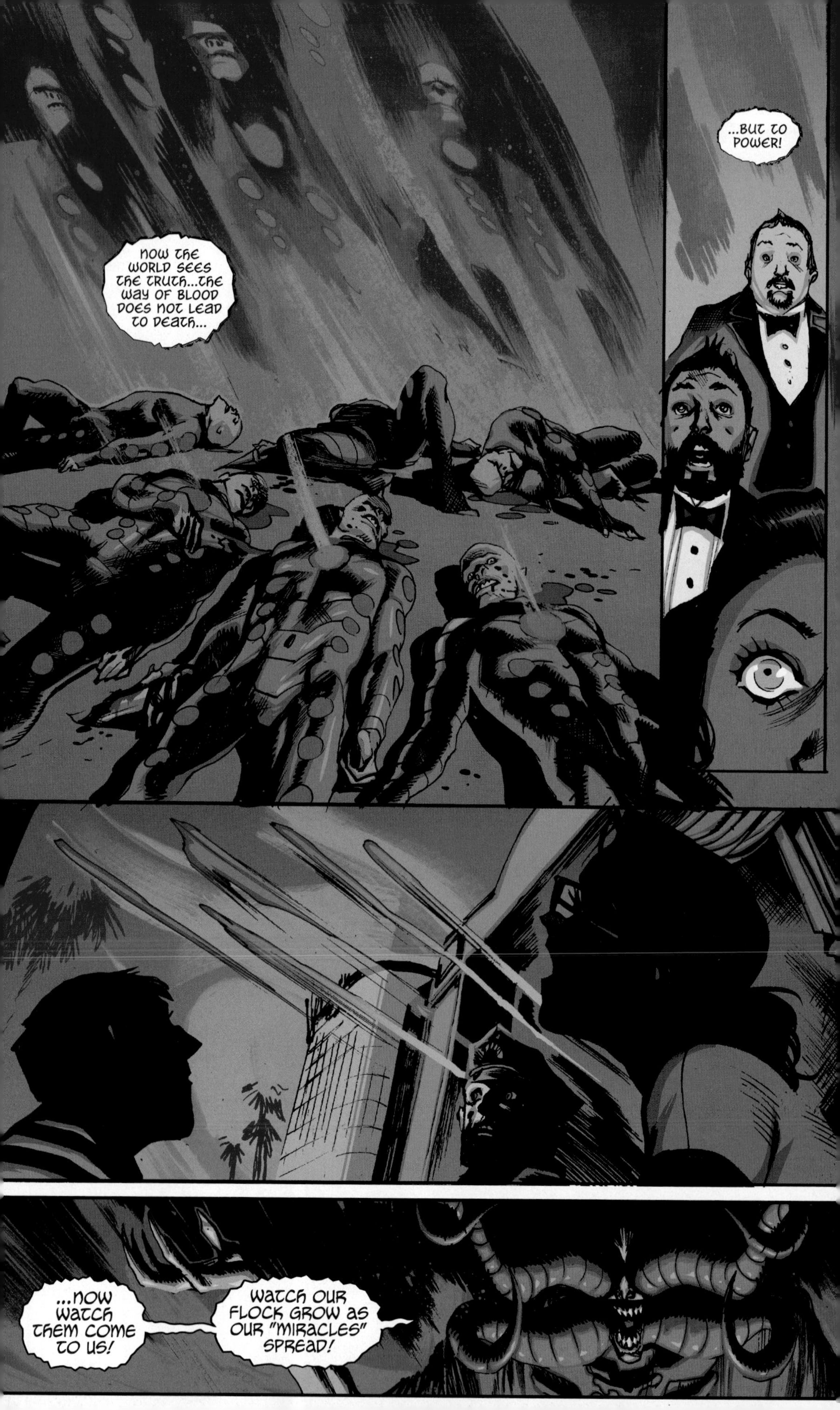
NOW THE WORLD SEES THE TRUTH...THE WAY OF BLOOD DOES NOT LEAD TO DEATH...
...BUT TO POWER!
...NOW WATCH THEM COME TO US!
WATCH OUR FLOCK GROW AS OUR "MIRACLES" SPREAD!

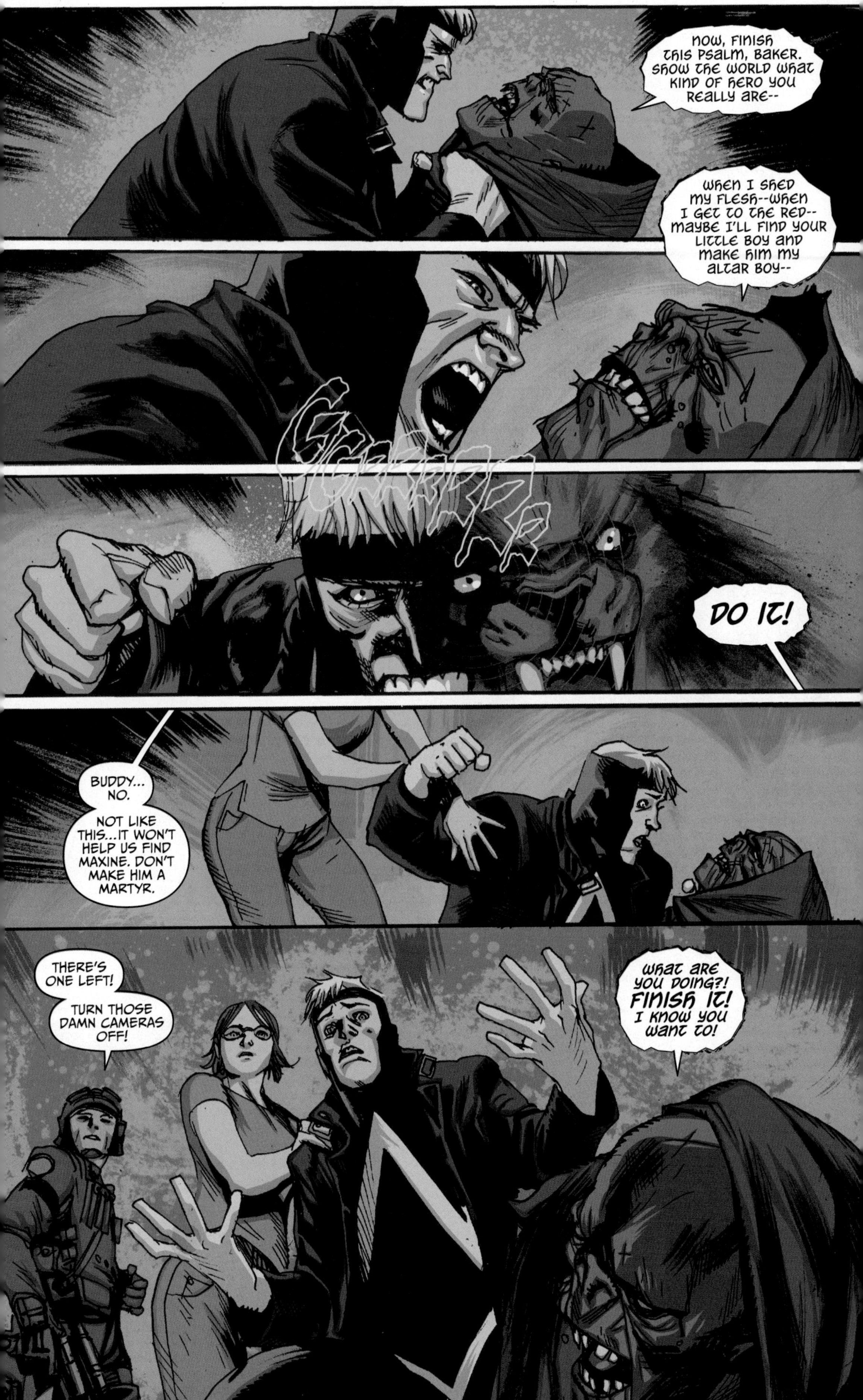
NOW, FINISH THIS PSALM, BAKER. SHOW THE WORLD WHAT KIND OF HERO YOU REALLY ARE--
WHEN I SHED MY FLESH--WHEN I GET TO THE RED--MAYBE I'LL FIND YOUR LITTLE BOY AND MAKE HIM MY ALTAR BOY--
DO IT!
BUDDY... NO.
NOT LIKE THIS...IT WON'T HELP US FIND MAXINE. DON'T MAKE HIM A MARTYR.
THERE'S ONE LEFT!
TURN THOSE DAMN CAMERAS OFF!
WHAT ARE YOU DOING?! FINISH IT! I KNOW YOU WANT TO!

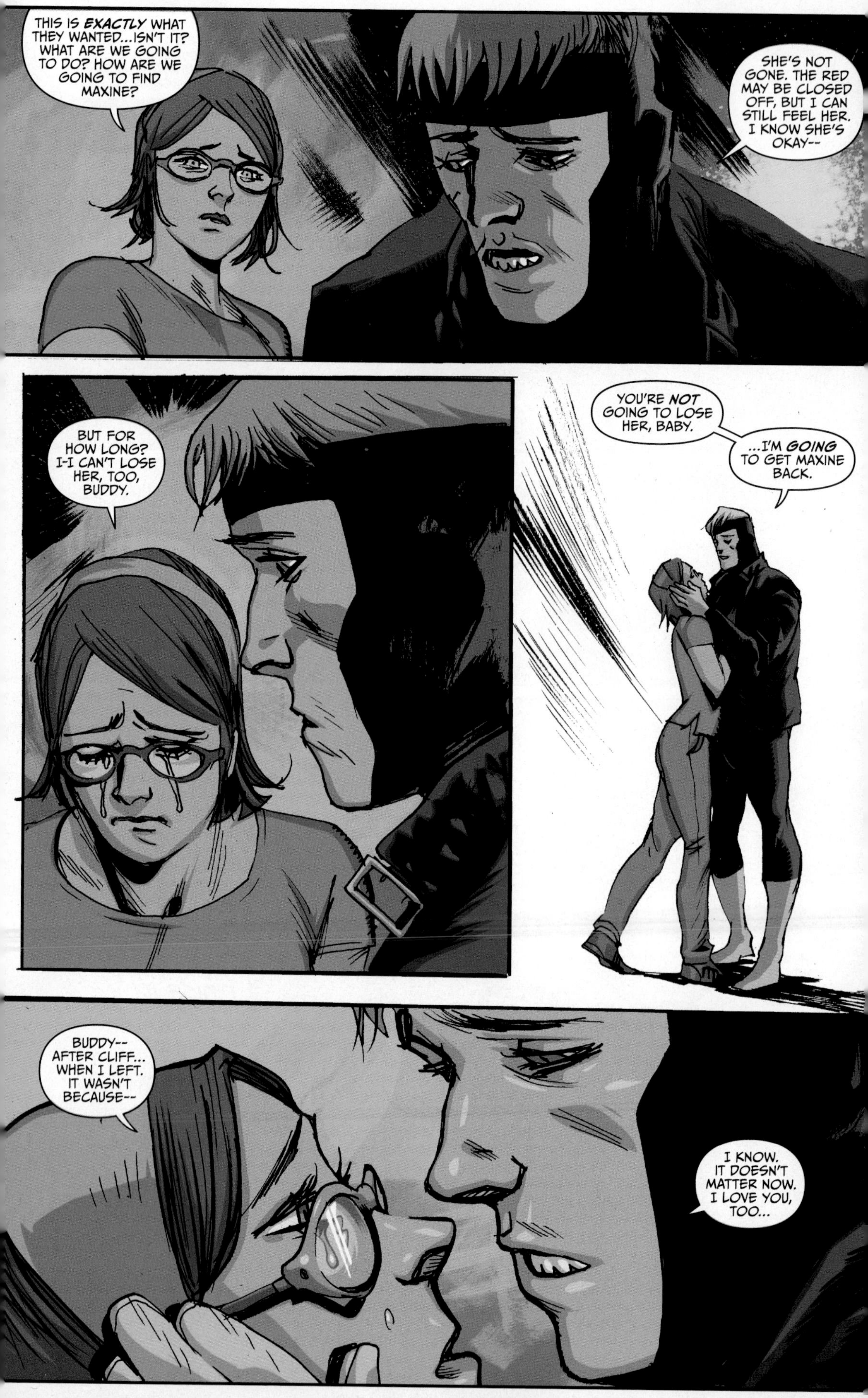
THIS IS EXACTLY WHAT THEY WANTED...ISN'T IT? WHAT ARE WE GOING TO DO? HOW ARE WE GOING TO FIND MAXINE?
SHE'S NOT GONE. THE RED MAY BE CLOSED OFF, BUT I CAN STILL FEEL HER. I KNOW SHE'S OKAY--
BUT FOR HOW LONG? I-I CAN'T LOSE HER, TOO, BUDDY.
YOU'RE NOT GOING TO LOSE HER, BABY.
...I'M GOING TO GET MAXINE BACK.
BUDDY-- AFTER CLIFF... WHEN I LEFT. IT WASN'T BECAUSE--
I KNOW. IT DOESN'T MATTER NOW. I LOVE YOU, TOO...

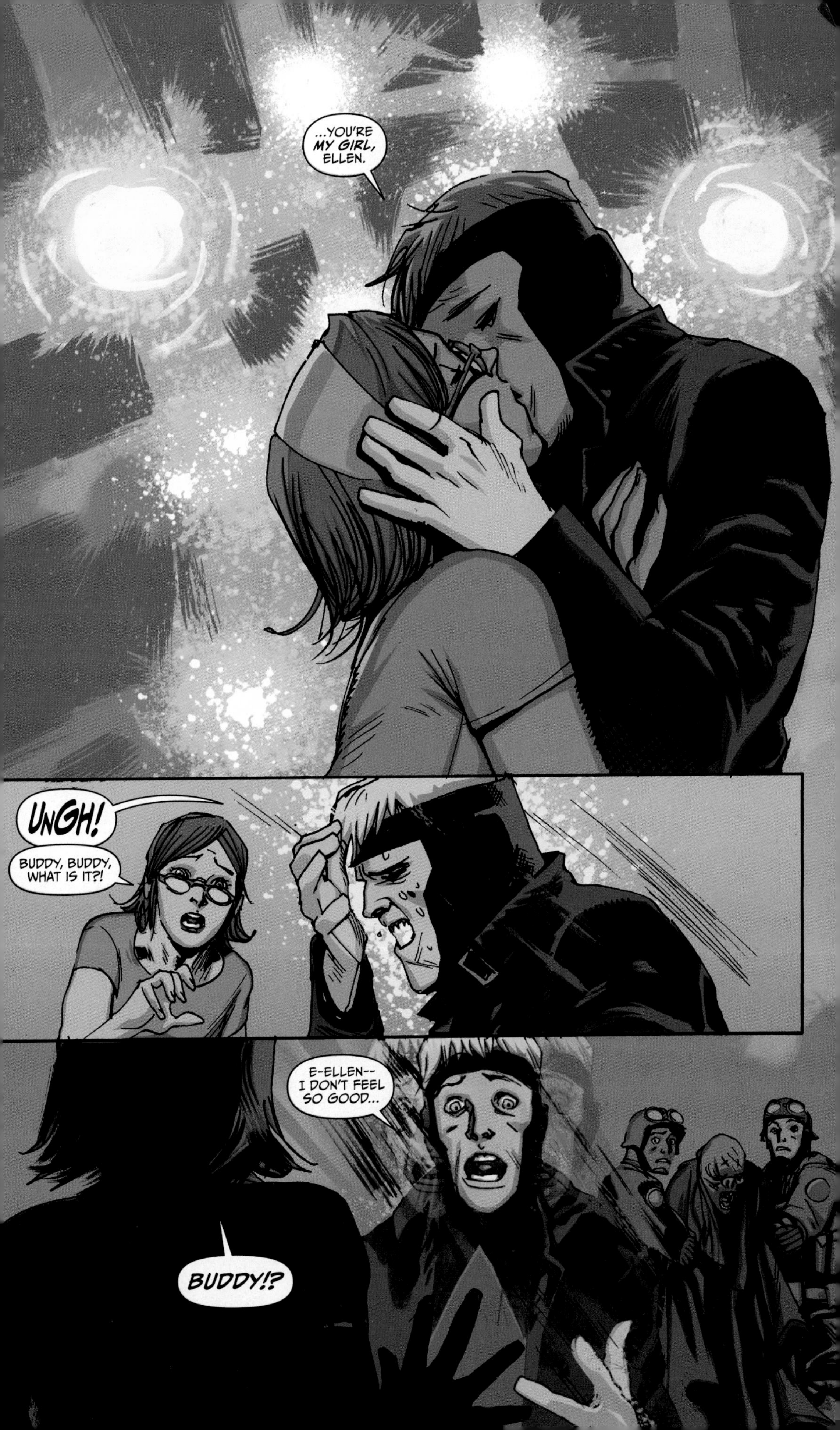
...YOU'RE MY GIRL, ELLEN.
UNGH!
BUDDY, BUDDY, WHAT IS IT?!
E-ELLEN-- I DON'T FEEL SO GOOD...
BUDDY!?

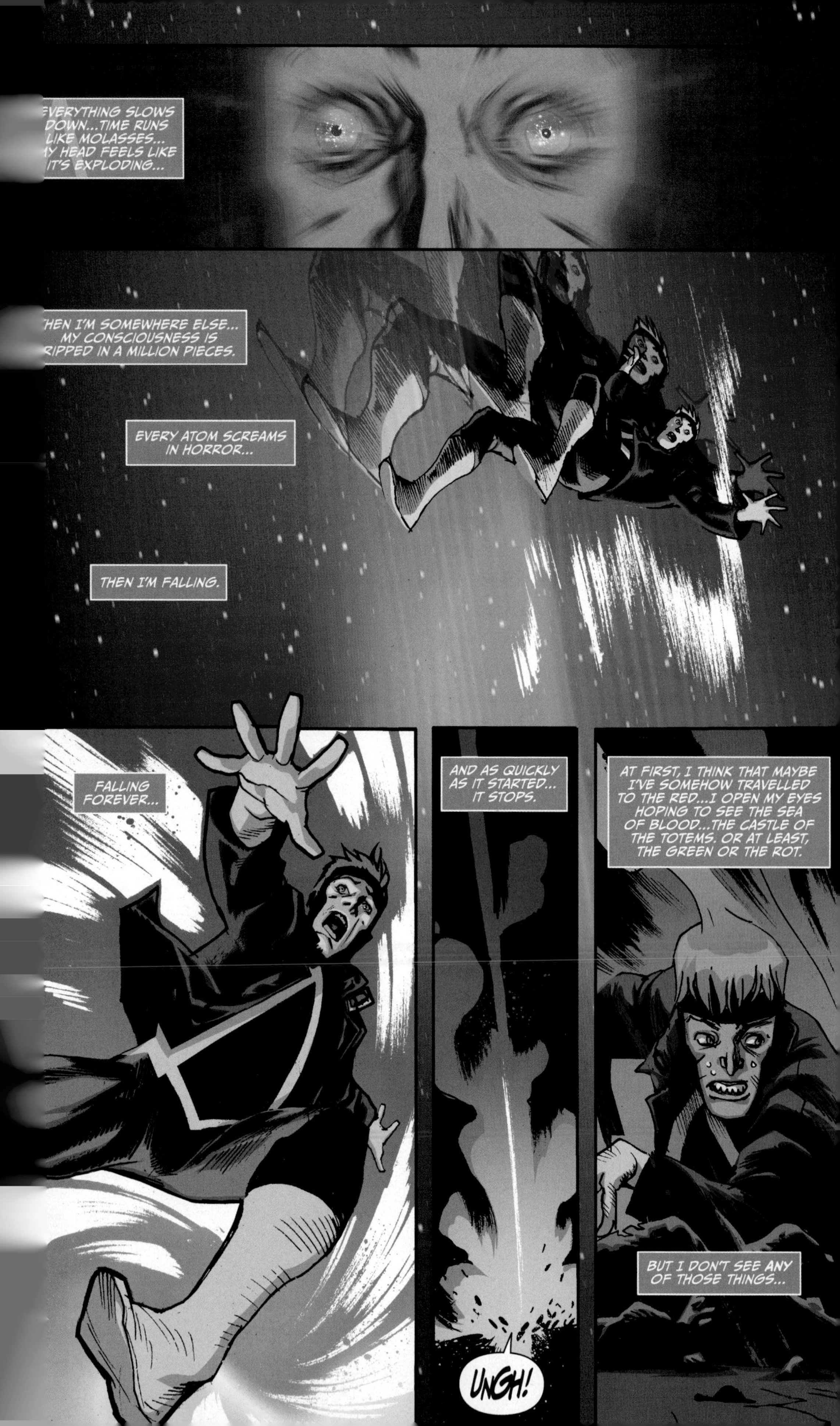
EVERYTHING SLOWS DOWN...TIME RUNS LIKE MOLASSES... MY HEAD FEELS LIKE IT'S EXPLODING...
THEN I'M SOMEWHERE ELSE... MY CONSCIOUSNESS IS RIPPED IN A MILLION PIECES.
EVERY ATOM SCREAMS IN HORROR...
THEN I'M FALLING.
FALLING FOREVER...
AND AS QUICKLY AS IT STARTED... IT STOPS.
UNGH!
AT FIRST, I THINK THAT MAYBE I'VE SOMEHOW TRAVELLED TO THE RED...I OPEN MY EYES HOPING TO SEE THE SEA OF BLOOD...THE CASTLE OF THE TOTEMS. OR AT LEAST, THE GREEN OR THE ROT.
BUT I DON'T SEE ANY OF THOSE THINGS...

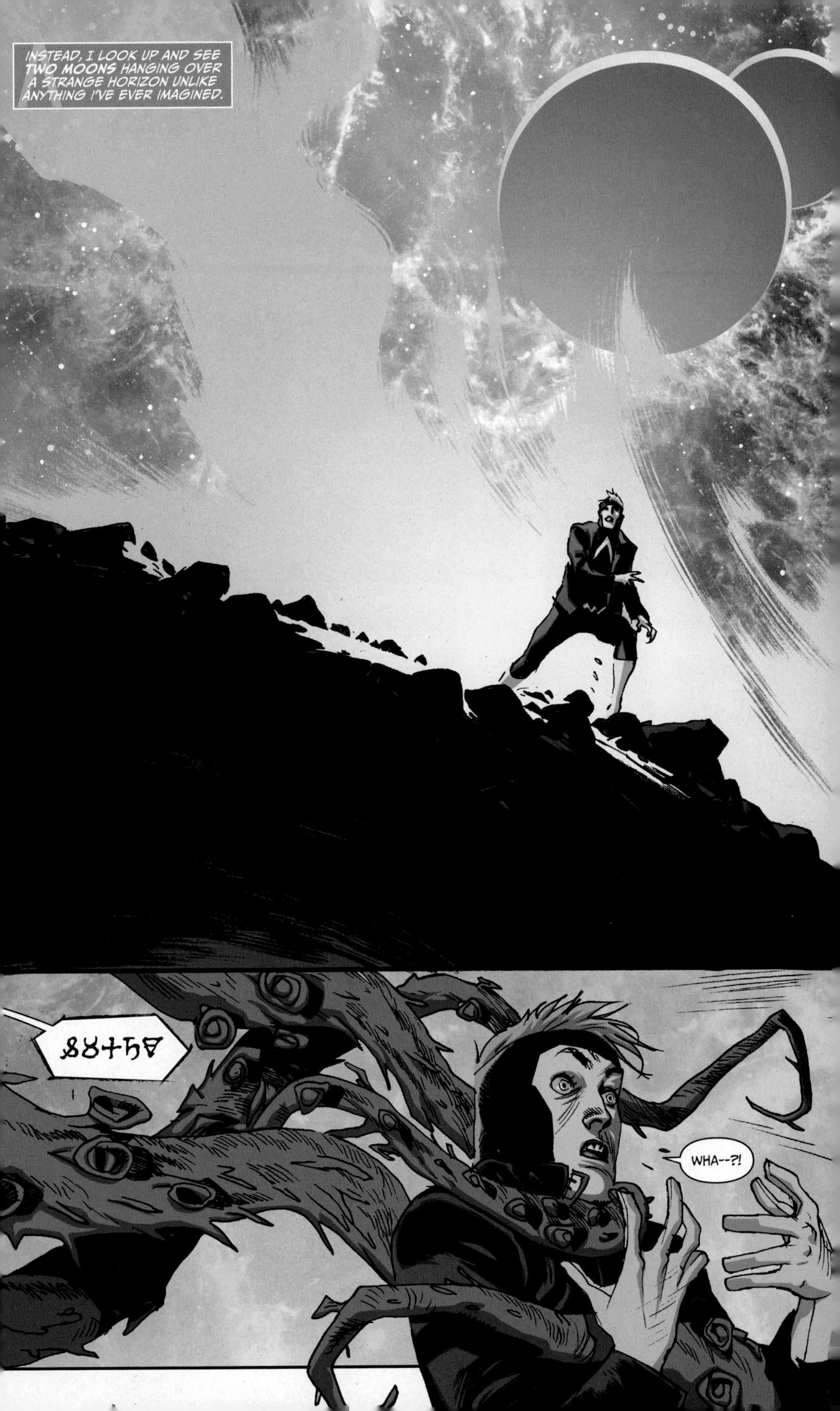
INSTEAD, I LOOK UP AND SEE TWO MOONS HANGING OVER A STRANGE HORIZON UNLIKE ANYTHING I'VE EVER IMAGINED.
WHA--?!

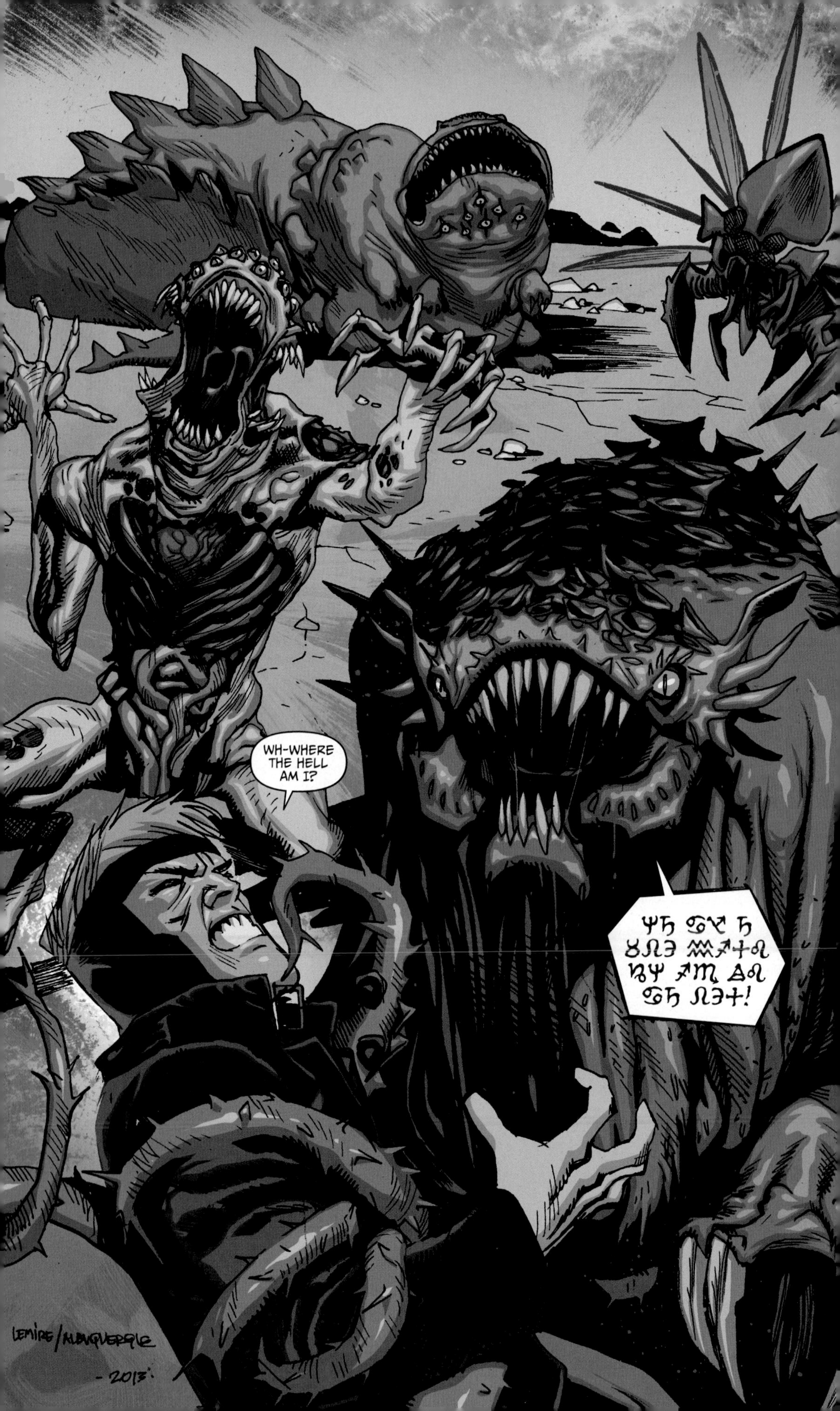
WH-WHERE THE HELL AM I?
LEMIRE/ALBUQUERQUE
- 2013.

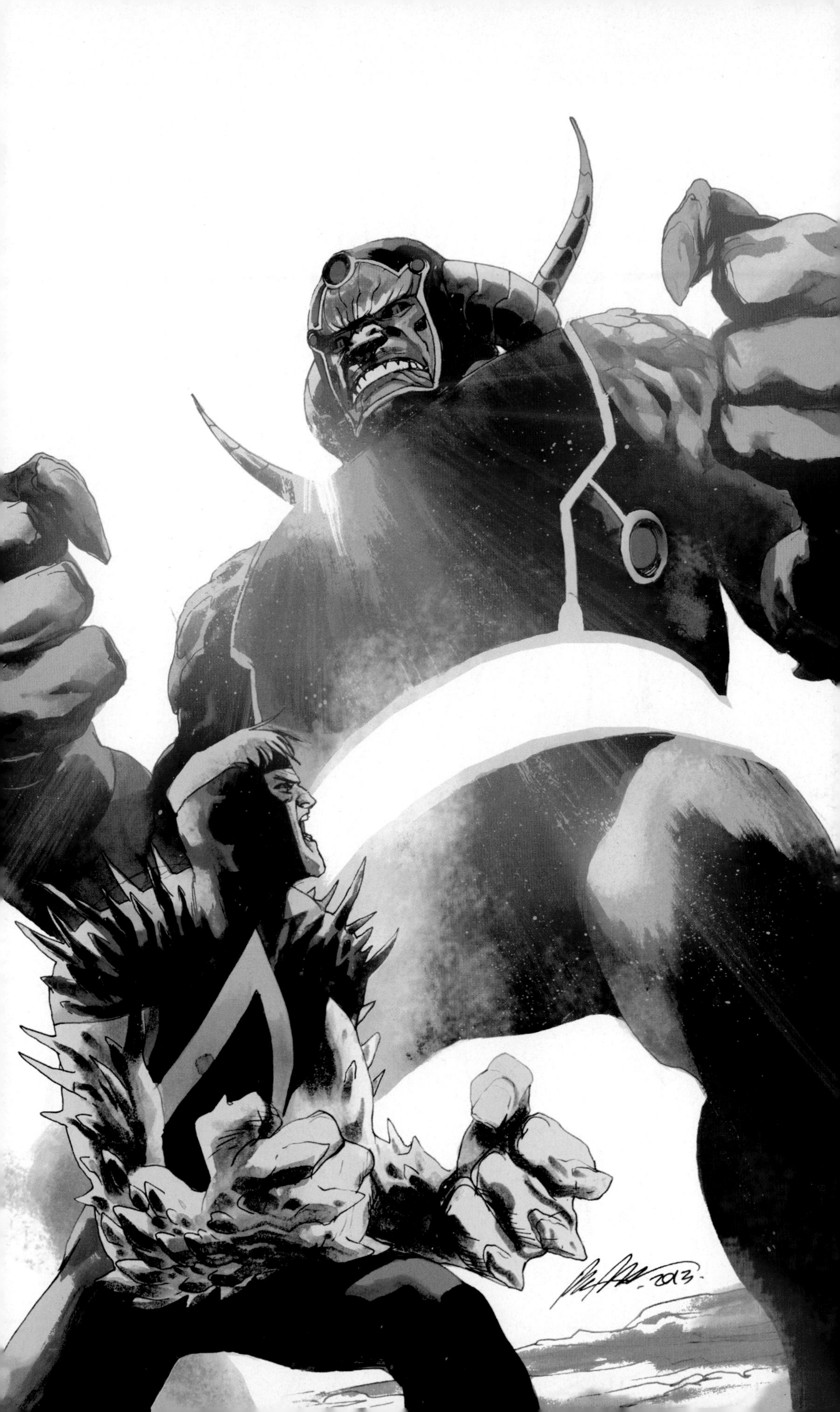

GODSEED

JEFF LEMIRE writer **CULLY HAMNER** artist

DAVE McCAIG colorist **JARED K. FLETCHER** letterer cover art by **RAFAEL ALBUQUERQUE**

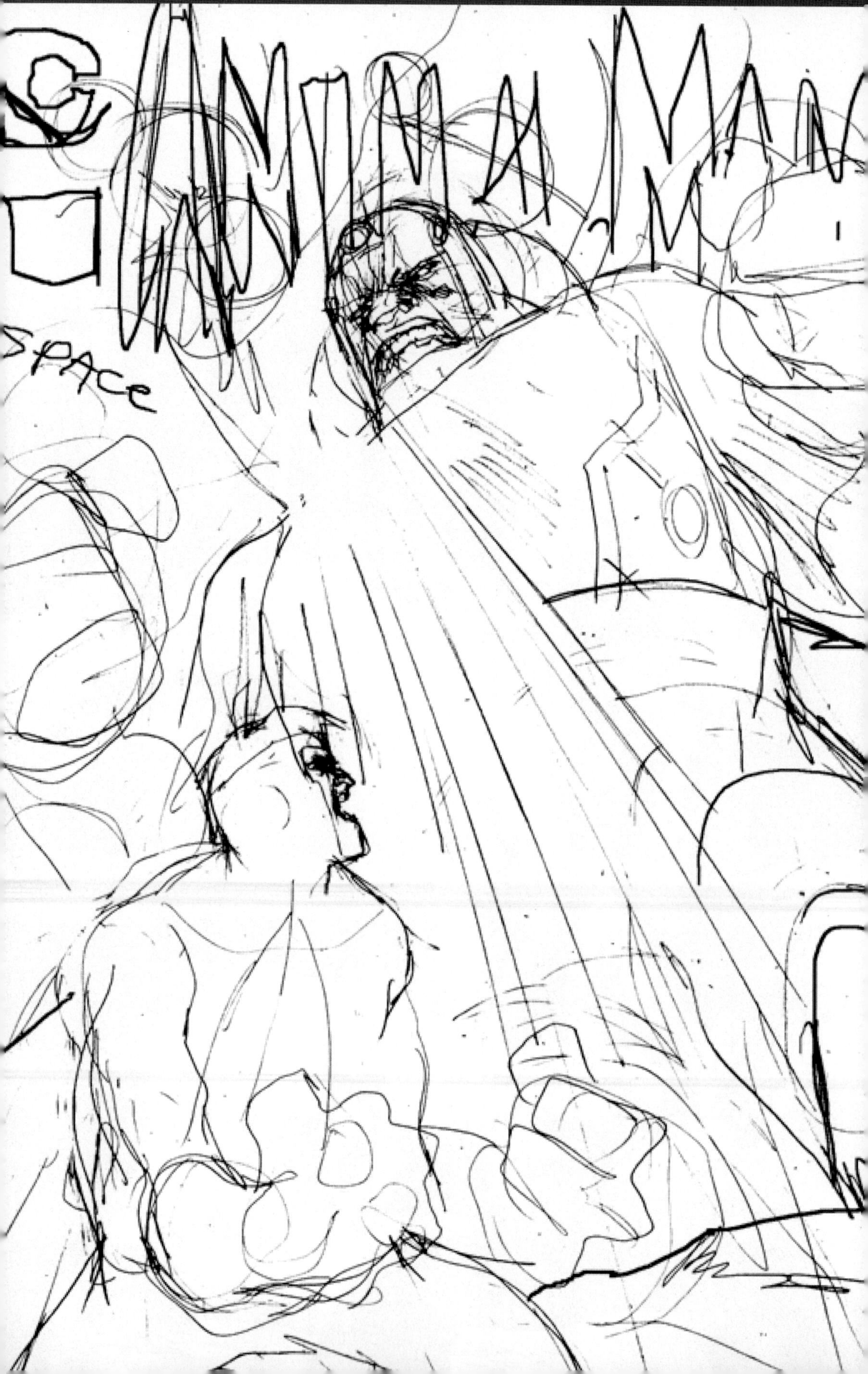
SPACE

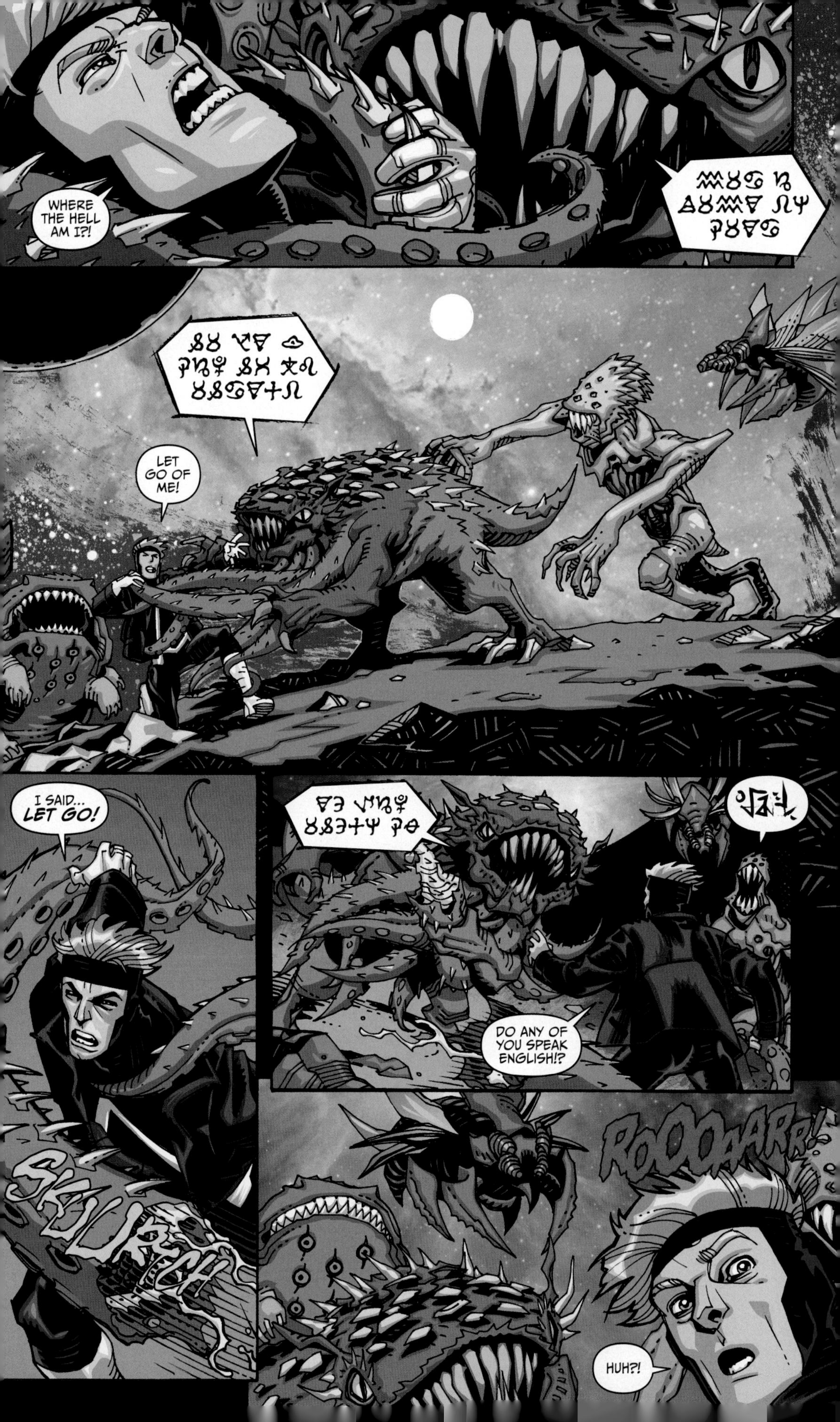
WHERE THE HELL AM I?!
LET GO OF ME!
I SAID... LET GO!
SKLURCH
DO ANY OF YOU SPEAK ENGLISH!?
ROOOAARR!
HUH?!

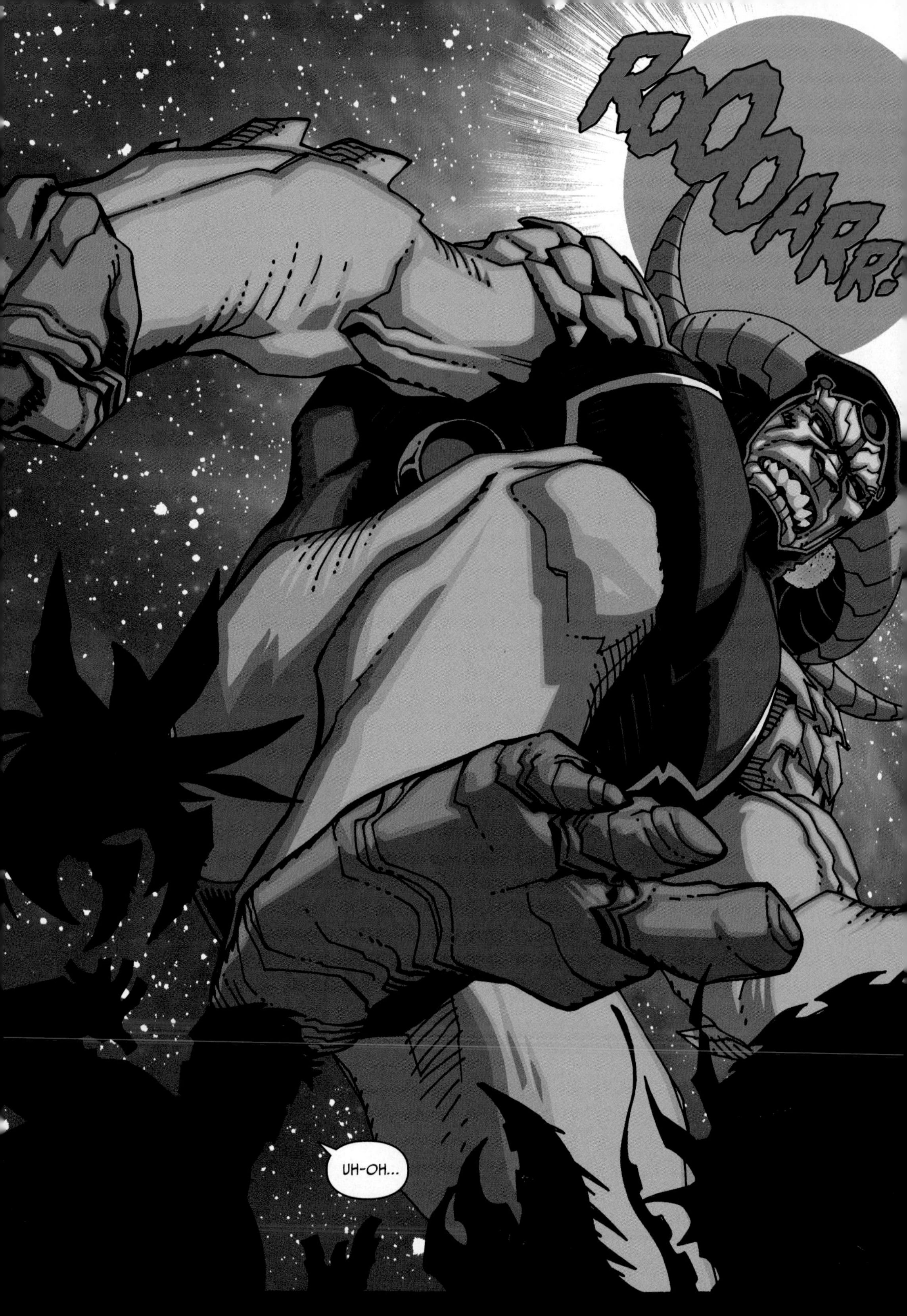
ROOOOARR!
UH-OH...

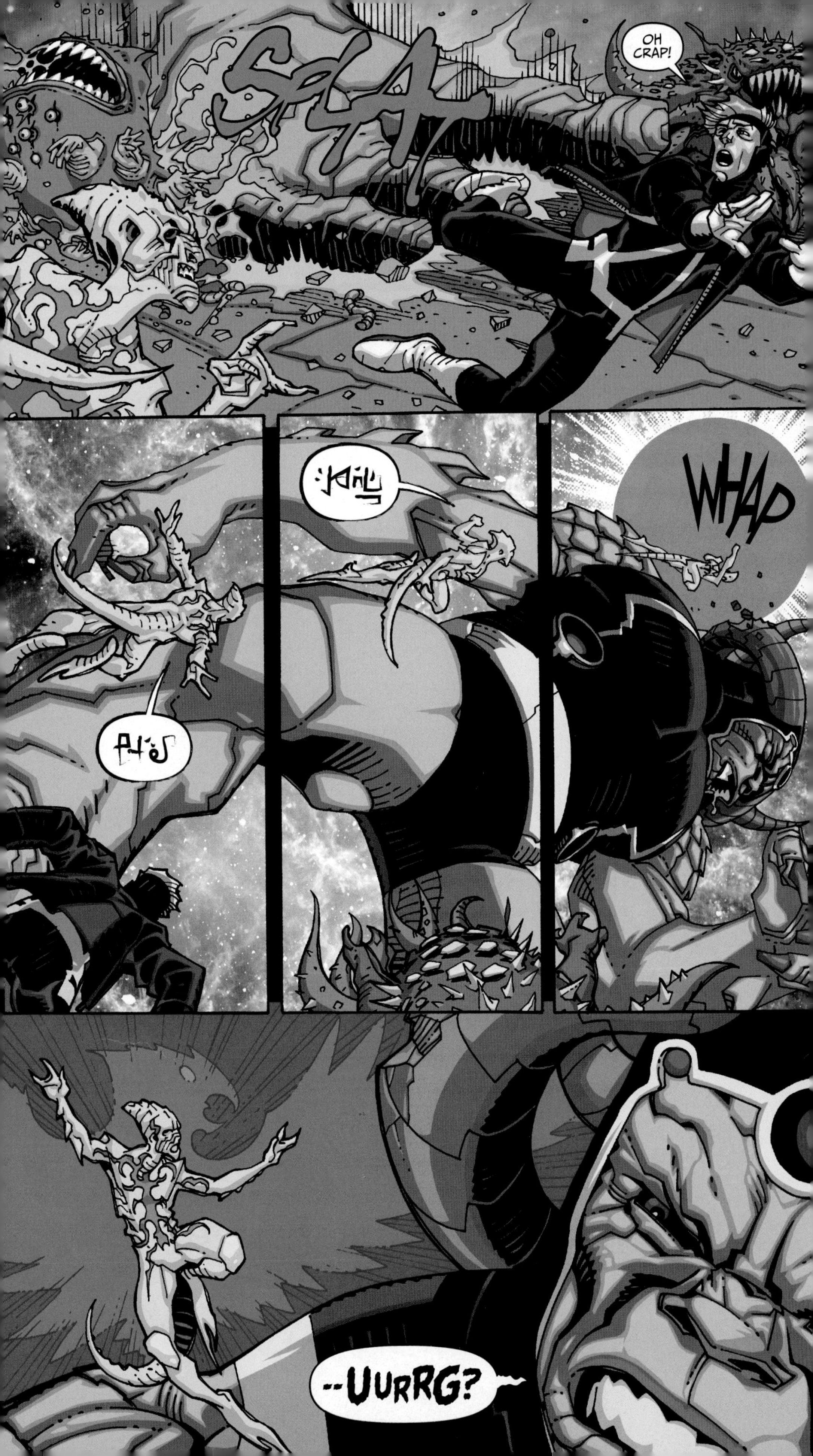
OH CRAP!
WHAP
--UURRG?

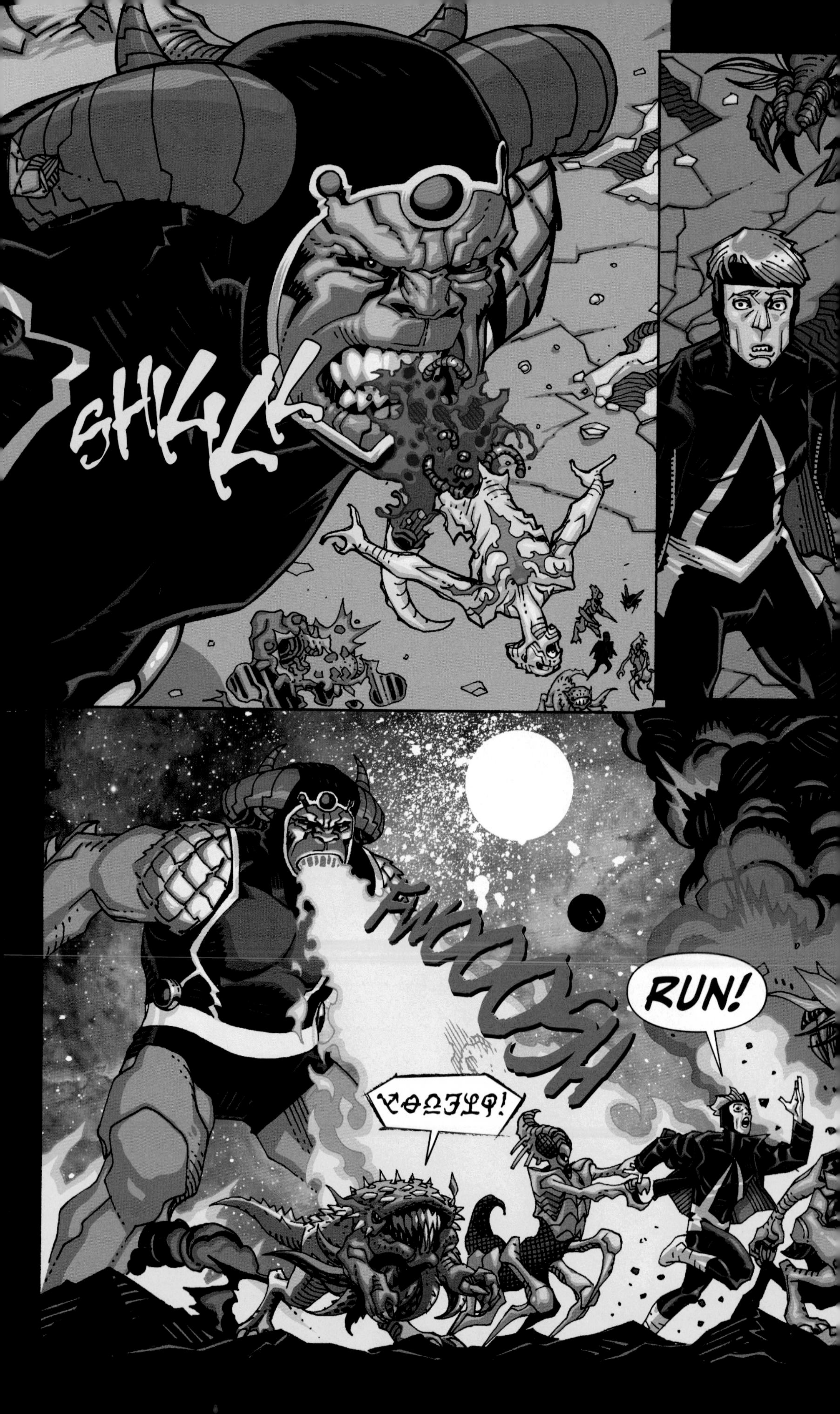
SHKK
FWOOOOSH
RUN!

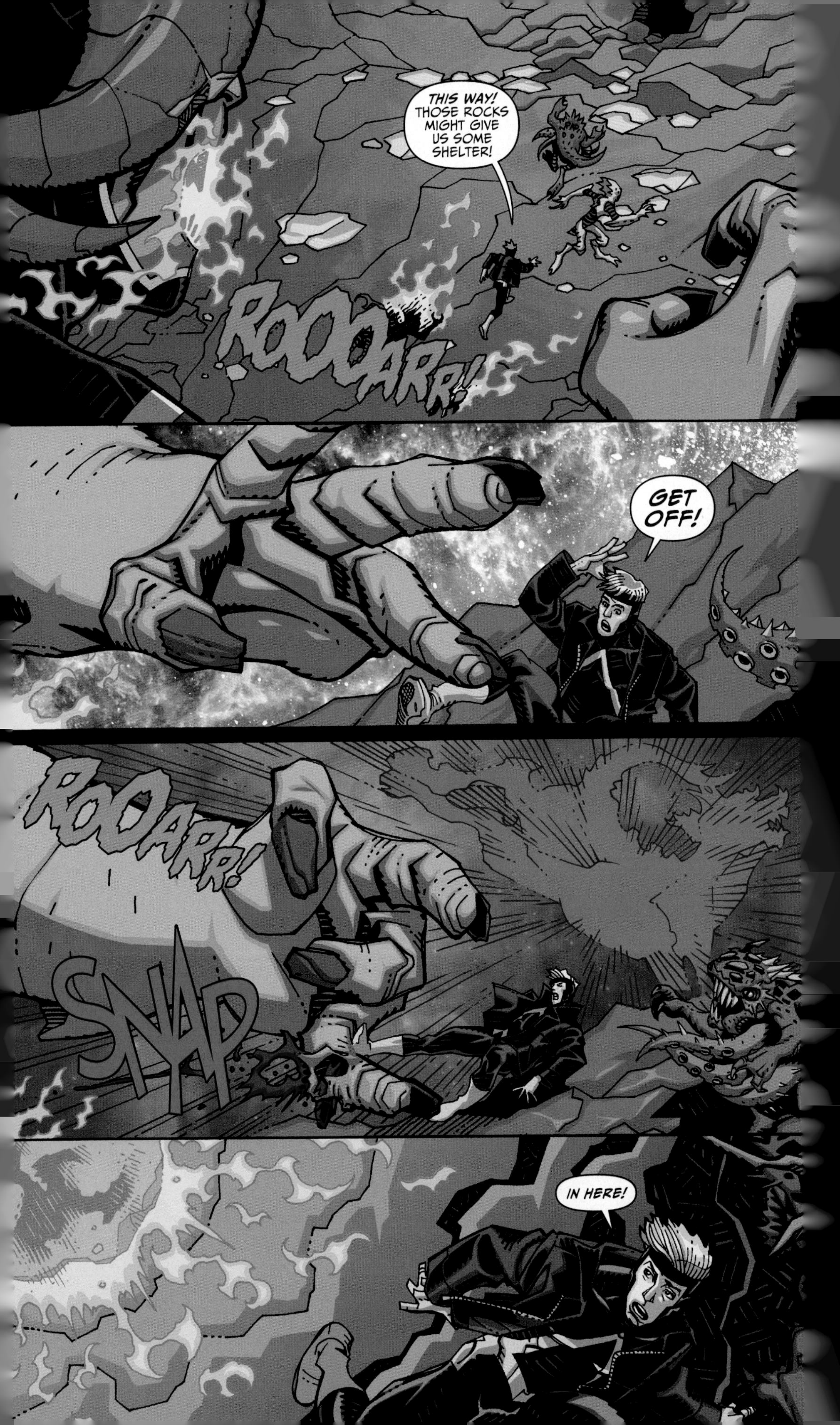
THIS WAY! THOSE ROCKS MIGHT GIVE US SOME SHELTER!
ROOOARRR!
GET OFF!
ROOARRR!
SNAP
IN HERE!

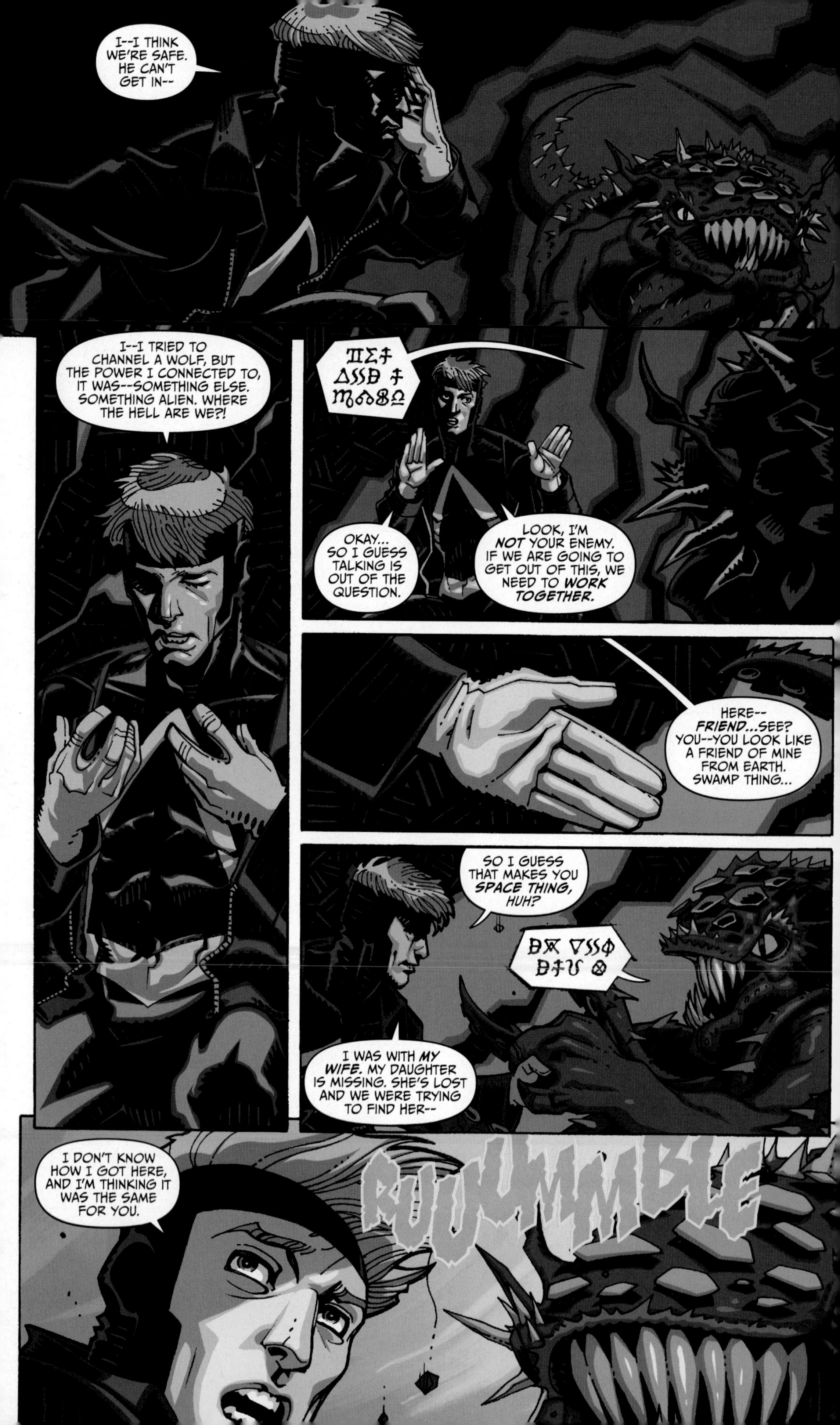
I--I THINK WE'RE SAFE. HE CAN'T GET IN--
I--I TRIED TO CHANNEL A WOLF, BUT THE POWER I CONNECTED TO, IT WAS--SOMETHING ELSE. SOMETHING ALIEN. WHERE THE HELL ARE WE?!
OKAY... SO I GUESS TALKING IS OUT OF THE QUESTION.
LOOK, I'M NOT YOUR ENEMY. IF WE ARE GOING TO GET OUT OF THIS, WE NEED TO WORK TOGETHER.
HERE-- FRIEND...SEE? YOU--YOU LOOK LIKE A FRIEND OF MINE FROM EARTH. SWAMP THING...
SO I GUESS THAT MAKES YOU SPACE THING, HUH?
I WAS WITH MY WIFE. MY DAUGHTER IS MISSING. SHE'S LOST AND WE WERE TRYING TO FIND HER--
I DON'T KNOW HOW I GOT HERE, AND I'M THINKING IT WAS THE SAME FOR YOU.
RUUMMBLE

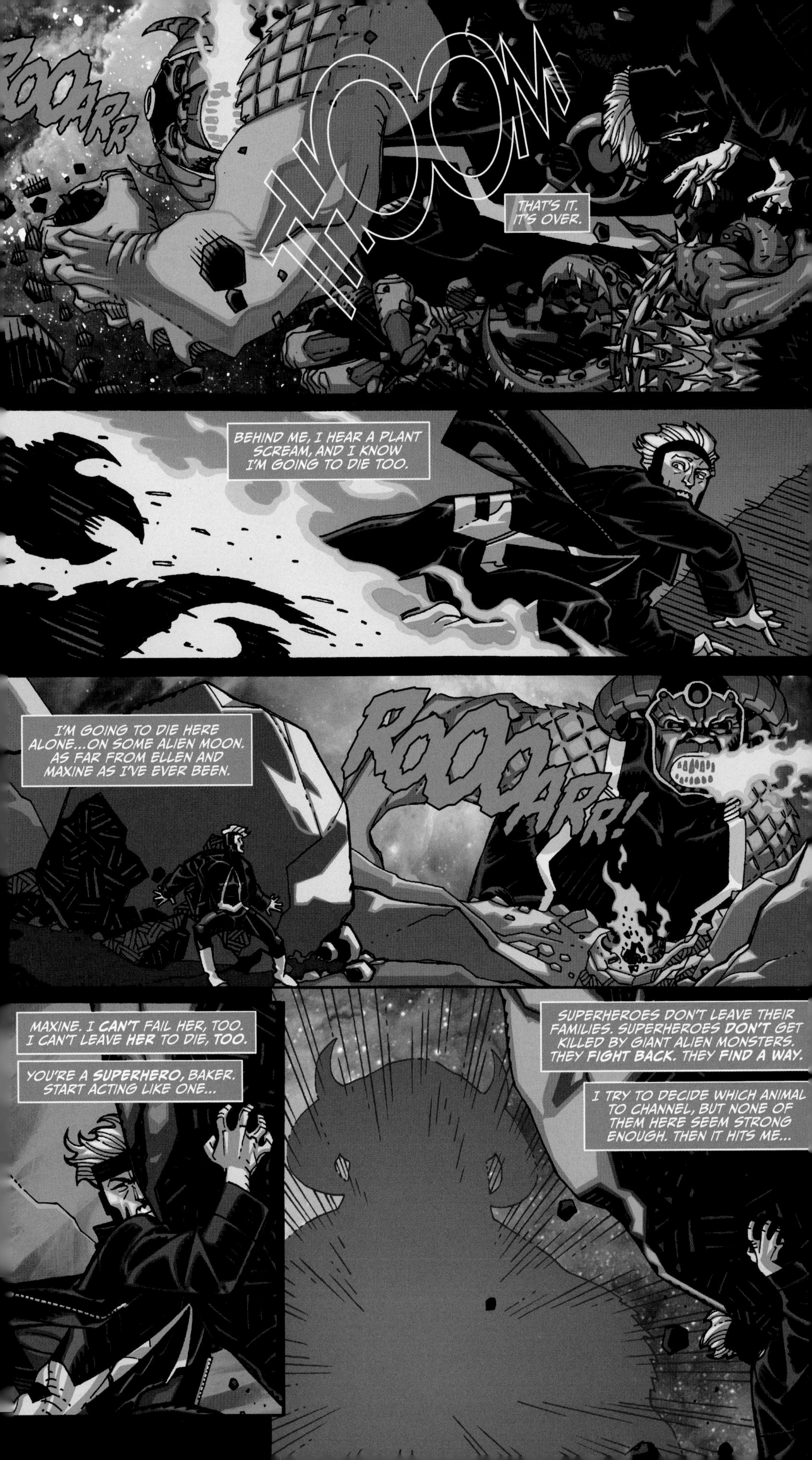
ROOOARR
THOOM
THAT'S IT. IT'S OVER.
BEHIND ME, I HEAR A PLANT SCREAM, AND I KNOW I'M GOING TO DIE TOO.
I'M GOING TO DIE HERE ALONE...ON SOME ALIEN MOON. AS FAR FROM ELLEN AND MAXINE AS I'VE EVER BEEN.
ROOOARR!
MAXINE. I CAN'T FAIL HER, TOO. I CAN'T LEAVE HER TO DIE, TOO.
YOU'RE A SUPERHERO, BAKER. START ACTING LIKE ONE...
SUPERHEROES DON'T LEAVE THEIR FAMILIES. SUPERHEROES DON'T GET KILLED BY GIANT ALIEN MONSTERS. THEY FIGHT BACK. THEY FIND A WAY.
I TRY TO DECIDE WHICH ANIMAL TO CHANNEL, BUT NONE OF THEM HERE SEEM STRONG ENOUGH. THEN IT HITS ME...

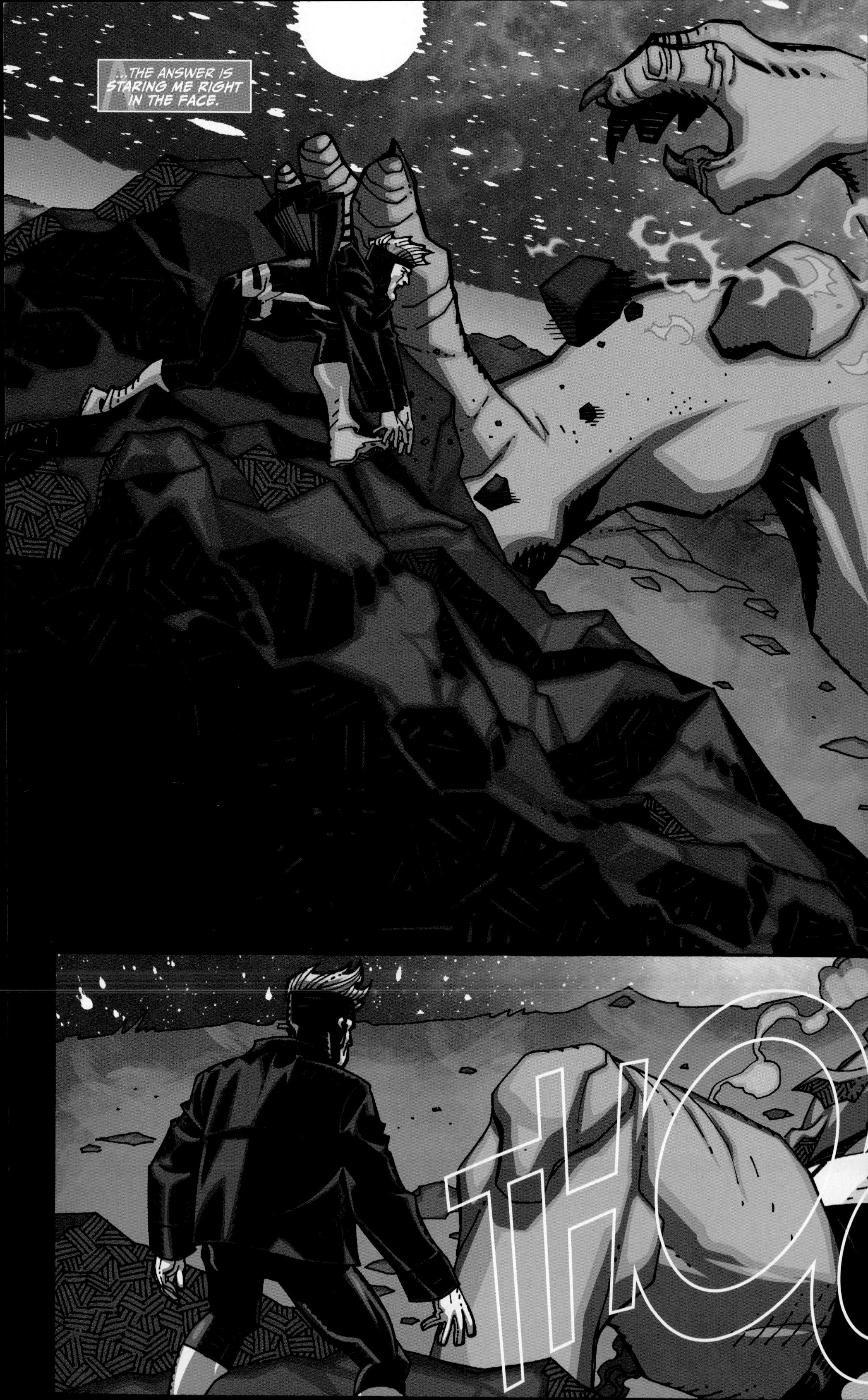
...THE ANSWER IS STARING ME RIGHT IN THE FACE.

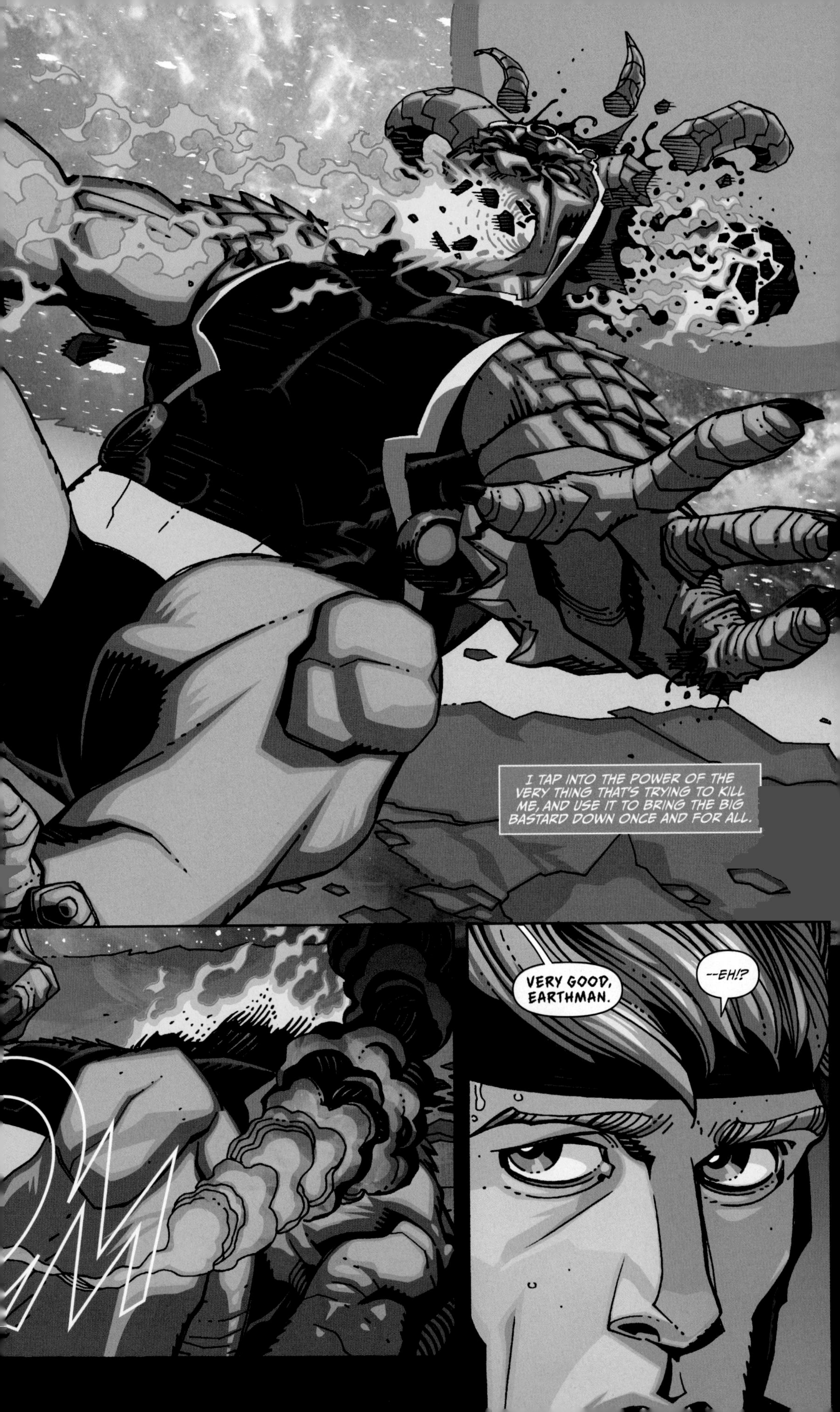
I TAP INTO THE POWER OF THE VERY THING THAT'S TRYING TO KILL ME, AND USE IT TO BRING THE BIG BASTARD DOWN ONCE AND FOR ALL.
VERY GOOD, EARTHMAN.
--EH!?

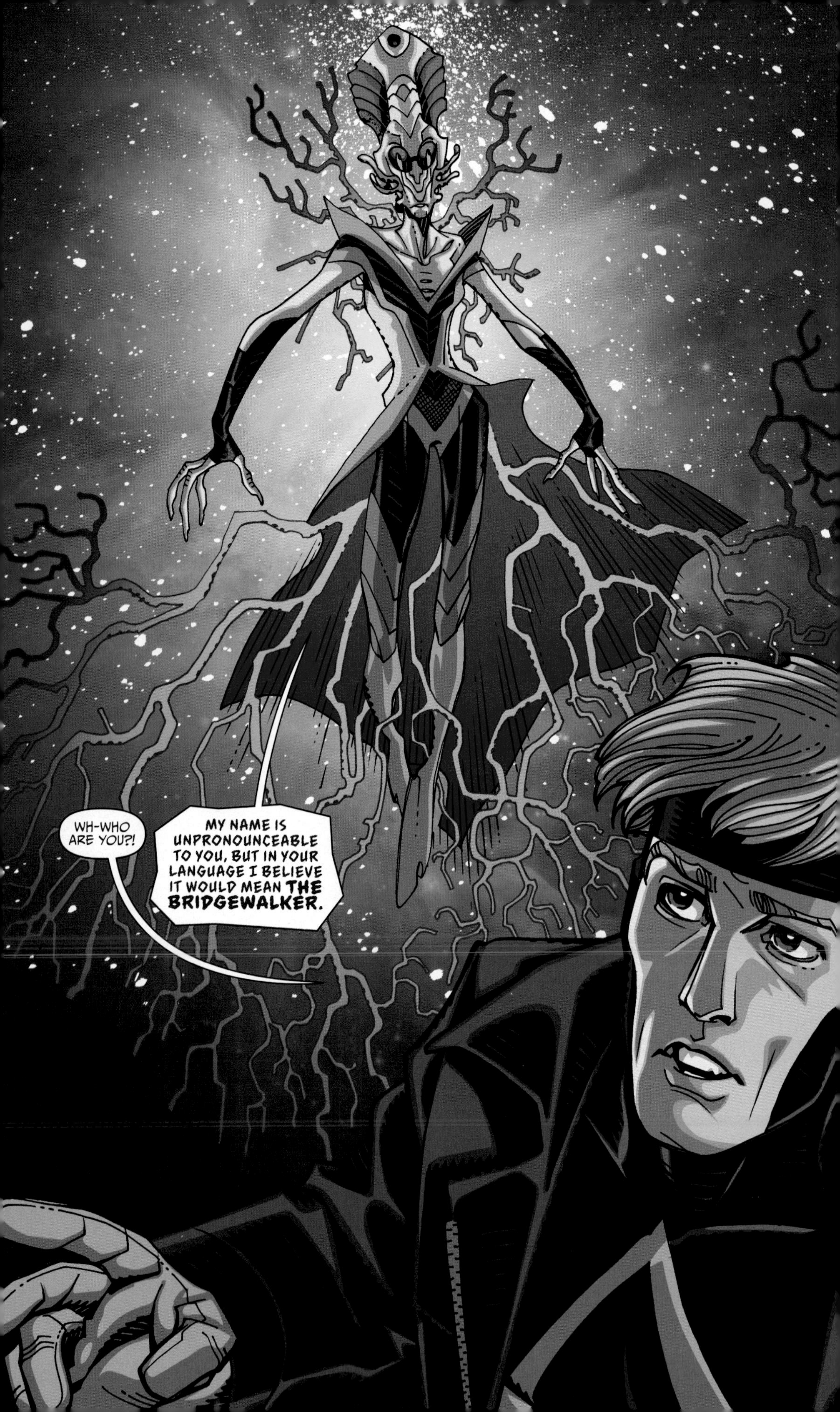
WH-WHO ARE YOU?!
MY NAME IS UNPRONOUNCEABLE TO YOU, BUT IN YOUR LANGUAGE I BELIEVE IT WOULD MEAN THE BRIDGEWALKER.

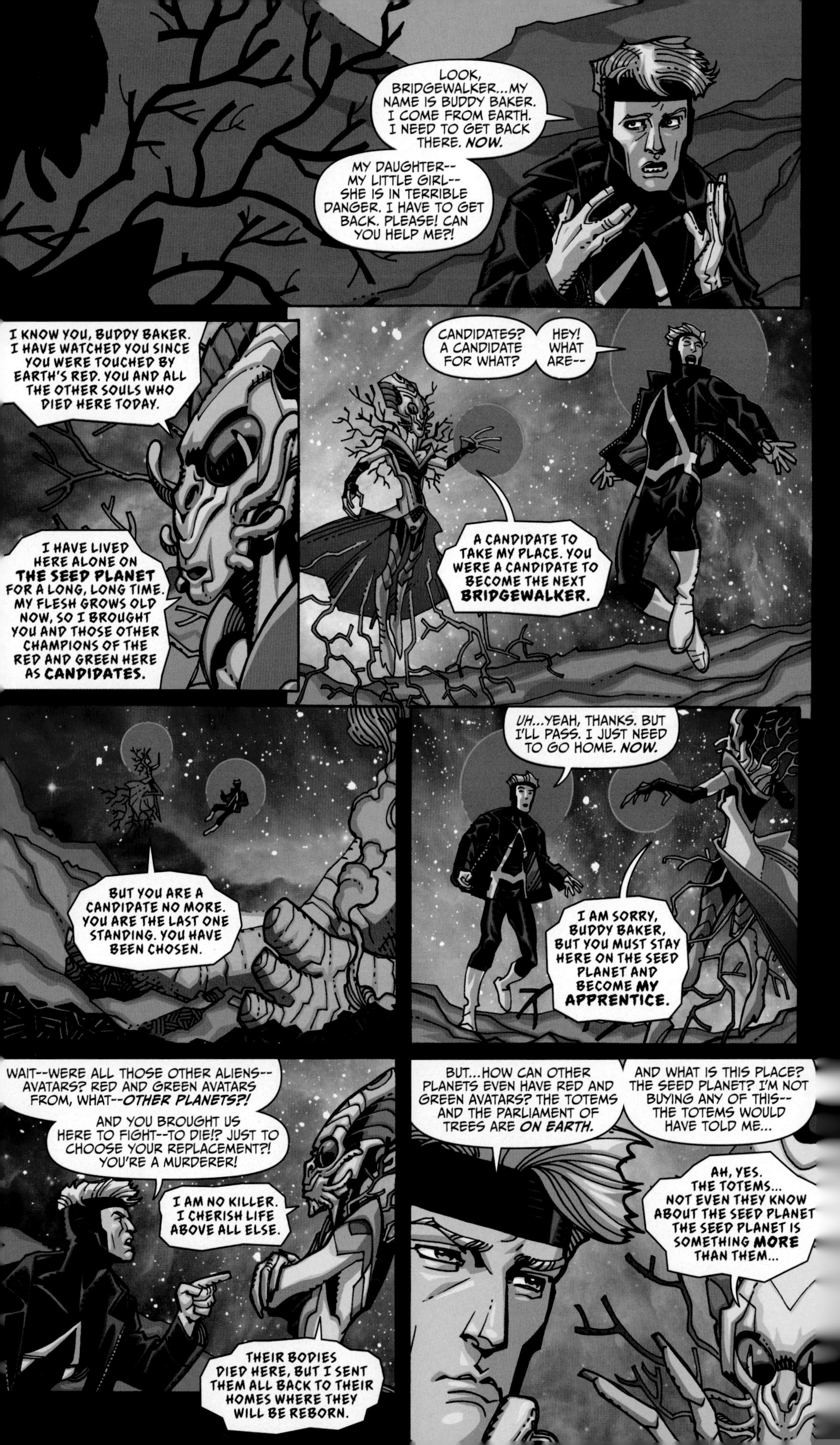
LOOK, BRIDGEWALKER...MY NAME IS BUDDY BAKER. I COME FROM EARTH. I NEED TO GET BACK THERE. NOW.
MY DAUGHTER-- MY LITTLE GIRL-- SHE IS IN TERRIBLE DANGER. I HAVE TO GET BACK. PLEASE! CAN YOU HELP ME?!
I KNOW YOU, BUDDY BAKER. I HAVE WATCHED YOU SINCE YOU WERE TOUCHED BY EARTH'S RED. YOU AND ALL THE OTHER SOULS WHO DIED HERE TODAY.
I HAVE LIVED HERE ALONE ON THE SEED PLANET FOR A LONG, LONG TIME. MY FLESH GROWS OLD NOW, SO I BROUGHT YOU AND THOSE OTHER CHAMPIONS OF THE RED AND GREEN HERE AS CANDIDATES.
HEY! WHAT ARE--
CANDIDATES? A CANDIDATE FOR WHAT?
A CANDIDATE TO TAKE MY PLACE. YOU WERE A CANDIDATE TO BECOME THE NEXT BRIDGEWALKER.
BUT YOU ARE A CANDIDATE NO MORE. YOU ARE THE LAST ONE STANDING. YOU HAVE BEEN CHOSEN.
UH...YEAH, THANKS. BUT I'LL PASS. I JUST NEED TO GO HOME. NOW.
I AM SORRY, BUDDY BAKER, BUT YOU MUST STAY HERE ON THE SEED PLANET AND BECOME MY APPRENTICE.
WAIT--WERE ALL THOSE OTHER ALIENS-- AVATARS? RED AND GREEN AVATARS FROM, WHAT--OTHER PLANETS?!
AND YOU BROUGHT US HERE TO FIGHT--TO DIE!? JUST TO CHOOSE YOUR REPLACEMENT?! YOU'RE A MURDERER!
I AM NO KILLER. I CHERISH LIFE ABOVE ALL ELSE.
THEIR BODIES DIED HERE, BUT I SENT THEM ALL BACK TO THEIR HOMES WHERE THEY WILL BE REBORN.
BUT...HOW CAN OTHER PLANETS EVEN HAVE RED AND GREEN AVATARS? THE TOTEMS AND THE PARLIAMENT OF TREES ARE ON EARTH.
AND WHAT IS THIS PLACE? THE SEED PLANET? I'M NOT BUYING ANY OF THIS-- THE TOTEMS WOULD HAVE TOLD ME...
AH, YES. THE TOTEMS... NOT EVEN THEY KNOW ABOUT THE SEED PLANET THE SEED PLANET IS SOMETHING MORE THAN THEM...

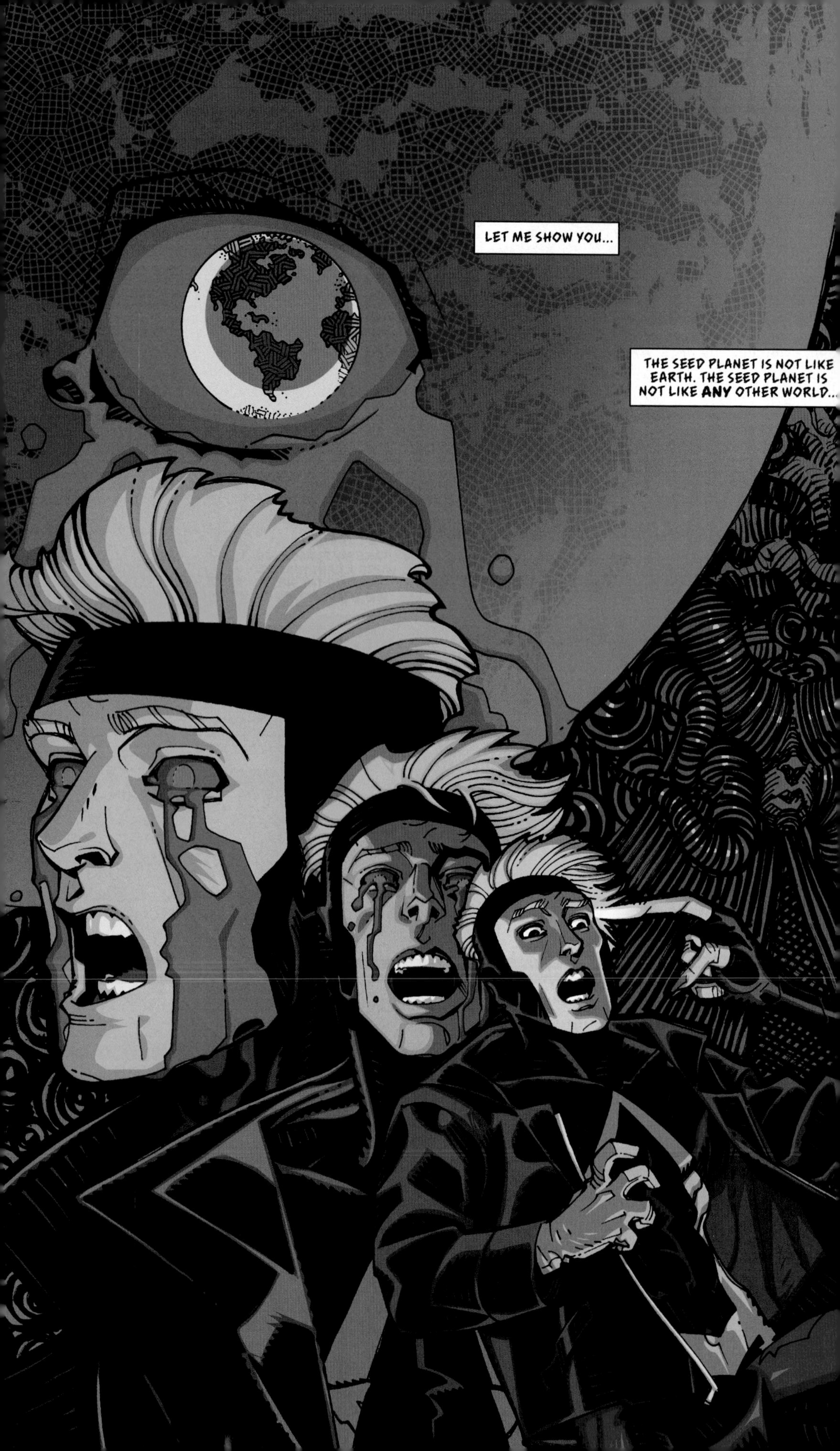
LET ME SHOW YOU...
THE SEED PLANET IS NOT LIKE EARTH. THE SEED PLANET IS NOT LIKE ANY OTHER WORLD...

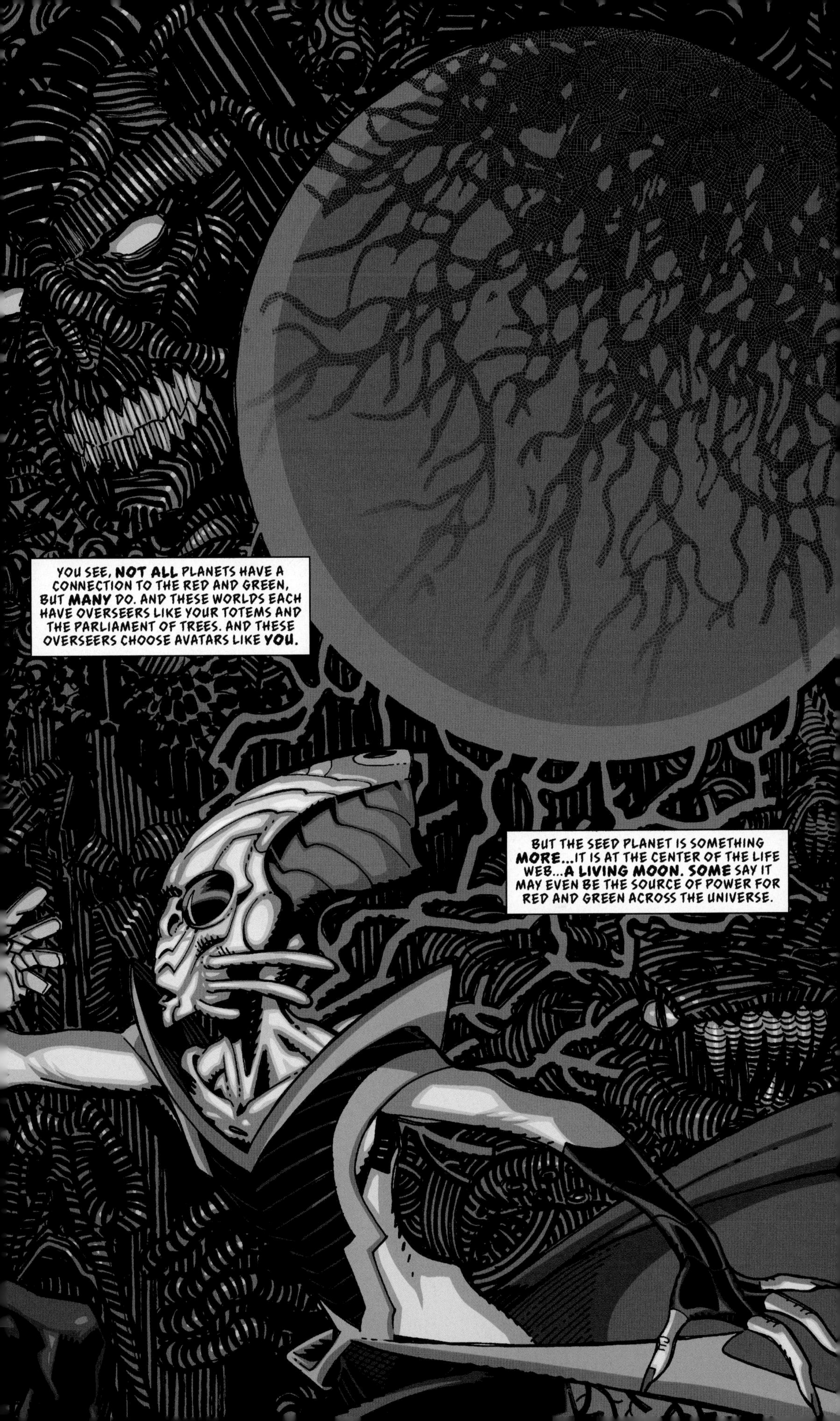
YOU SEE, NOT ALL PLANETS HAVE A CONNECTION TO THE RED AND GREEN, BUT MANY DO. AND THESE WORLDS EACH HAVE OVERSEERS LIKE YOUR TOTEMS AND THE PARLIAMENT OF TREES. AND THESE OVERSEERS CHOOSE AVATARS LIKE YOU.
BUT THE SEED PLANET IS SOMETHING MORE...IT IS AT THE CENTER OF THE LIFE WEB...A LIVING MOON. SOME SAY IT MAY EVEN BE THE SOURCE OF POWER FOR RED AND GREEN ACROSS THE UNIVERSE.

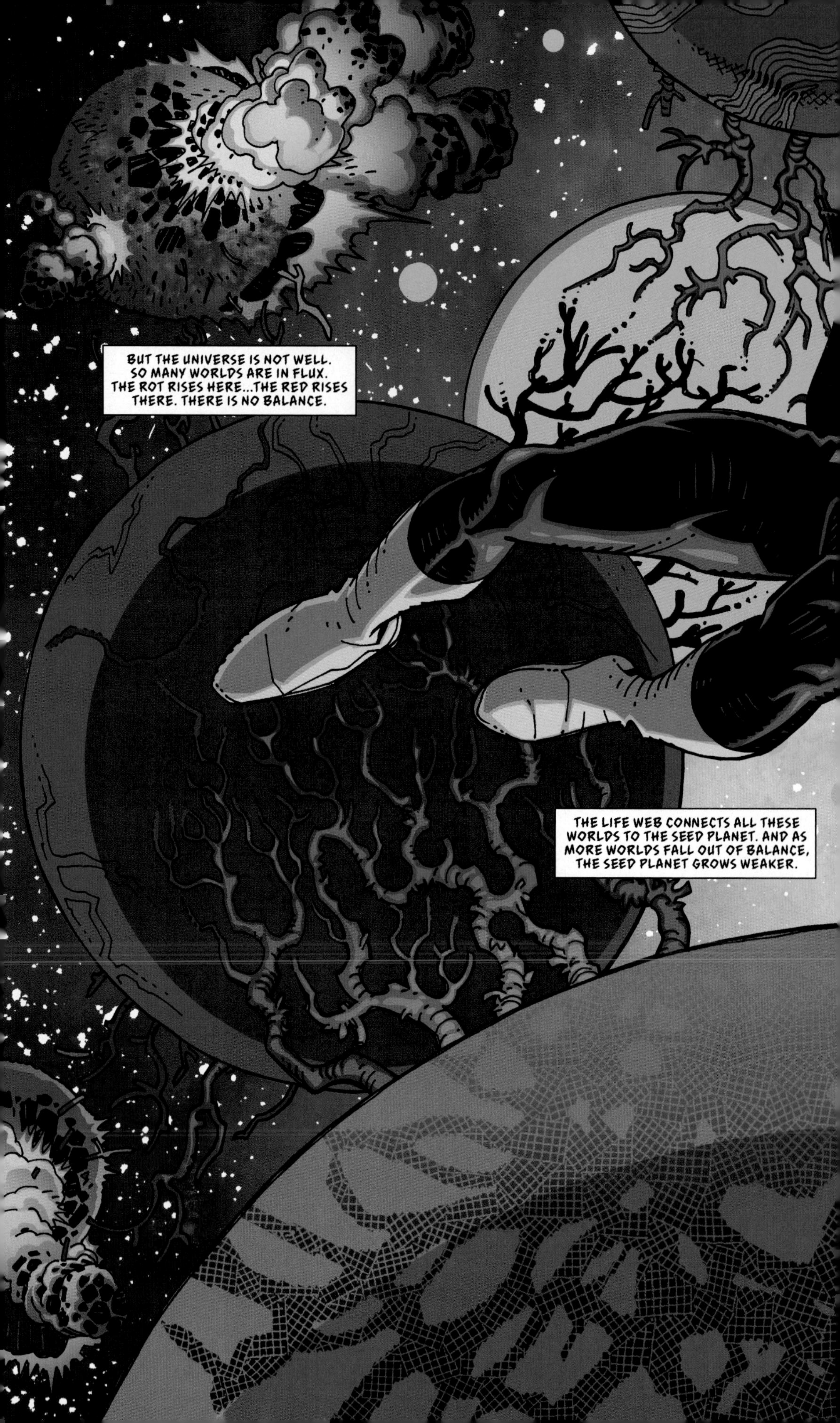
BUT THE UNIVERSE IS NOT WELL. SO MANY WORLDS ARE IN FLUX. THE ROT RISES HERE...THE RED RISES THERE. THERE IS NO BALANCE.
THE LIFE WEB CONNECTS ALL THESE WORLDS TO THE SEED PLANET. AND AS MORE WORLDS FALL OUT OF BALANCE, THE SEED PLANET GROWS WEAKER.

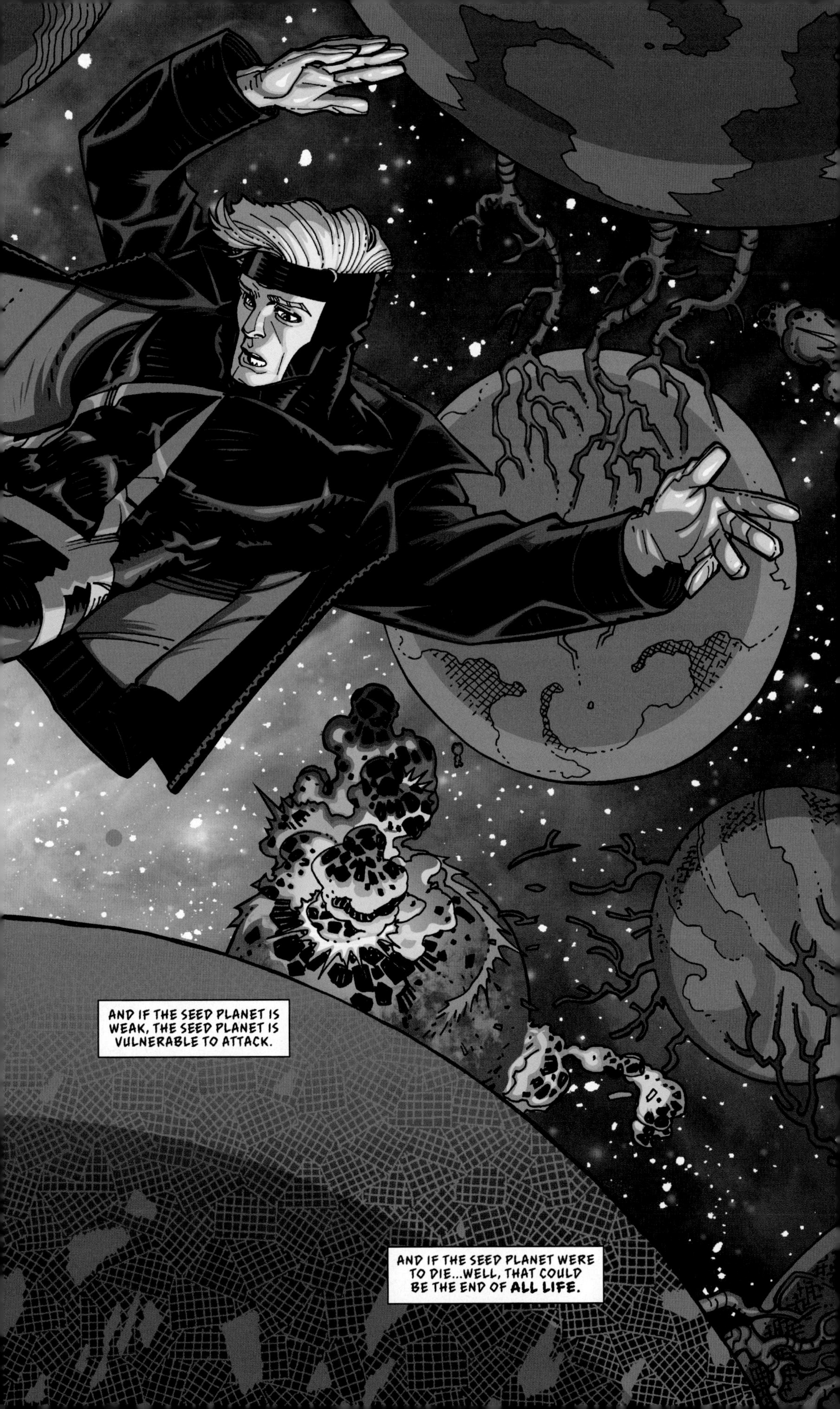
AND IF THE SEED PLANET IS
WEAK, THE SEED PLANET IS
VULNERABLE TO ATTACK.
AND IF THE SEED PLANET WERE
TO DIE...WELL, THAT COULD
BE THE END OF **ALL LIFE**.

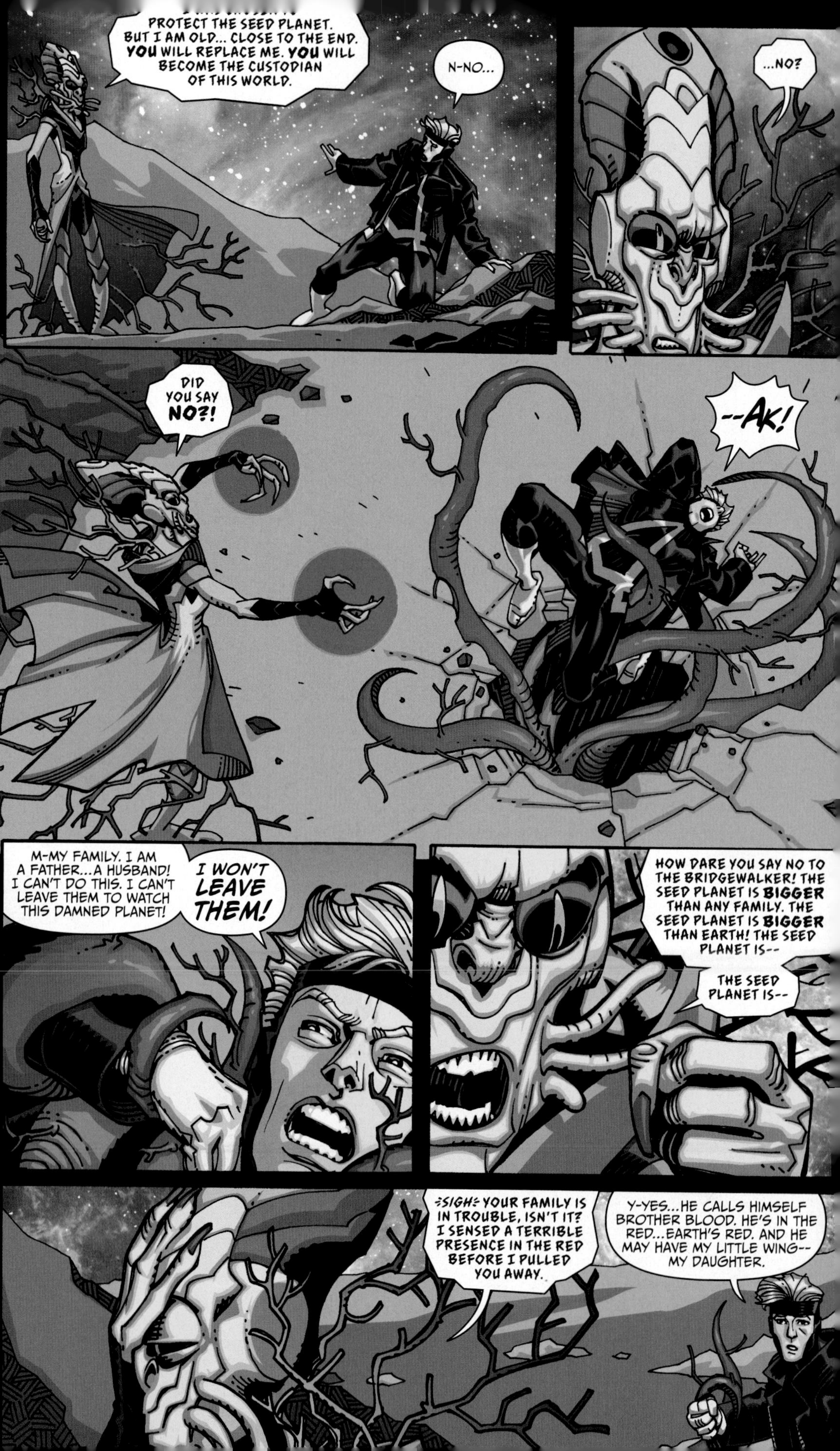
PROTECT THE SEED PLANET. BUT I AM OLD... CLOSE TO THE END. YOU WILL REPLACE ME. YOU WILL BECOME THE CUSTODIAN OF THIS WORLD.
N-NO...
...NO?
DID YOU SAY NO?!
--AK!
M-MY FAMILY. I AM A FATHER... A HUSBAND! I CAN'T DO THIS. I CAN'T LEAVE THEM TO WATCH THIS DAMNED PLANET!
I WON'T LEAVE THEM!
HOW DARE YOU SAY NO TO THE BRIDGEWALKER! THE SEED PLANET IS BIGGER THAN ANY FAMILY. THE SEED PLANET IS BIGGER THAN EARTH! THE SEED PLANET IS--
THE SEED PLANET IS--
=SIGH= YOUR FAMILY IS IN TROUBLE, ISN'T IT? I SENSED A TERRIBLE PRESENCE IN THE RED BEFORE I PULLED YOU AWAY.
Y-YES... HE CALLS HIMSELF BROTHER BLOOD. HE'S IN THE RED... EARTH'S RED. AND HE MAY HAVE MY LITTLE WING-- MY DAUGHTER.

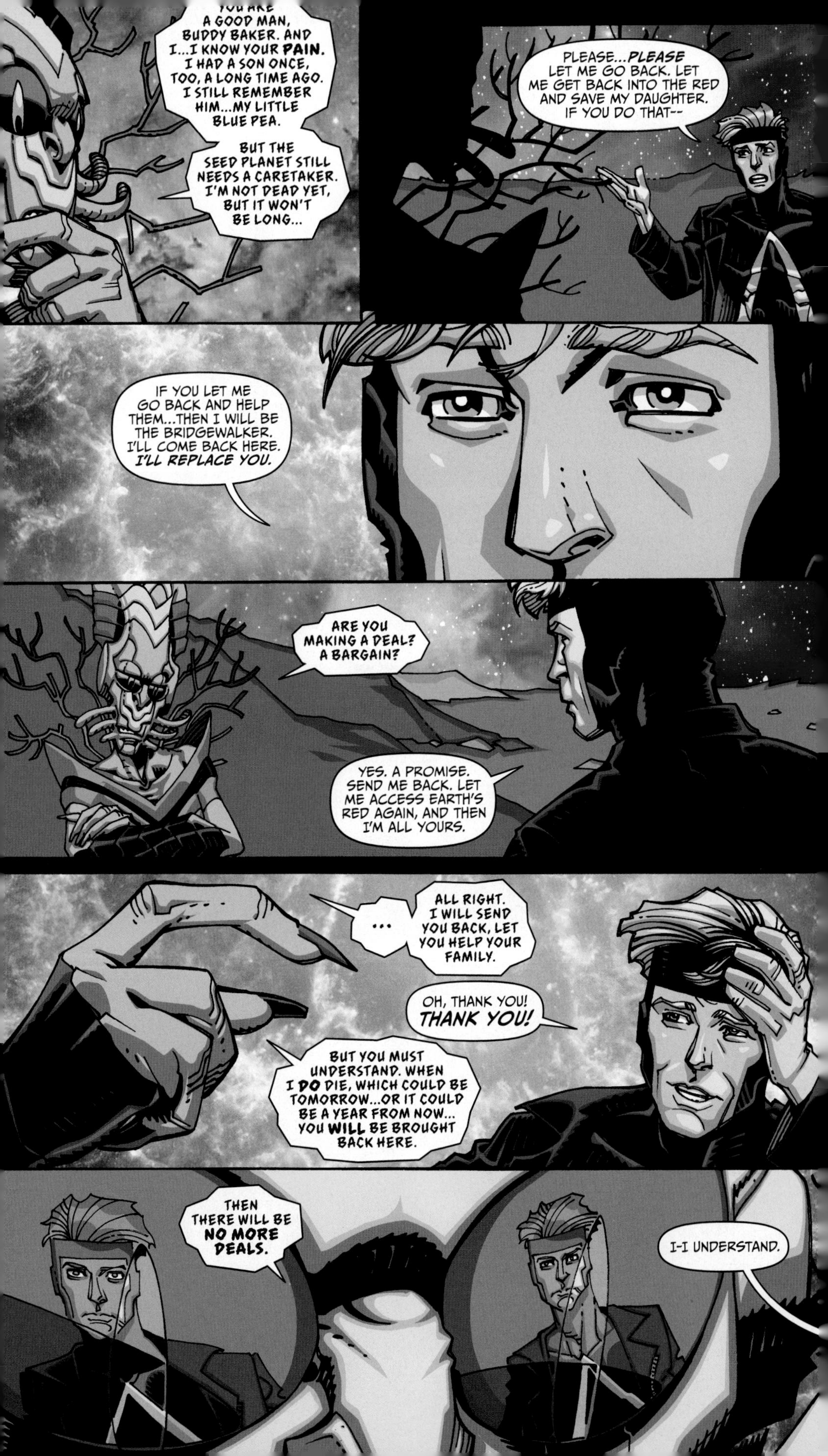

YOU ARE A GOOD MAN, BUDDY BAKER. AND I...I KNOW YOUR **PAIN.** I HAD A SON ONCE, TOO, A LONG TIME AGO. I STILL REMEMBER HIM...MY LITTLE BLUE PEA.
BUT THE SEED PLANET STILL NEEDS A CARETAKER. I'M NOT DEAD YET, BUT IT WON'T BE LONG...
PLEASE...***PLEASE*** LET ME GO BACK. LET ME GET BACK INTO THE RED AND SAVE MY DAUGHTER. IF YOU DO THAT--
IF YOU LET ME GO BACK AND HELP THEM...THEN I WILL BE THE BRIDGEWALKER. I'LL COME BACK HERE. ***I'LL REPLACE YOU.***
ARE YOU MAKING A DEAL? A BARGAIN?
YES. A PROMISE. SEND ME BACK. LET ME ACCESS EARTH'S RED AGAIN, AND THEN I'M ALL YOURS.
...
ALL RIGHT. I WILL SEND YOU BACK, LET YOU HELP YOUR FAMILY.
OH, THANK YOU! ***THANK YOU!***
BUT YOU MUST UNDERSTAND. WHEN I **DO** DIE, WHICH COULD BE TOMORROW...OR IT COULD BE A YEAR FROM NOW... YOU **WILL** BE BROUGHT BACK HERE.
THEN THERE WILL BE **NO MORE DEALS.**
I-I UNDERSTAND.

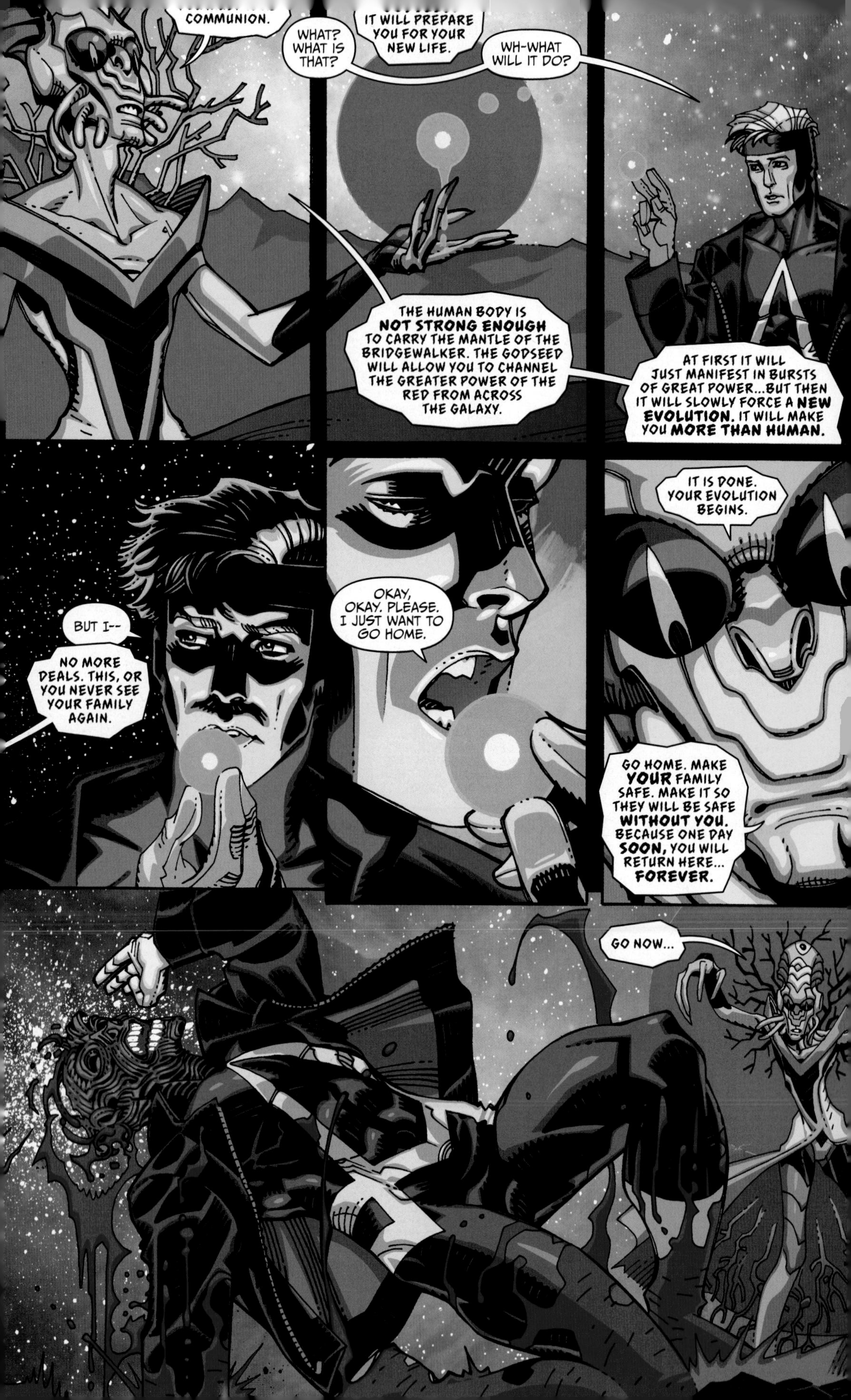
COMMUNION.
WHAT? WHAT IS THAT?
IT WILL PREPARE YOU FOR YOUR NEW LIFE.
WH-WHAT WILL IT DO?
THE HUMAN BODY IS NOT STRONG ENOUGH TO CARRY THE MANTLE OF THE BRIDGEWALKER. THE GODSEED WILL ALLOW YOU TO CHANNEL THE GREATER POWER OF THE RED FROM ACROSS THE GALAXY.
AT FIRST IT WILL JUST MANIFEST IN BURSTS OF GREAT POWER...BUT THEN IT WILL SLOWLY FORCE A NEW EVOLUTION. IT WILL MAKE YOU MORE THAN HUMAN.
BUT I--
NO MORE DEALS. THIS, OR YOU NEVER SEE YOUR FAMILY AGAIN.
OKAY, OKAY. PLEASE. I JUST WANT TO GO HOME.
IT IS DONE. YOUR EVOLUTION BEGINS.
GO HOME. MAKE YOUR FAMILY SAFE. MAKE IT SO THEY WILL BE SAFE WITHOUT YOU. BECAUSE ONE DAY SOON, YOU WILL RETURN HERE... FOREVER.
GO NOW...

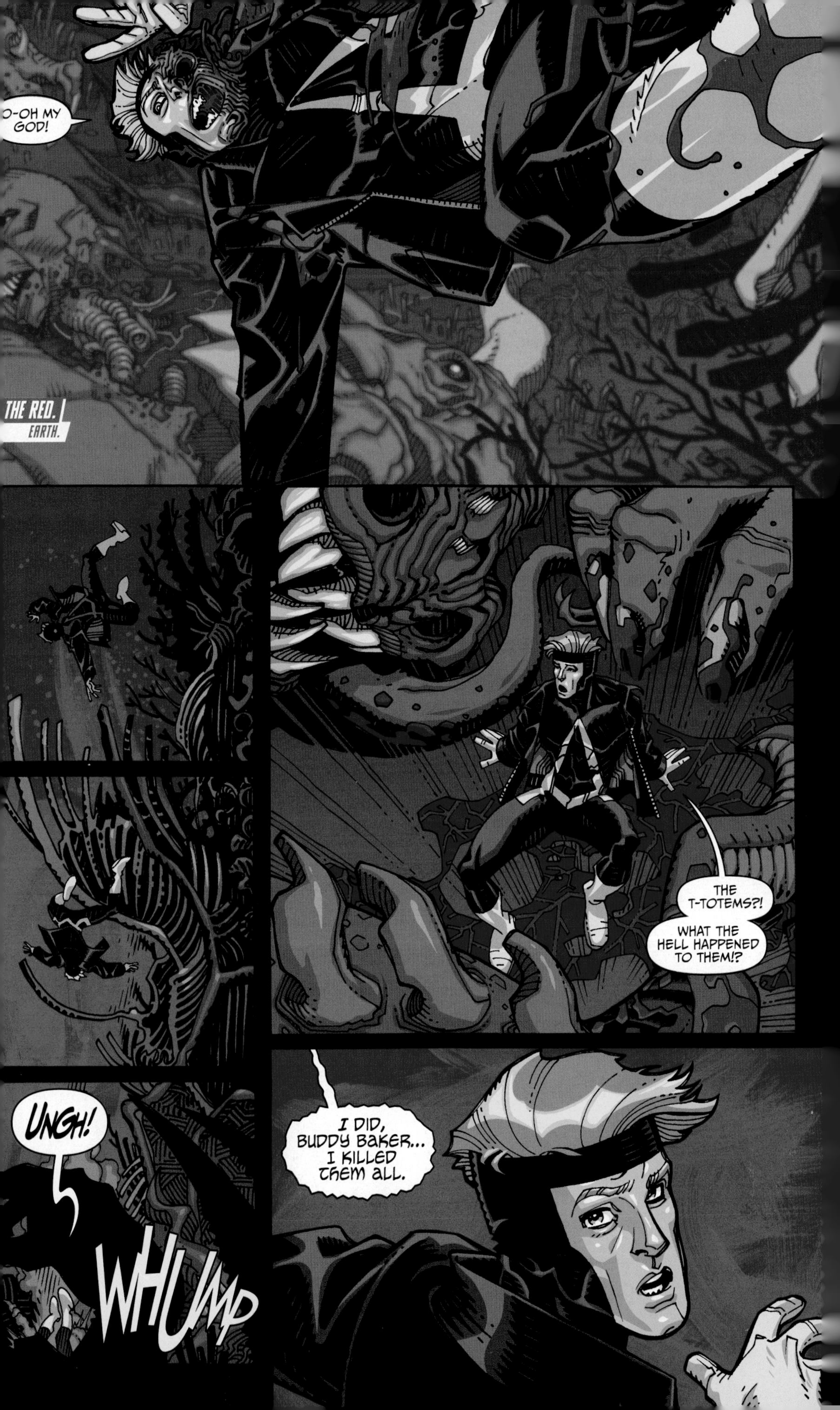
O-OH MY GOD!
THE RED.
EARTH.
THE T-TOTEMS?!
WHAT THE HELL HAPPENED TO THEM!?
UNGH!
WHUMP
I DID, BUDDY BAKER... I KILLED THEM ALL.

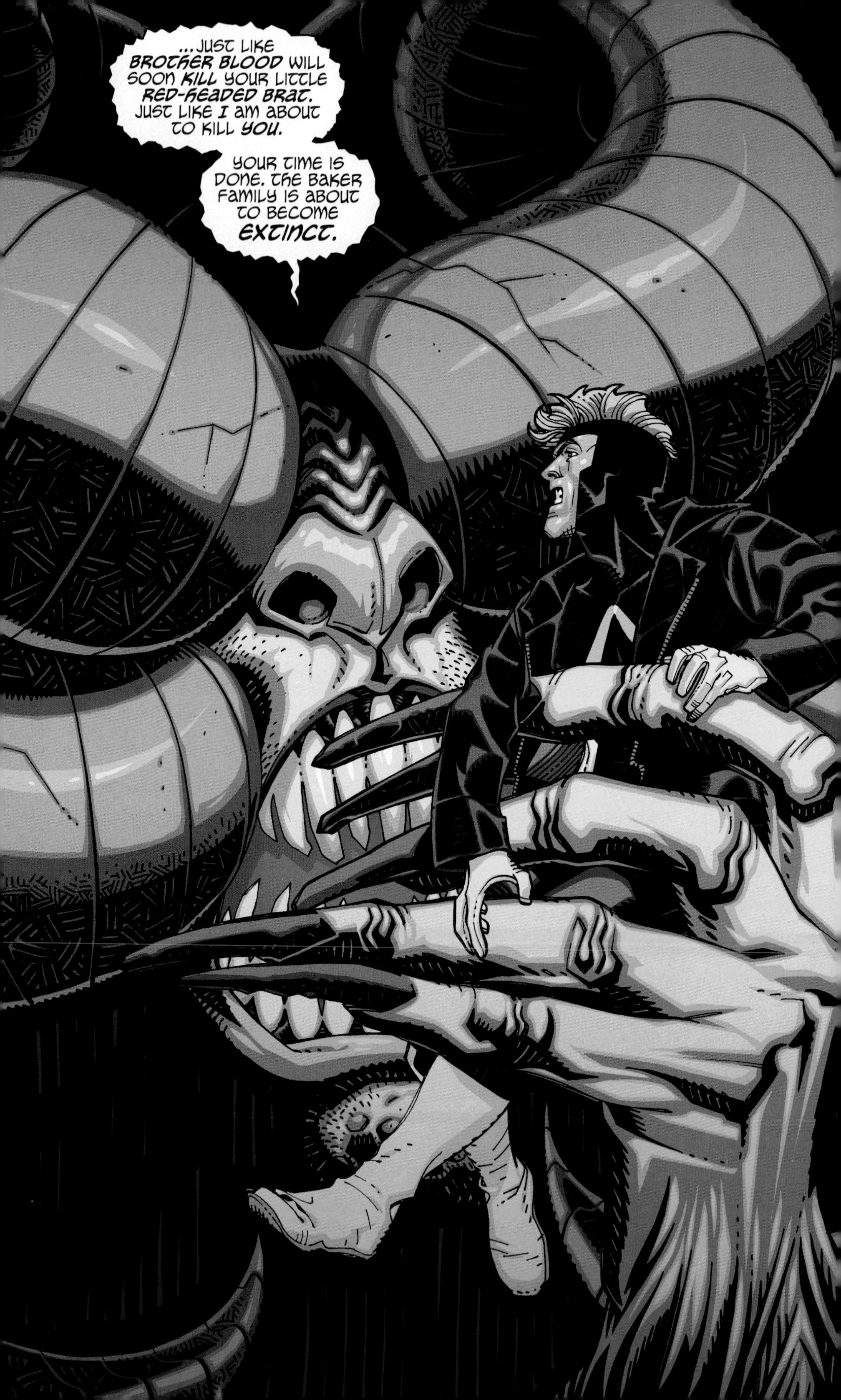
...JUST LIKE BROTHER BLOOD WILL SOON KILL YOUR LITTLE RED-HEADED BRAT. JUST LIKE I AM ABOUT TO KILL YOU.
YOUR TIME IS DONE. THE BAKER FAMILY IS ABOUT TO BECOME EXTINCT.

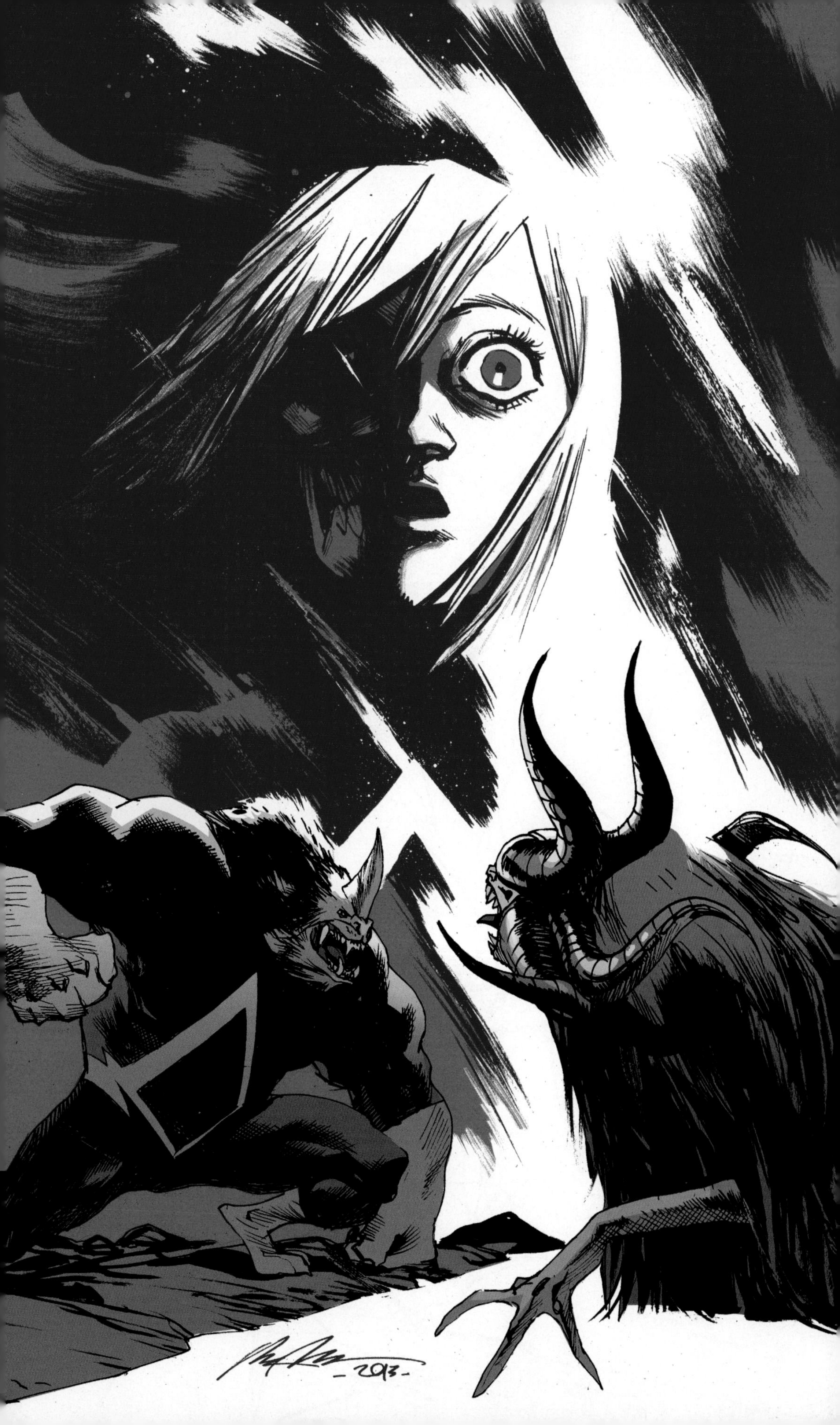

EVOLVE OR DIE PART 1
JEFF LEMIRE writer **RAFAEL ALBUQUERQUE** artist, interior and cover
JOHN KALISZ colorist **JARED K. FLETCHER** letterer

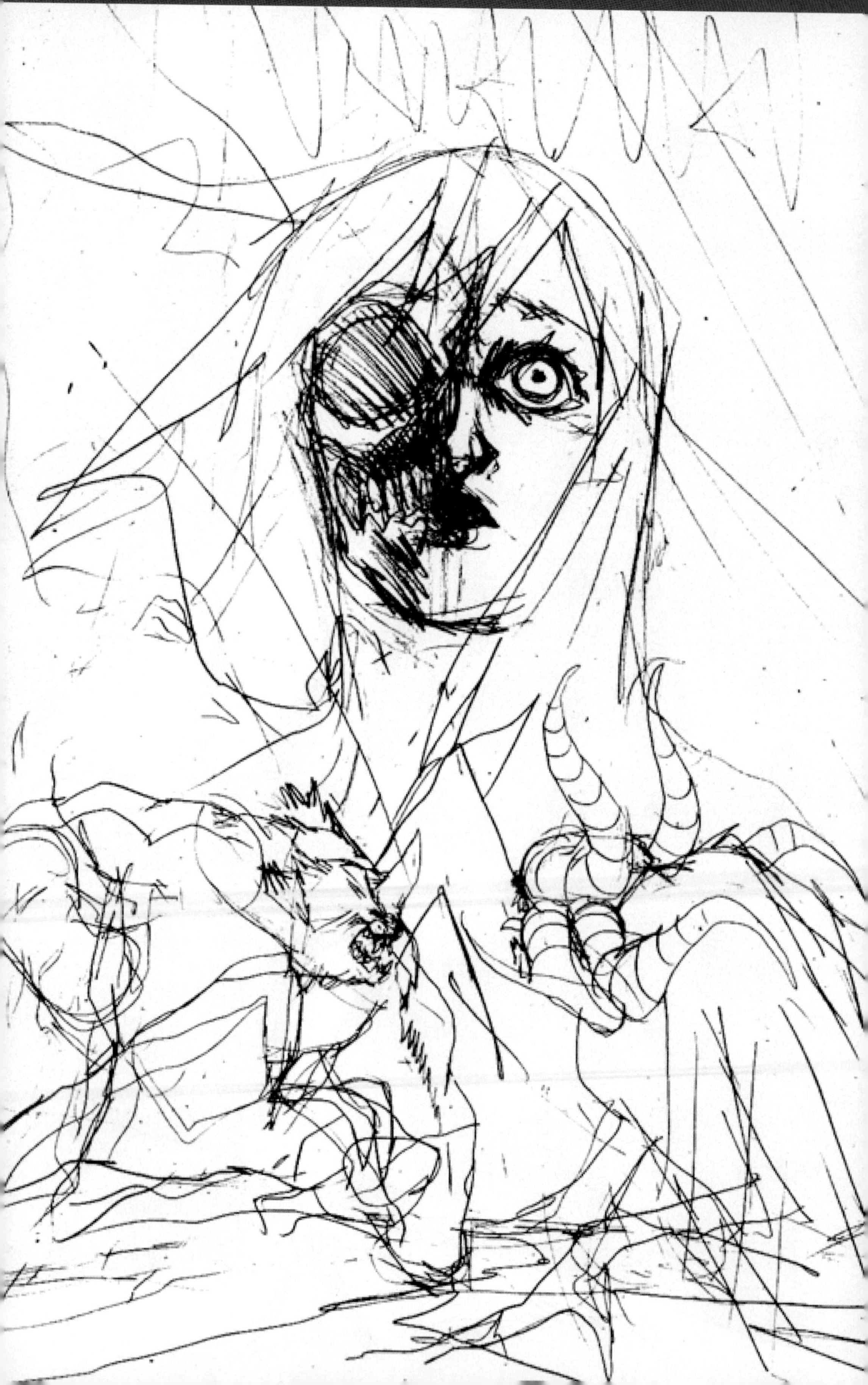

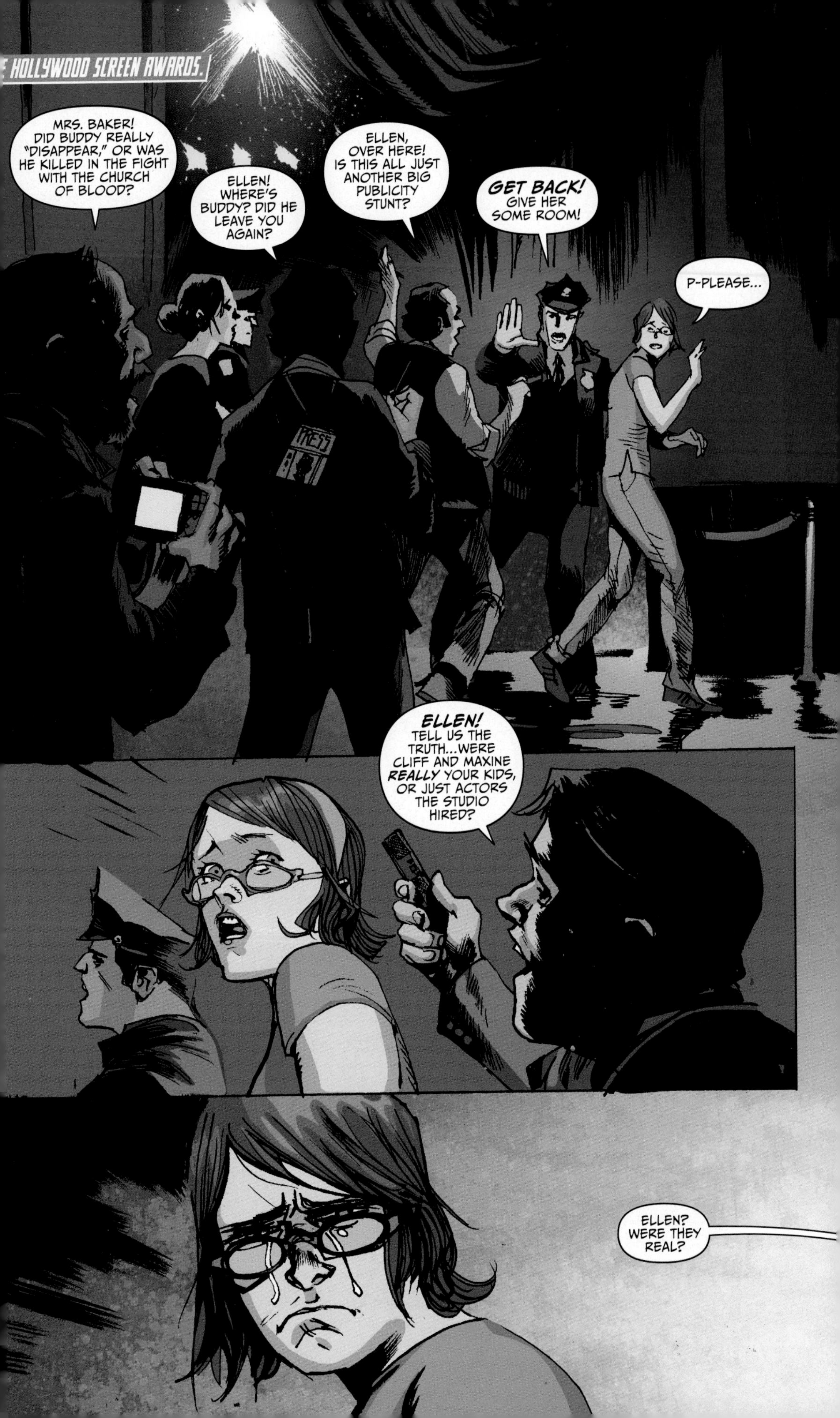
HOLLYWOOD SCREEN AWARDS.
MRS. BAKER! DID BUDDY REALLY "DISAPPEAR," OR WAS HE KILLED IN THE FIGHT WITH THE CHURCH OF BLOOD?
ELLEN! WHERE'S BUDDY? DID HE LEAVE YOU AGAIN?
ELLEN, OVER HERE! IS THIS ALL JUST ANOTHER BIG PUBLICITY STUNT?
GET BACK! GIVE HER SOME ROOM!
P-PLEASE...
PRESS
ELLEN! TELL US THE TRUTH...WERE CLIFF AND MAXINE REALLY YOUR KIDS, OR JUST ACTORS THE STUDIO HIRED?
ELLEN? WERE THEY REAL?

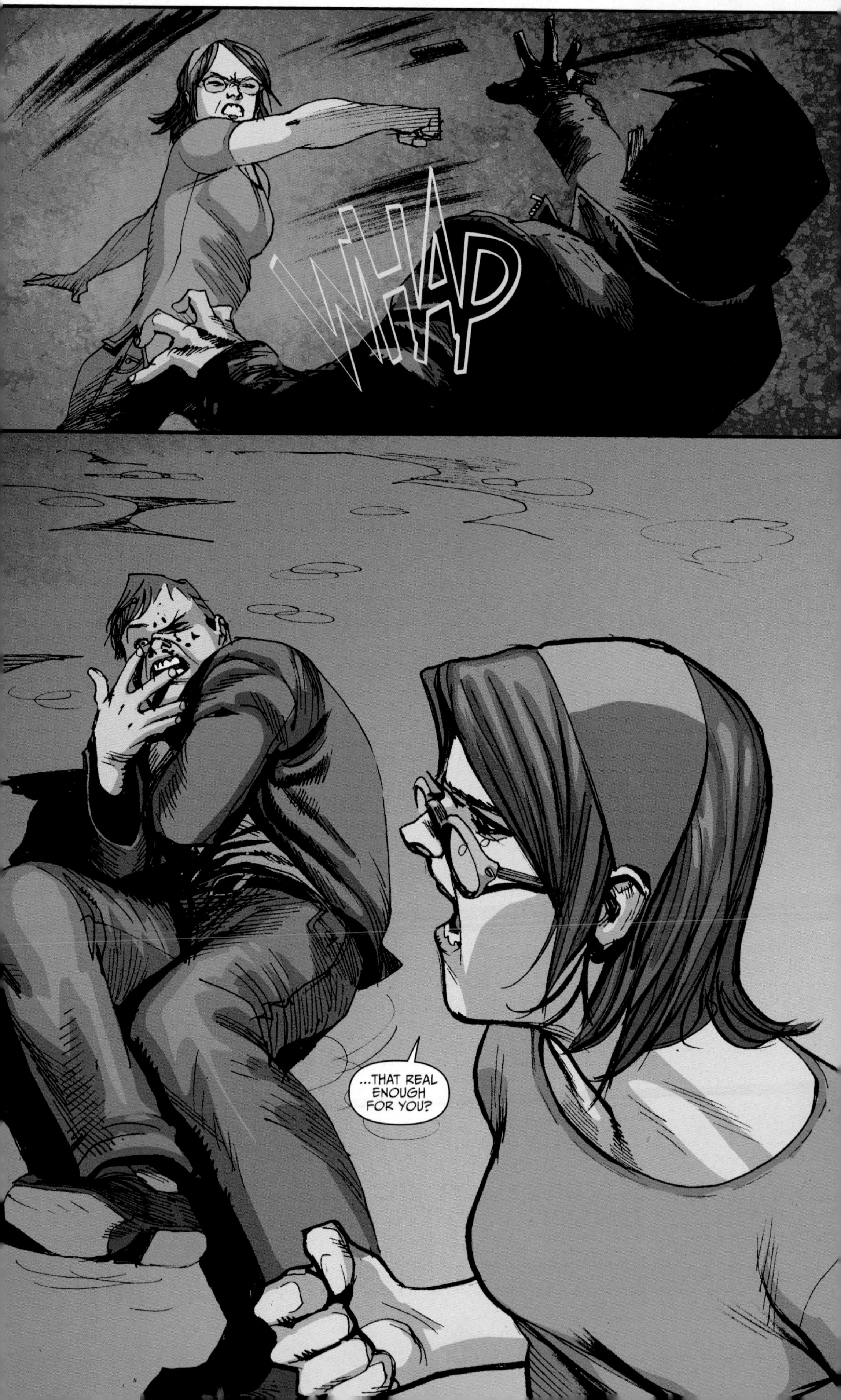
WHAP
...THAT REAL ENOUGH FOR YOU?

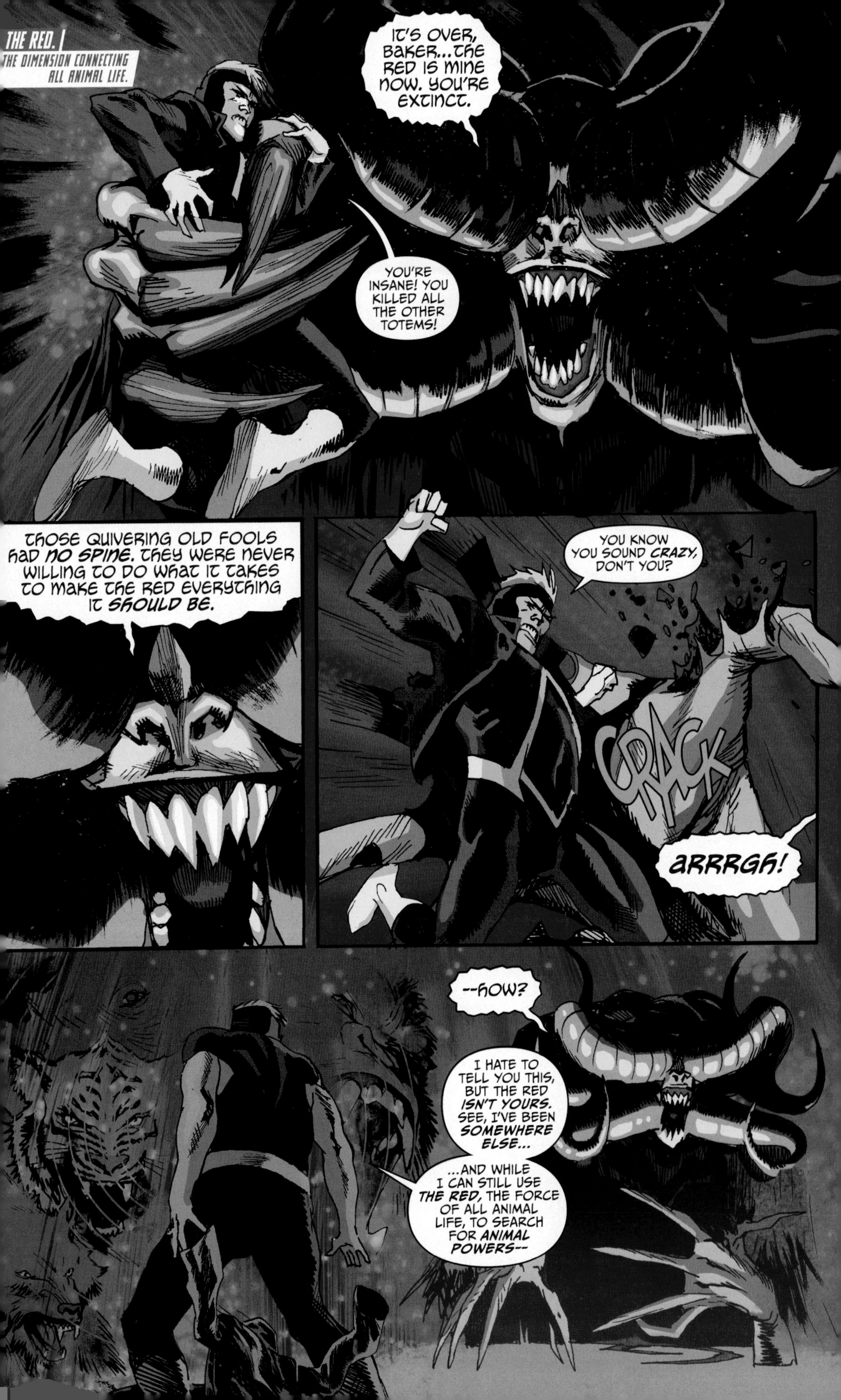
THE RED.
THE DIMENSION CONNECTING ALL ANIMAL LIFE.
IT'S OVER, BAKER...THE RED IS MINE NOW. YOU'RE EXTINCT.
YOU'RE INSANE! YOU KILLED ALL THE OTHER TOTEMS!
THOSE QUIVERING OLD FOOLS HAD NO SPINE. THEY WERE NEVER WILLING TO DO WHAT IT TAKES TO MAKE THE RED EVERYTHING IT SHOULD BE.
YOU KNOW YOU SOUND CRAZY, DON'T YOU?
CRACK
ARRRGH!
--HOW?
I HATE TO TELL YOU THIS, BUT THE RED ISN'T YOURS. SEE, I'VE BEEN SOMEWHERE ELSE...
...AND WHILE I CAN STILL USE THE RED, THE FORCE OF ALL ANIMAL LIFE, TO SEARCH FOR ANIMAL POWERS--

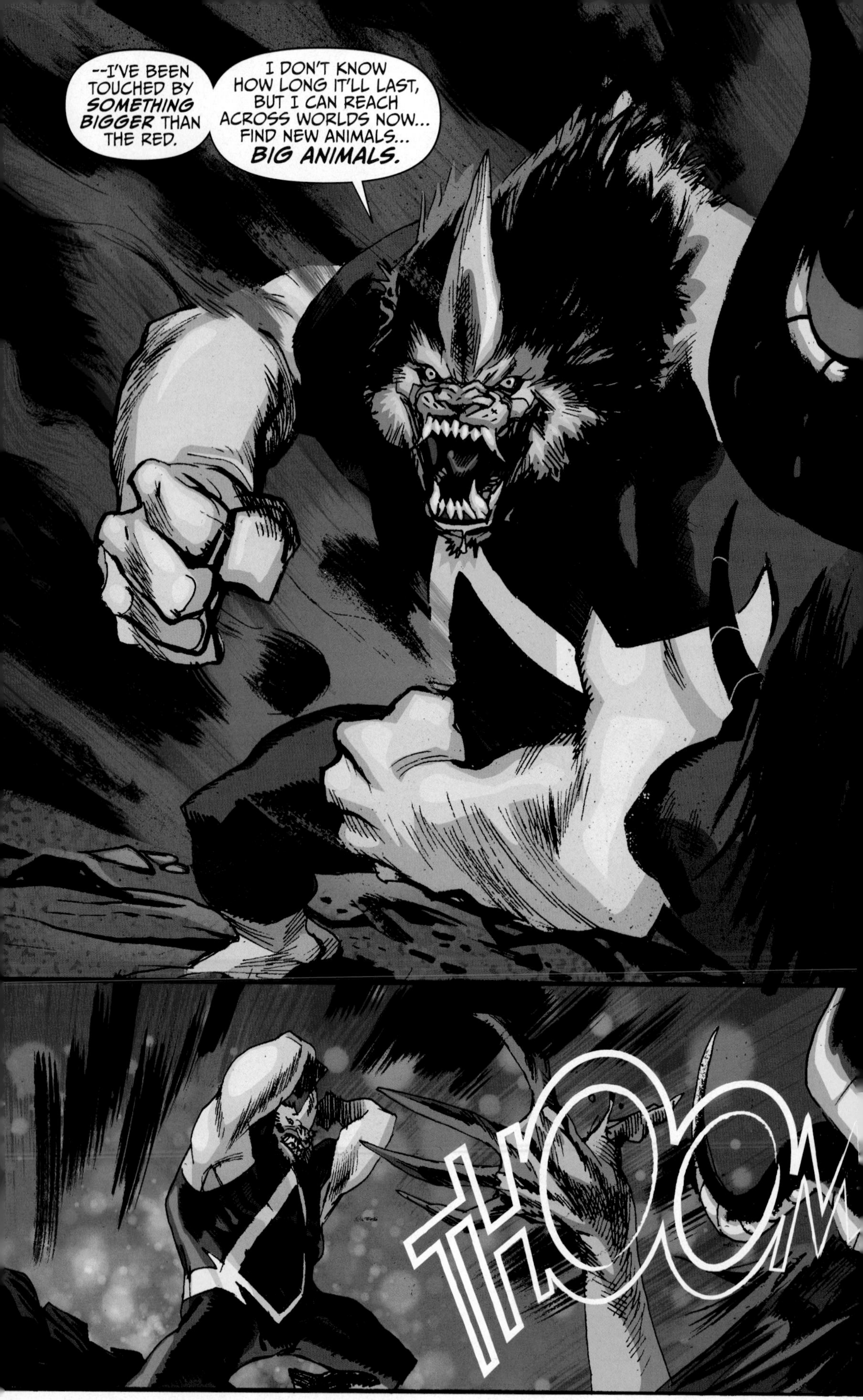
--I'VE BEEN TOUCHED BY SOMETHING BIGGER THAN THE RED.
I DON'T KNOW HOW LONG IT'LL LAST, BUT I CAN REACH ACROSS WORLDS NOW... FIND NEW ANIMALS... BIG ANIMALS.
THOOM

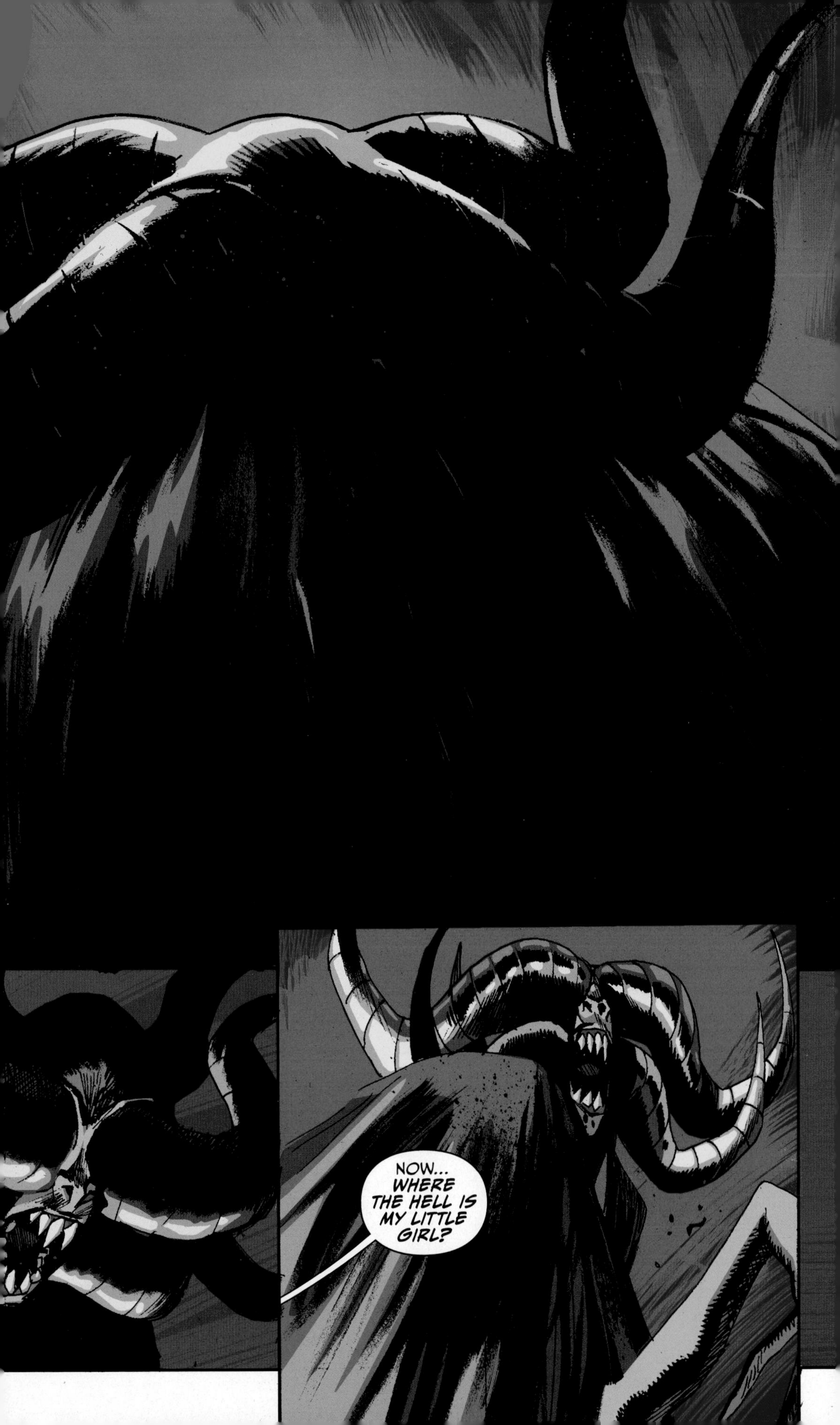
NOW... WHERE THE HELL IS MY LITTLE GIRL?

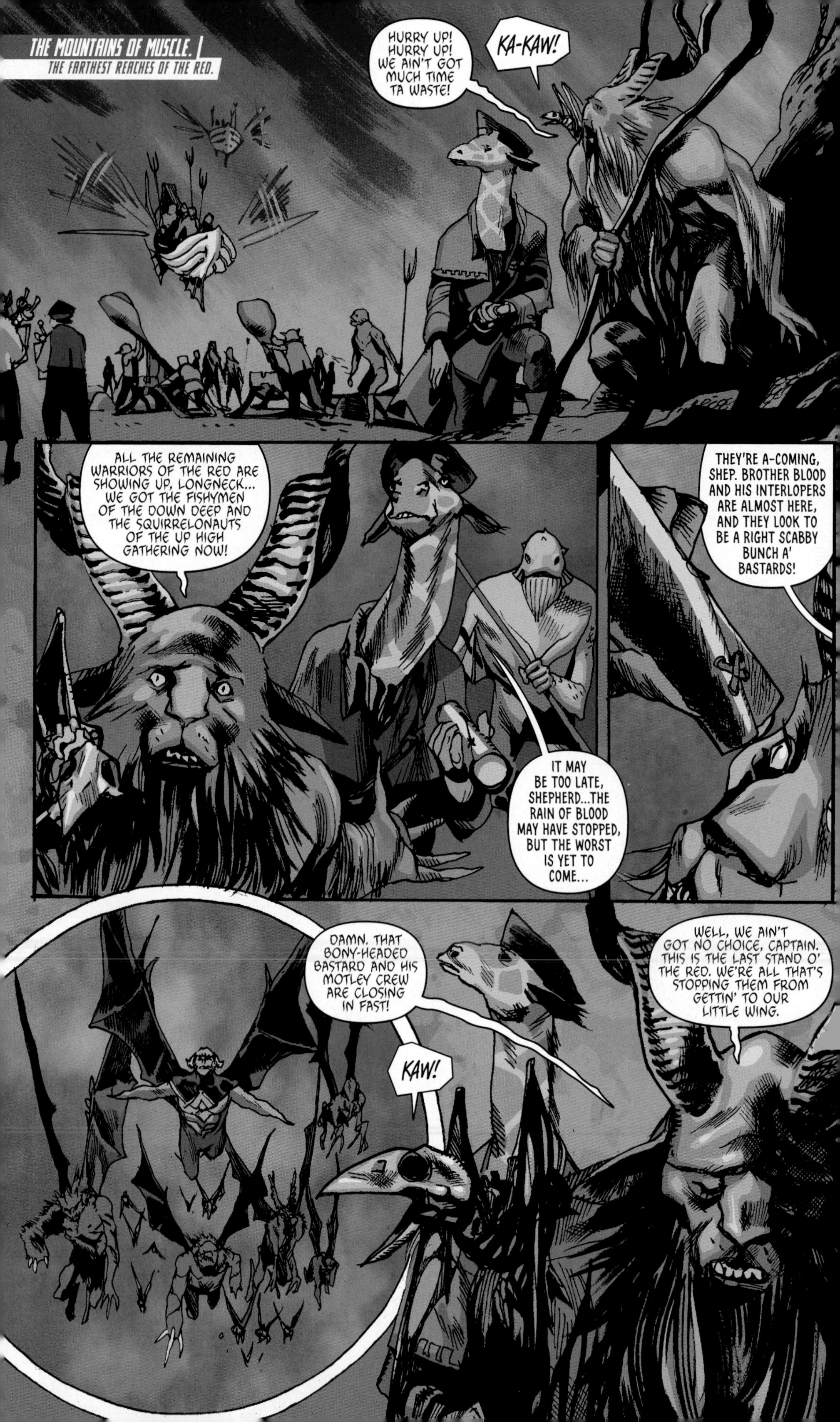
THE MOUNTAINS OF MUSCLE.
THE FARTHEST REACHES OF THE RED.
HURRY UP! HURRY UP! WE AIN'T GOT MUCH TIME TA WASTE!
KA-KAW!
ALL THE REMAINING WARRIORS OF THE RED ARE SHOWING UP, LONGNECK... WE GOT THE FISHYMEN OF THE DOWN DEEP AND THE SQUIRRELONAUTS OF THE UP HIGH GATHERING NOW!
IT MAY BE TOO LATE, SHEPHERD...THE RAIN OF BLOOD MAY HAVE STOPPED, BUT THE WORST IS YET TO COME...
THEY'RE A-COMING, SHEP. BROTHER BLOOD AND HIS INTERLOPERS ARE ALMOST HERE, AND THEY LOOK TO BE A RIGHT SCABBY BUNCH A' BASTARDS!
DAMN. THAT BONY-HEADED BASTARD AND HIS MOTLEY CREW ARE CLOSING IN FAST!
KAW!
WELL, WE AIN'T GOT NO CHOICE, CAPTAIN. THIS IS THE LAST STAND O' THE RED. WE'RE ALL THAT'S STOPPING THEM FROM GETTIN' TO OUR LITTLE WING.

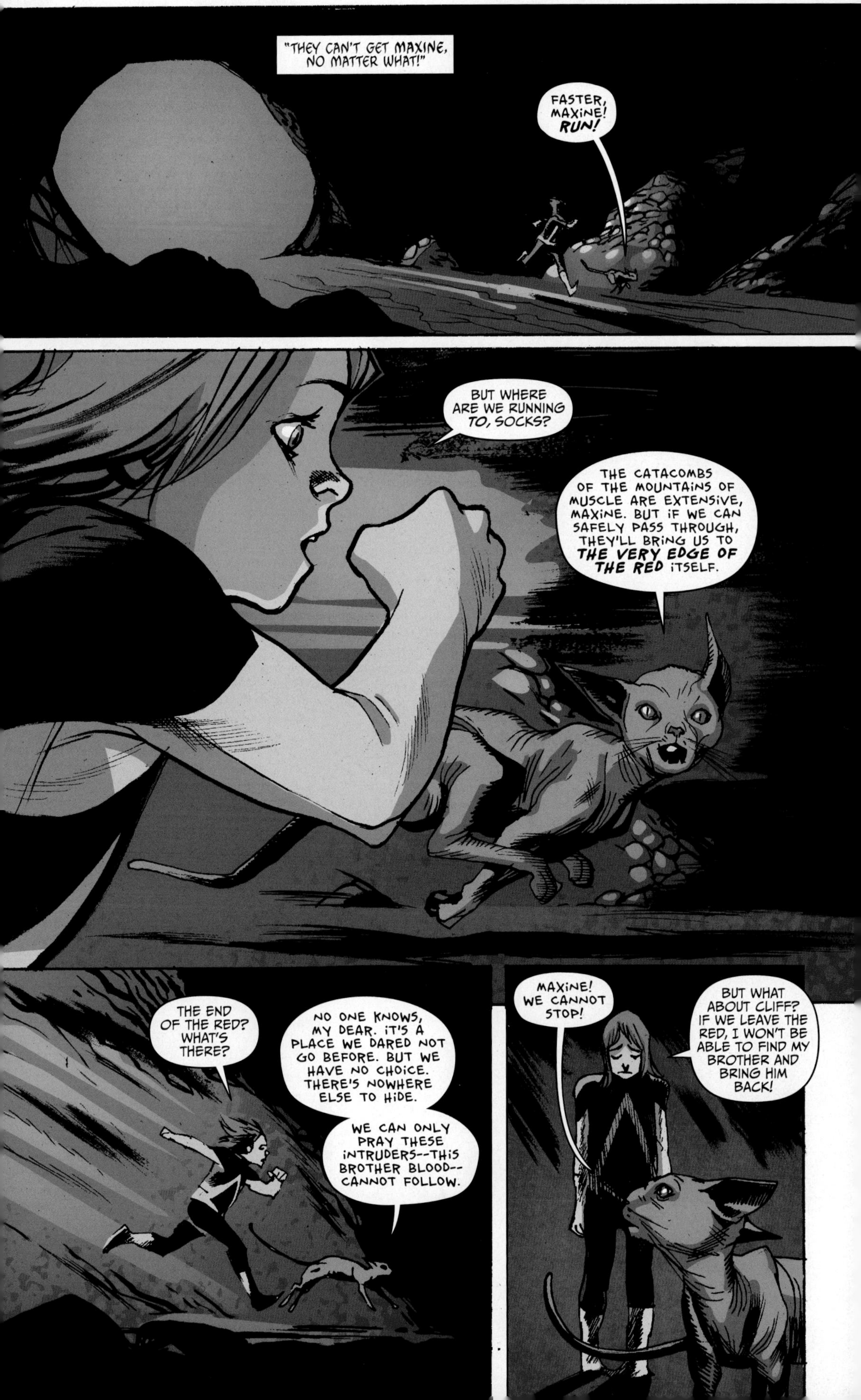
"THEY CAN'T GET MAXINE, NO MATTER WHAT!"
FASTER, MAXINE! RUN!
BUT WHERE ARE WE RUNNING TO, SOCKS?
THE CATACOMBS OF THE MOUNTAINS OF MUSCLE ARE EXTENSIVE, MAXINE. BUT IF WE CAN SAFELY PASS THROUGH, THEY'LL BRING US TO THE VERY EDGE OF THE RED ITSELF.
THE END OF THE RED? WHAT'S THERE?
NO ONE KNOWS, MY DEAR. IT'S A PLACE WE DARED NOT GO BEFORE. BUT WE HAVE NO CHOICE. THERE'S NOWHERE ELSE TO HIDE.
WE CAN ONLY PRAY THESE INTRUDERS--THIS BROTHER BLOOD--CANNOT FOLLOW.
MAXINE! WE CANNOT STOP!
BUT WHAT ABOUT CLIFF? IF WE LEAVE THE RED, I WON'T BE ABLE TO FIND MY BROTHER AND BRING HIM BACK!

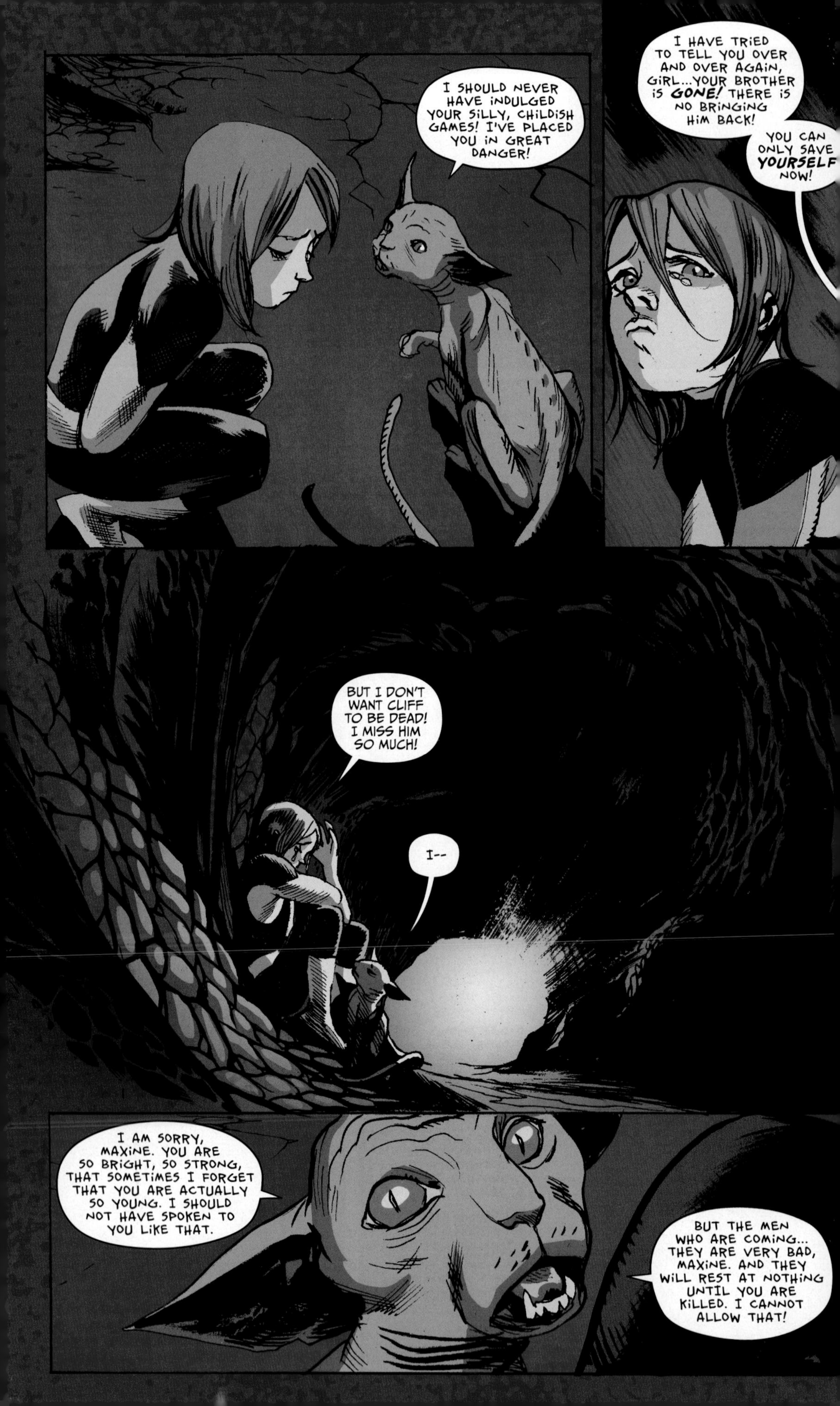
I SHOULD NEVER HAVE INDULGED YOUR SILLY, CHILDISH GAMES! I'VE PLACED YOU IN GREAT DANGER!
I HAVE TRIED TO TELL YOU OVER AND OVER AGAIN, GIRL...YOUR BROTHER IS GONE! THERE IS NO BRINGING HIM BACK!
YOU CAN ONLY SAVE YOURSELF NOW!
BUT I DON'T WANT CLIFF TO BE DEAD! I MISS HIM SO MUCH!
I--
I AM SORRY, MAXINE. YOU ARE SO BRIGHT, SO STRONG, THAT SOMETIMES I FORGET THAT YOU ARE ACTUALLY SO YOUNG. I SHOULD NOT HAVE SPOKEN TO YOU LIKE THAT.
BUT THE MEN WHO ARE COMING... THEY ARE VERY BAD, MAXINE. AND THEY WILL REST AT NOTHING UNTIL YOU ARE KILLED. I CANNOT ALLOW THAT!

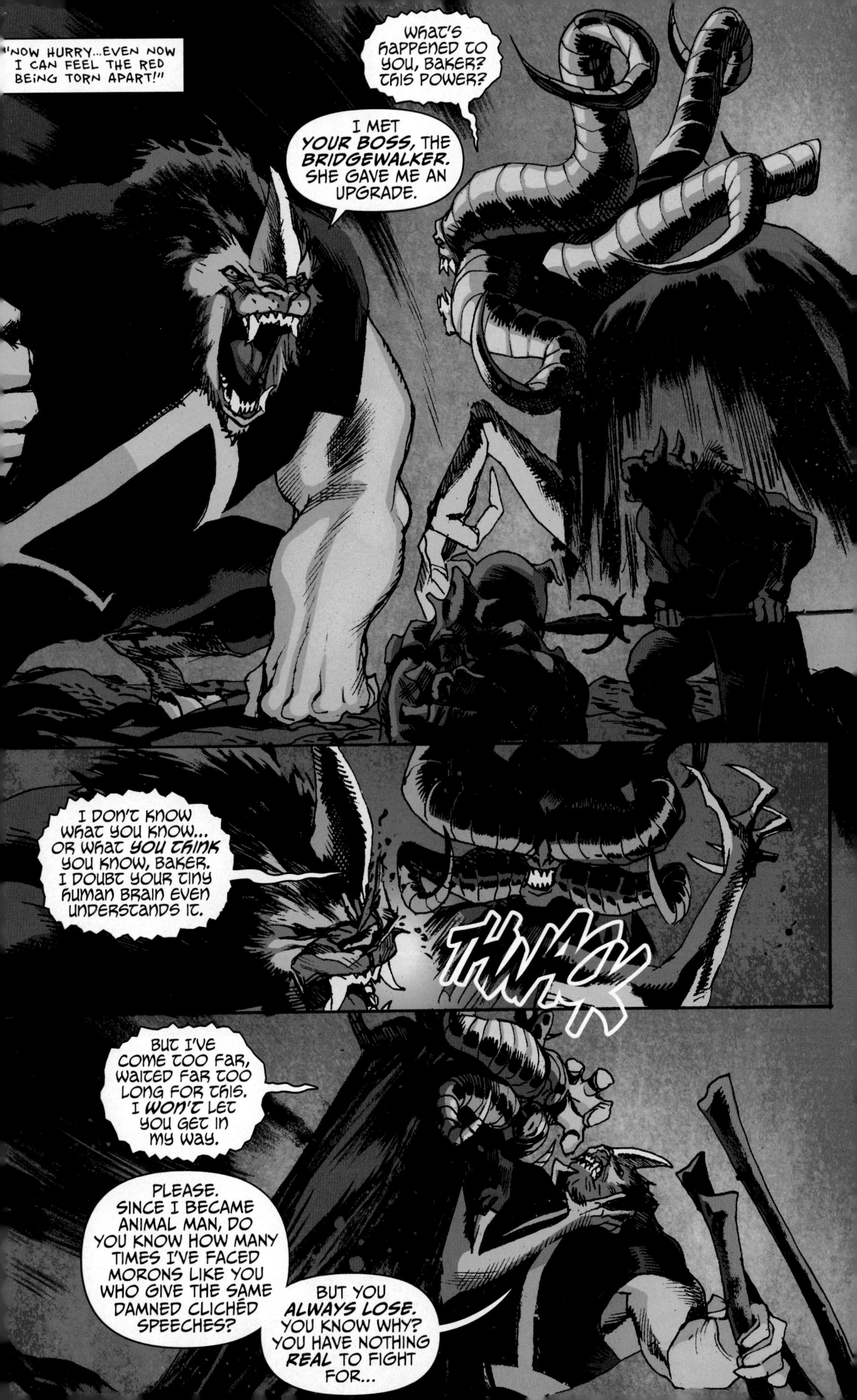
"NOW HURRY...EVEN NOW I CAN FEEL THE RED BEING TORN APART!"
WHAT'S HAPPENED TO YOU, BAKER? THIS POWER?
I MET YOUR BOSS, THE BRIDGEWALKER. SHE GAVE ME AN UPGRADE.
I DON'T KNOW WHAT YOU KNOW... OR WHAT YOU THINK YOU KNOW, BAKER. I DOUBT YOUR TINY HUMAN BRAIN EVEN UNDERSTANDS IT.
THWACK
BUT I'VE COME TOO FAR, WAITED FAR TOO LONG FOR THIS. I WON'T LET YOU GET IN MY WAY.
PLEASE. SINCE I BECAME ANIMAL MAN, DO YOU KNOW HOW MANY TIMES I'VE FACED MORONS LIKE YOU WHO GIVE THE SAME DAMNED CLICHÉD SPEECHES?
BUT YOU ALWAYS LOSE. YOU KNOW WHY? YOU HAVE NOTHING REAL TO FIGHT FOR...

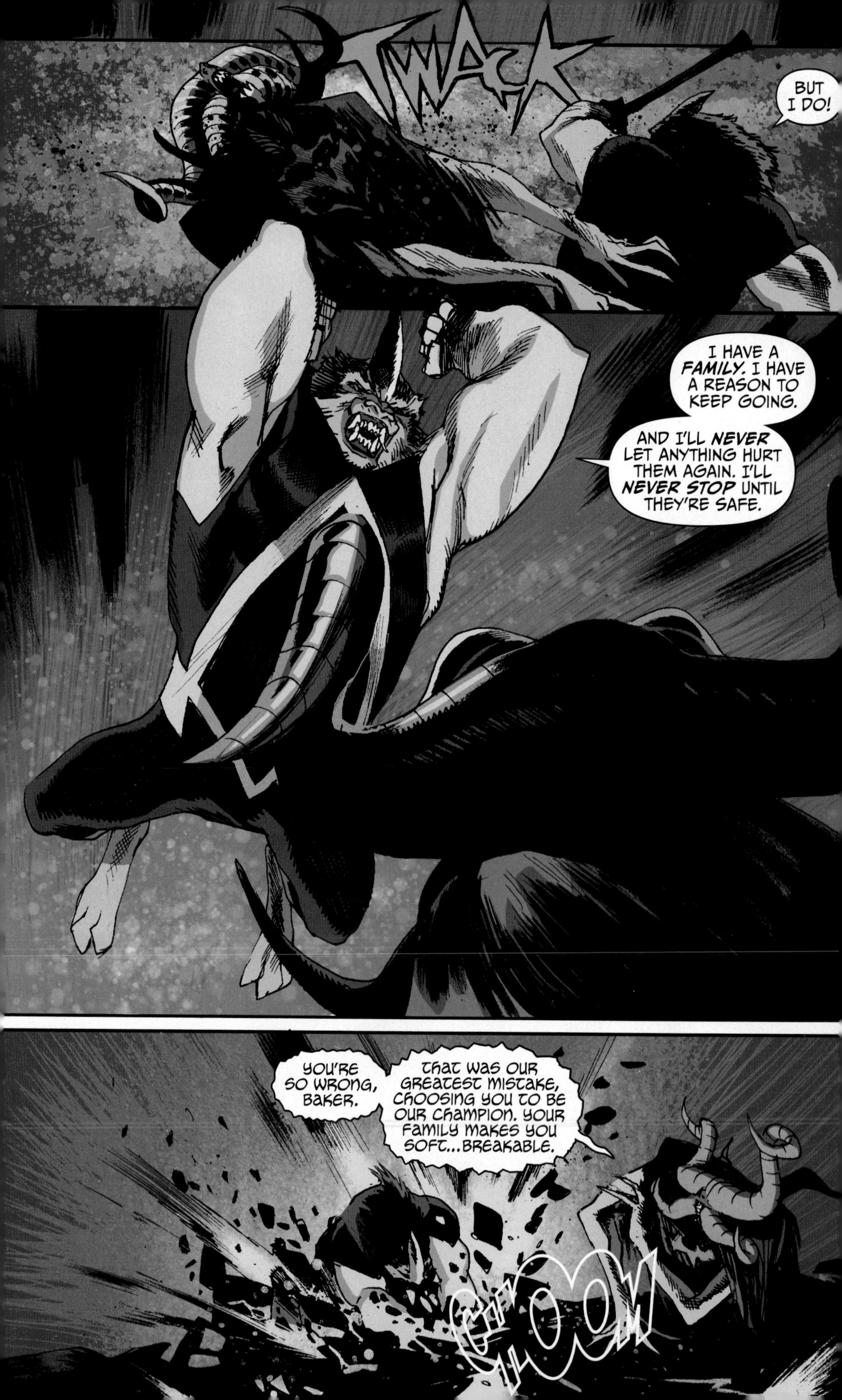
TWACK
BUT I DO!
I HAVE A *FAMILY.* I HAVE A REASON TO KEEP GOING.
AND I'LL ***NEVER*** LET ANYTHING HURT THEM AGAIN. I'LL ***NEVER STOP*** UNTIL THEY'RE SAFE.
YOU'RE SO WRONG, BAKER.
THAT WAS OUR GREATEST MISTAKE, CHOOSING YOU TO BE OUR CHAMPION. YOUR FAMILY MAKES YOU SOFT...BREAKABLE.
GOOM

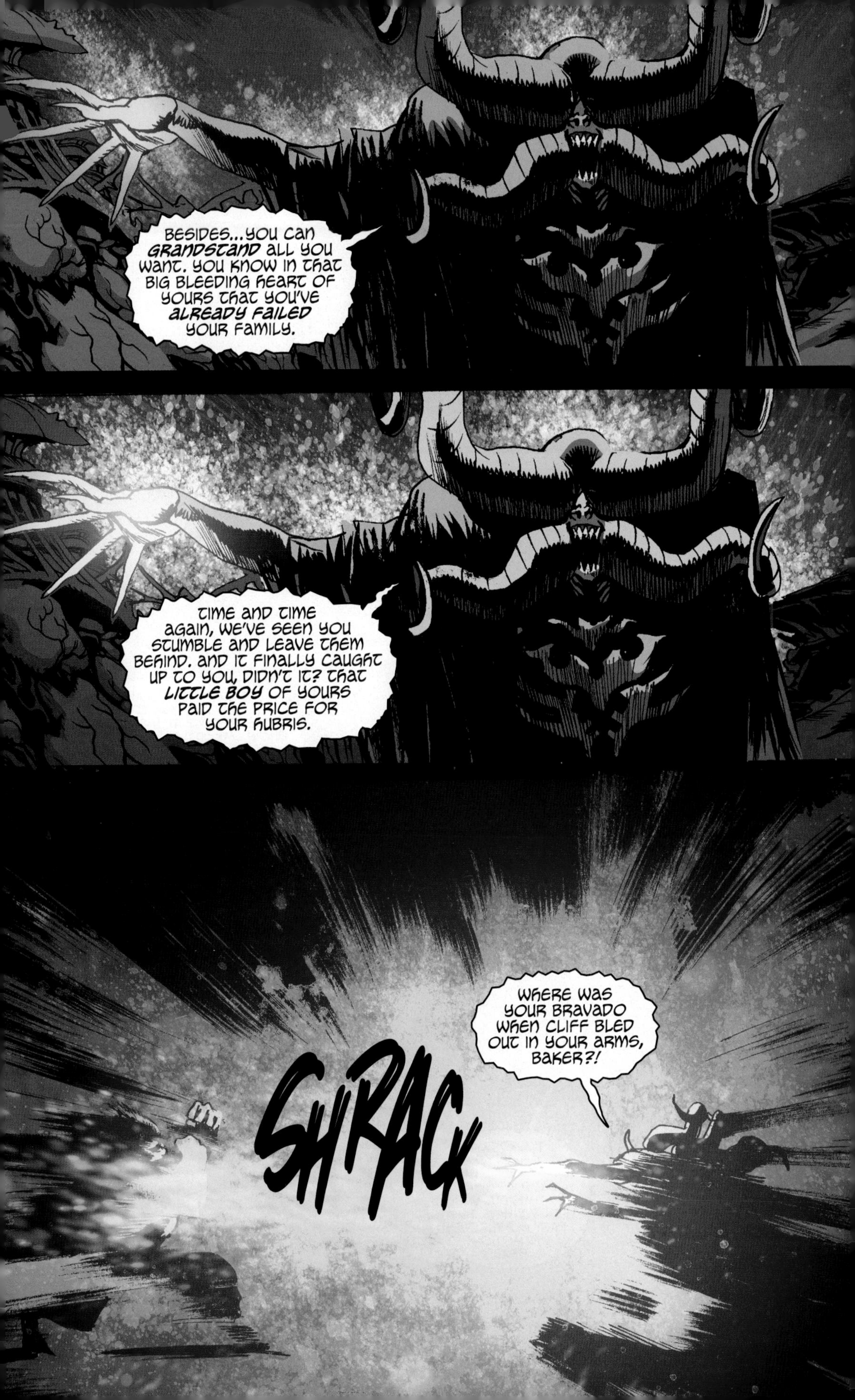
BESIDES...YOU CAN GRANDSTAND ALL YOU WANT. YOU KNOW IN THAT BIG BLEEDING HEART OF YOURS THAT YOU'VE ALREADY FAILED YOUR FAMILY.
TIME AND TIME AGAIN, WE'VE SEEN YOU STUMBLE AND LEAVE THEM BEHIND. AND IT FINALLY CAUGHT UP TO YOU, DIDN'T IT? THAT LITTLE BOY OF YOURS PAID THE PRICE FOR YOUR HUBRIS.
WHERE WAS YOUR BRAVADO WHEN CLIFF BLED OUT IN YOUR ARMS, BAKER?!
SHRACK

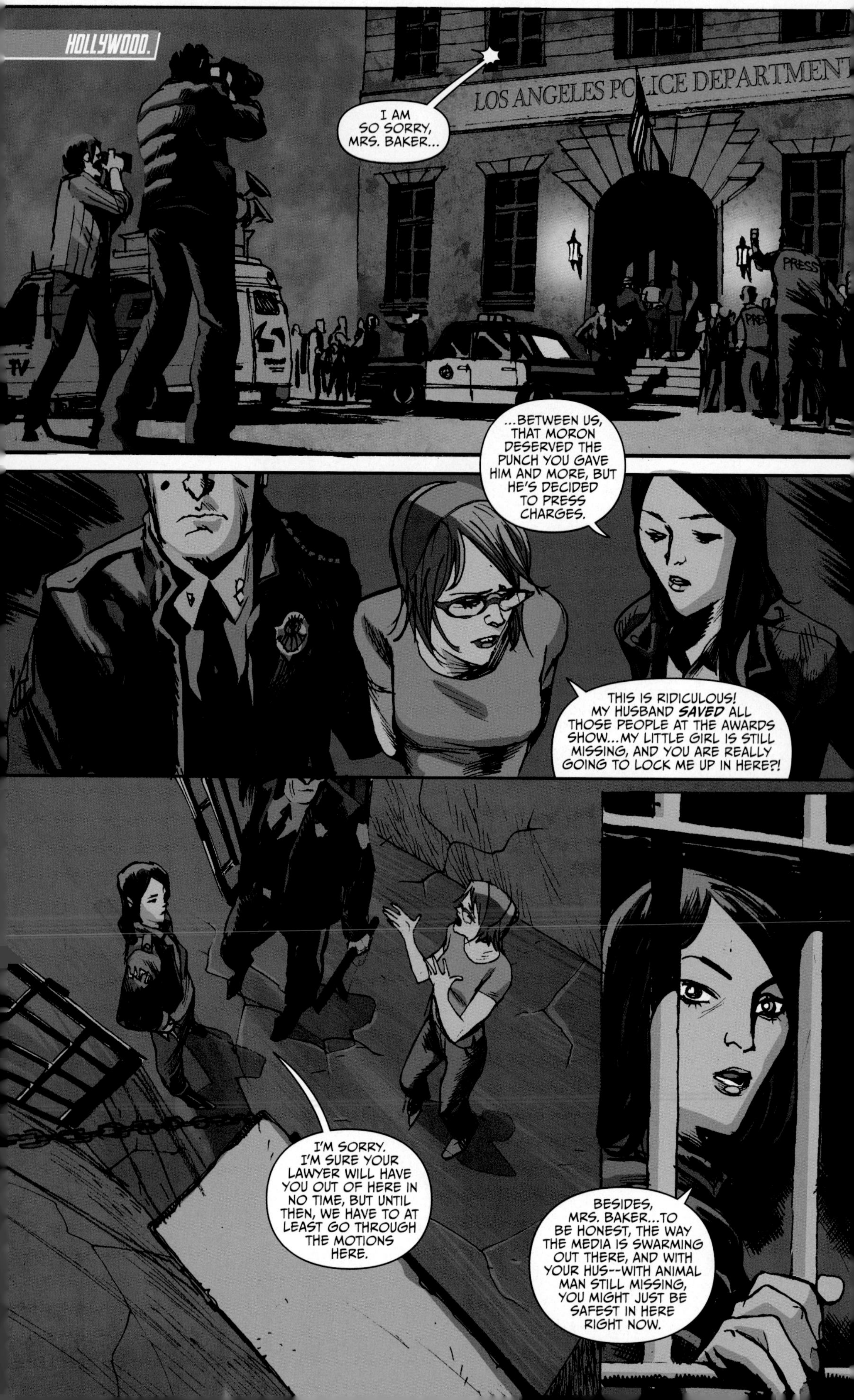
HOLLYWOOD.
LOS ANGELES POLICE DEPARTMENT
I AM SO SORRY, MRS. BAKER...
...BETWEEN US, THAT MORON DESERVED THE PUNCH YOU GAVE HIM AND MORE, BUT HE'S DECIDED TO PRESS CHARGES.
THIS IS RIDICULOUS! MY HUSBAND SAVED ALL THOSE PEOPLE AT THE AWARDS SHOW...MY LITTLE GIRL IS STILL MISSING, AND YOU ARE REALLY GOING TO LOCK ME UP IN HERE?!
I'M SORRY. I'M SURE YOUR LAWYER WILL HAVE YOU OUT OF HERE IN NO TIME, BUT UNTIL THEN, WE HAVE TO AT LEAST GO THROUGH THE MOTIONS HERE.
BESIDES, MRS. BAKER...TO BE HONEST, THE WAY THE MEDIA IS SWARMING OUT THERE, AND WITH YOUR HUS--WITH ANIMAL MAN STILL MISSING, YOU MIGHT JUST BE SAFEST IN HERE RIGHT NOW.

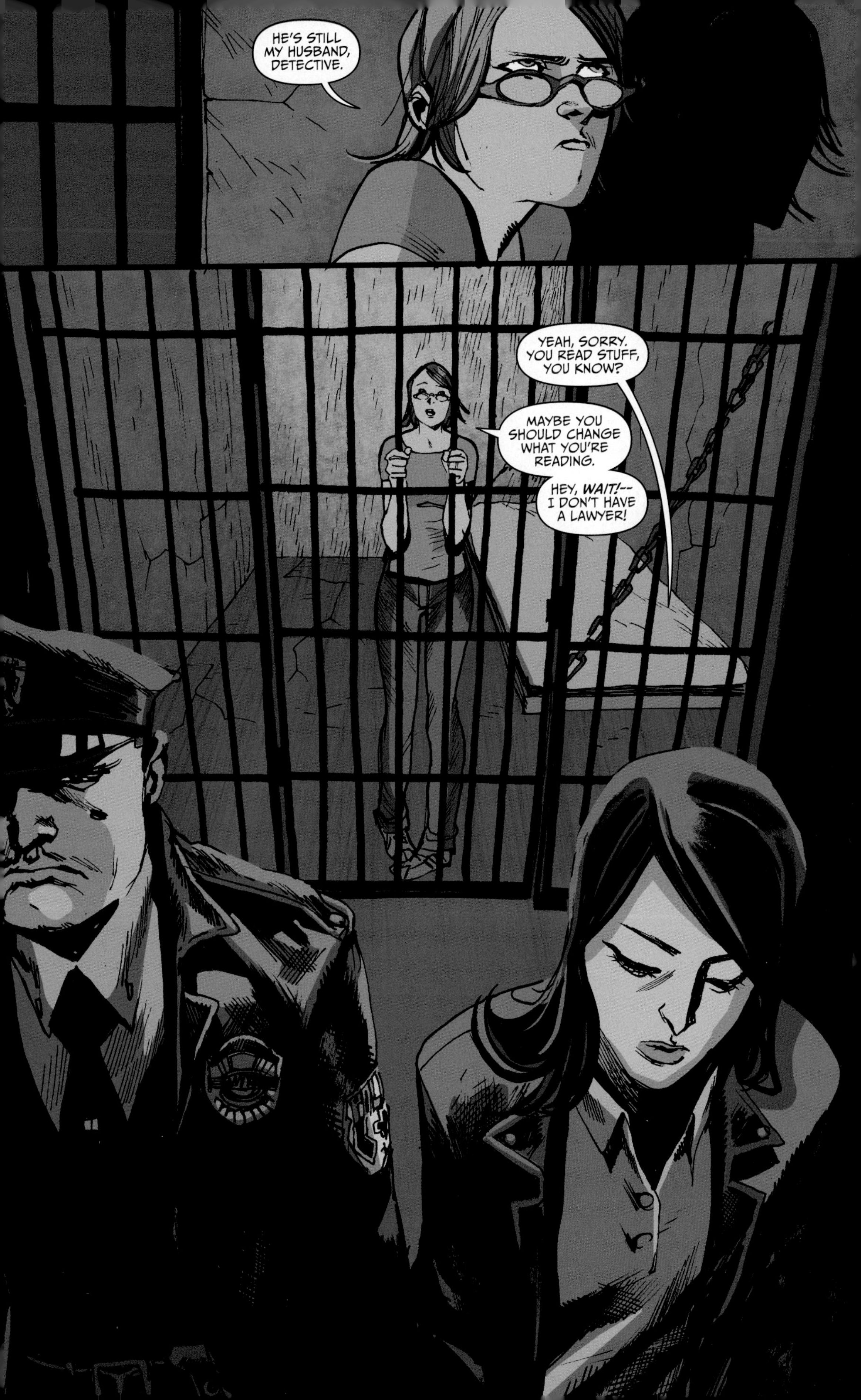
HE'S STILL MY HUSBAND, DETECTIVE.
YEAH, SORRY. YOU READ STUFF, YOU KNOW?
MAYBE YOU SHOULD CHANGE WHAT YOU'RE READING.
HEY, *WAIT!*-- I DON'T HAVE A LAWYER!

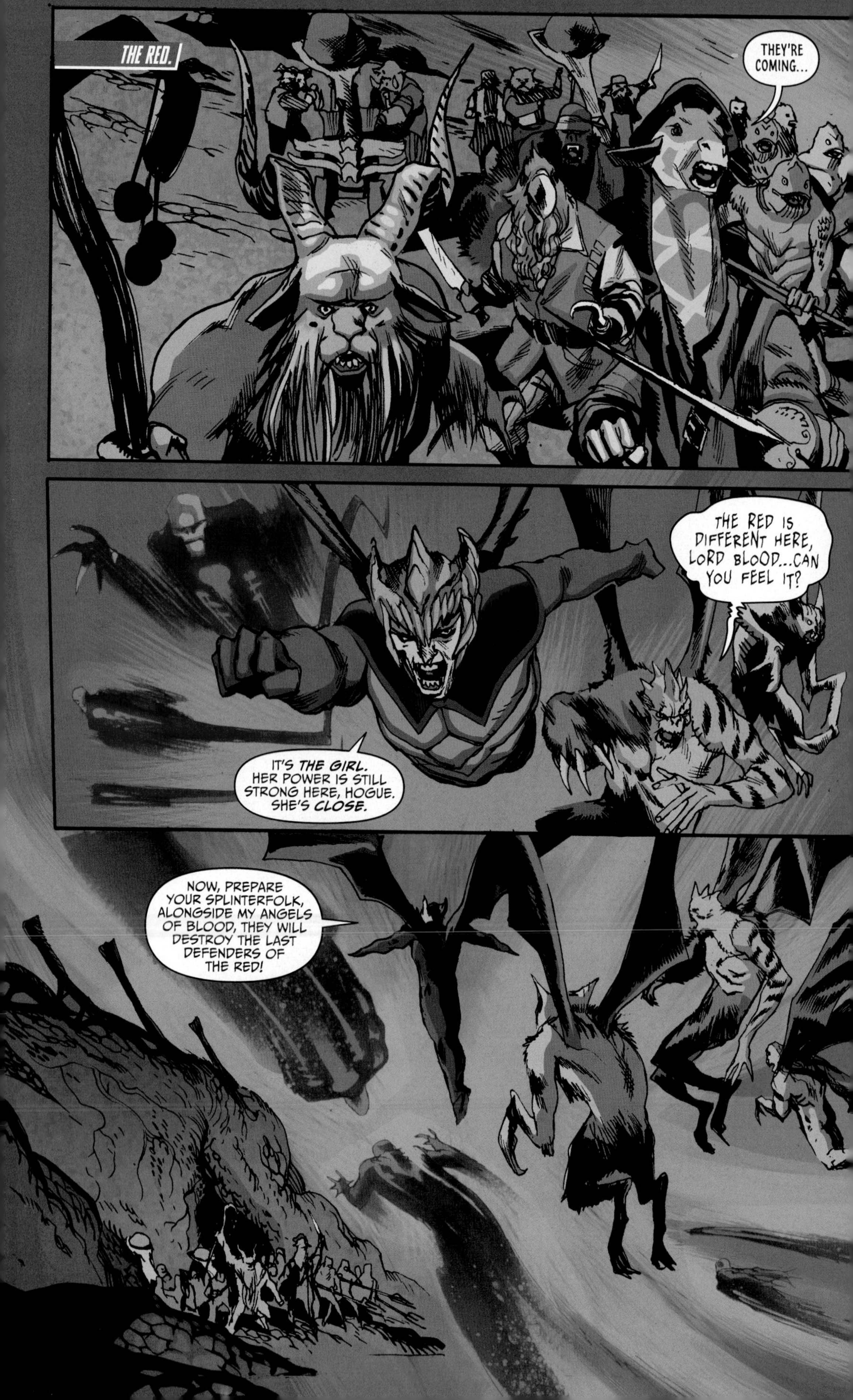
THE RED.
THEY'RE COMING...
THE RED IS DIFFERENT HERE, LORD BLOOD...CAN YOU FEEL IT?
IT'S THE GIRL. HER POWER IS STILL STRONG HERE, HOGUE. SHE'S CLOSE.
NOW, PREPARE YOUR SPLINTERFOLK, ALONGSIDE MY ANGELS OF BLOOD, THEY WILL DESTROY THE LAST DEFENDERS OF THE RED!

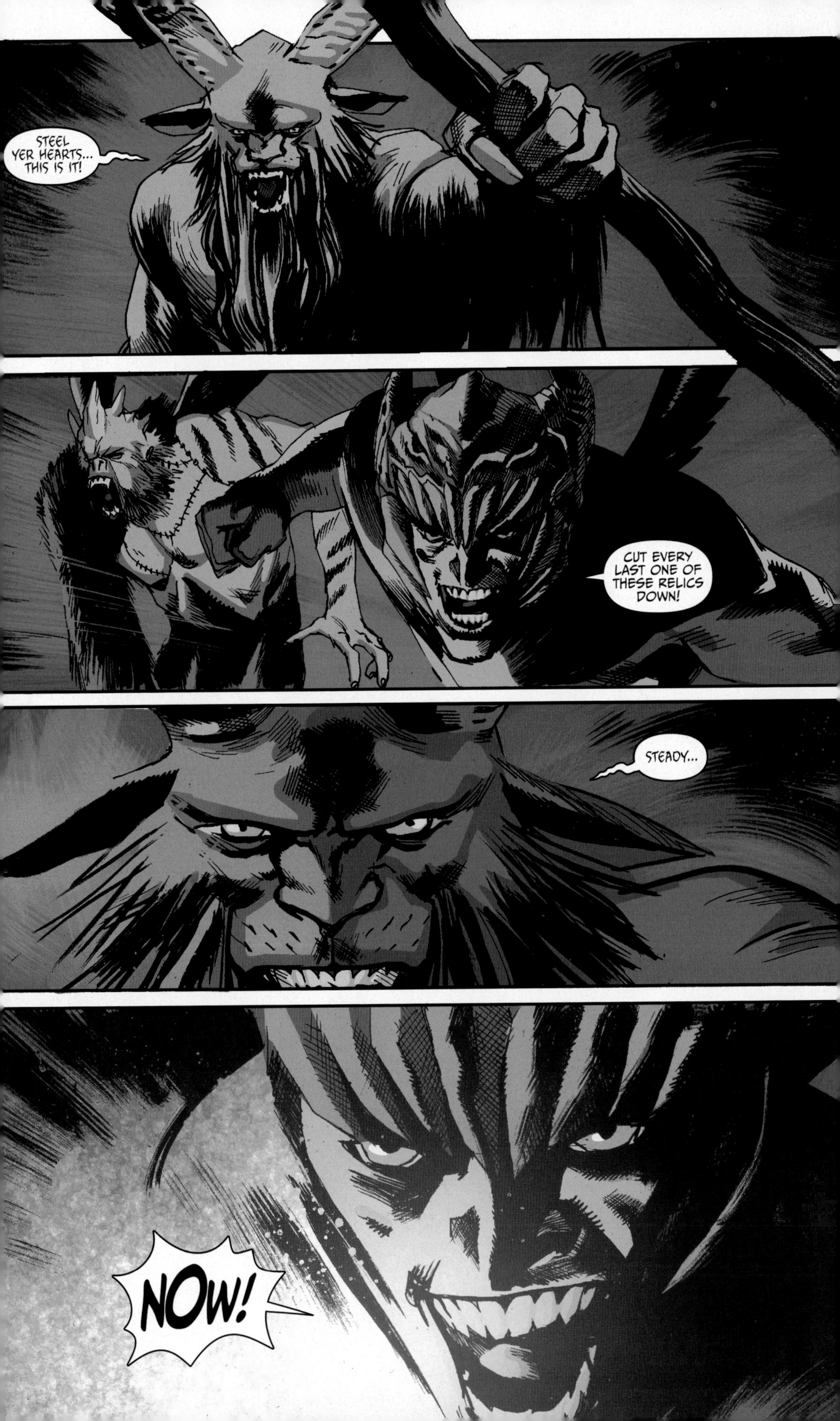
STEEL YER HEARTS... THIS IS IT!
CUT EVERY LAST ONE OF THESE RELICS DOWN!
STEADY...
NOW!

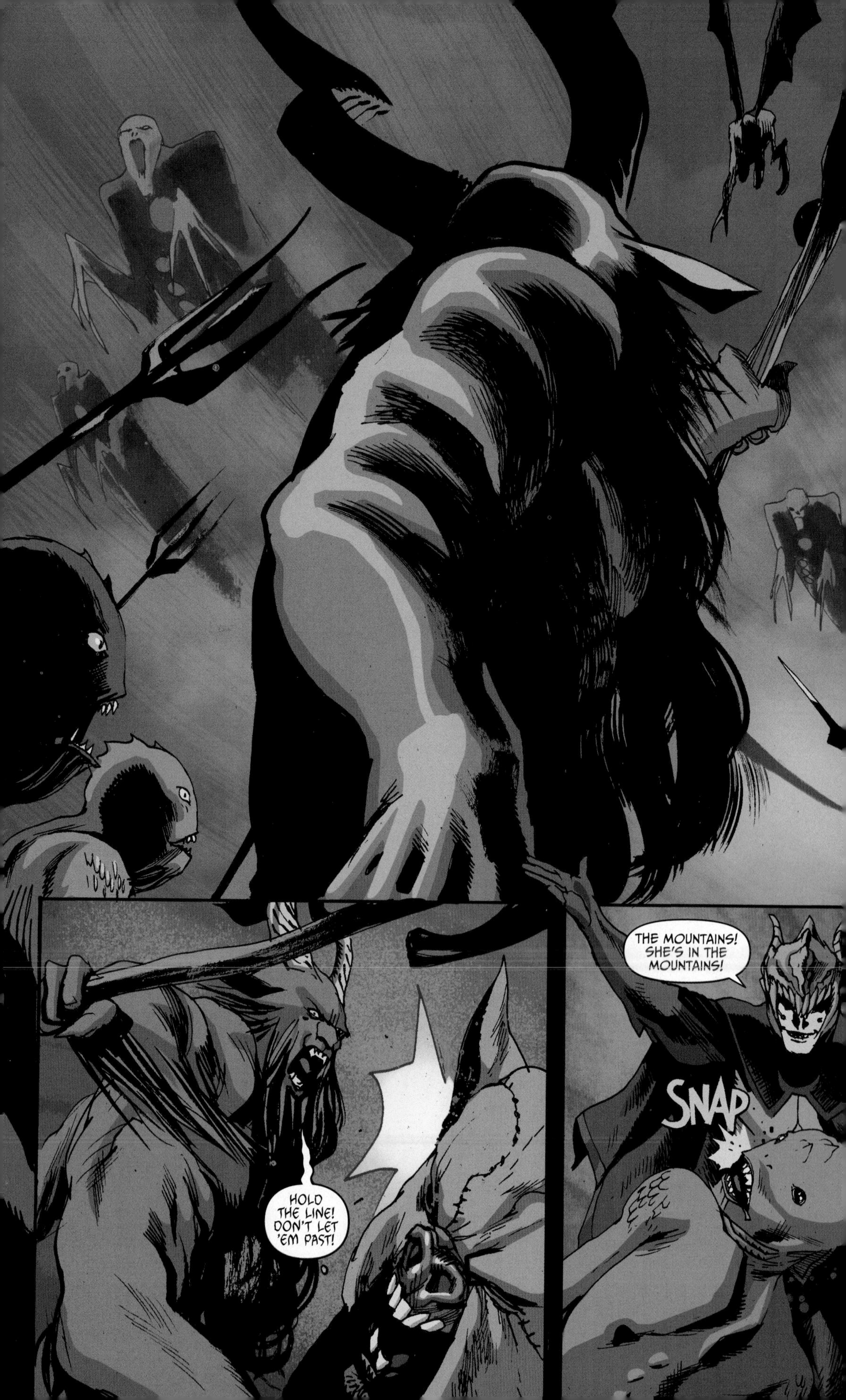
HOLD THE LINE! DON'T LET 'EM PAST!
THE MOUNTAINS! SHE'S IN THE MOUNTAINS!
SNAP

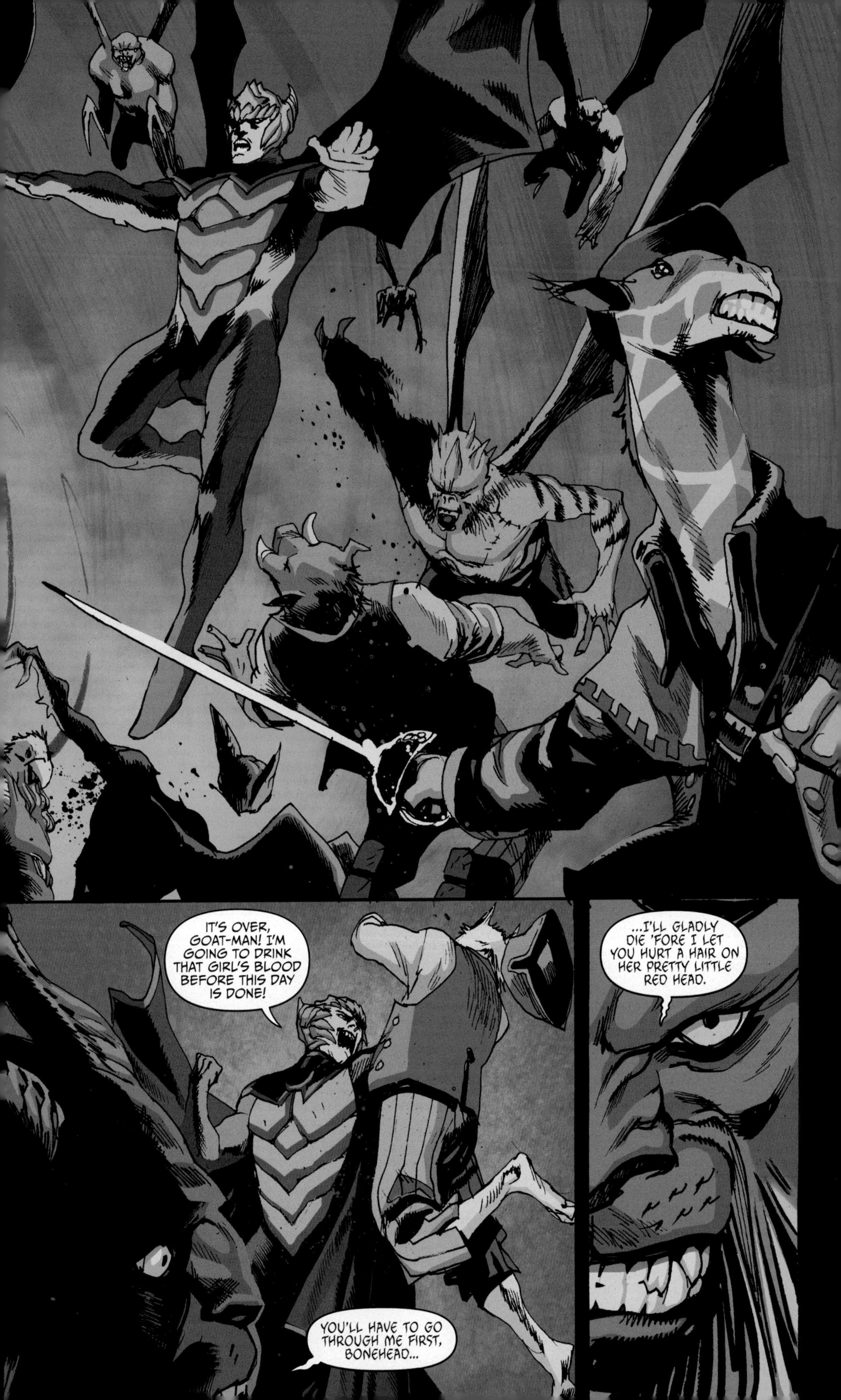
IT'S OVER, GOAT-MAN! I'M GOING TO DRINK THAT GIRL'S BLOOD BEFORE THIS DAY IS DONE!
YOU'LL HAVE TO GO THROUGH ME FIRST, BONEHEAD...
...I'LL GLADLY DIE 'FORE I LET YOU HURT A HAIR ON HER PRETTY LITTLE RED HEAD.

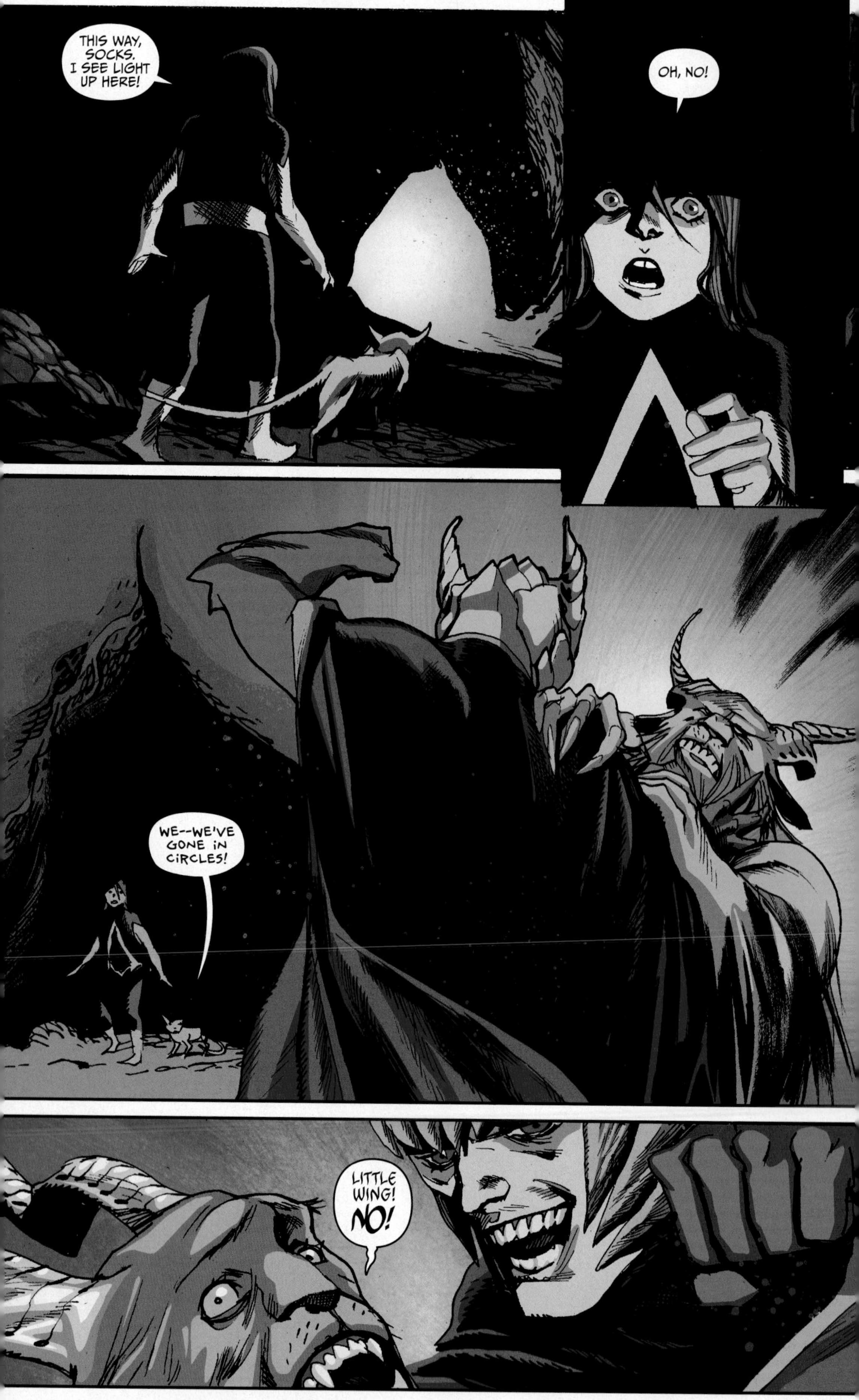
THIS WAY, SOCKS. I SEE LIGHT UP HERE!
OH, NO!
WE--WE'VE GONE IN CIRCLES!
LITTLE WING! NO!

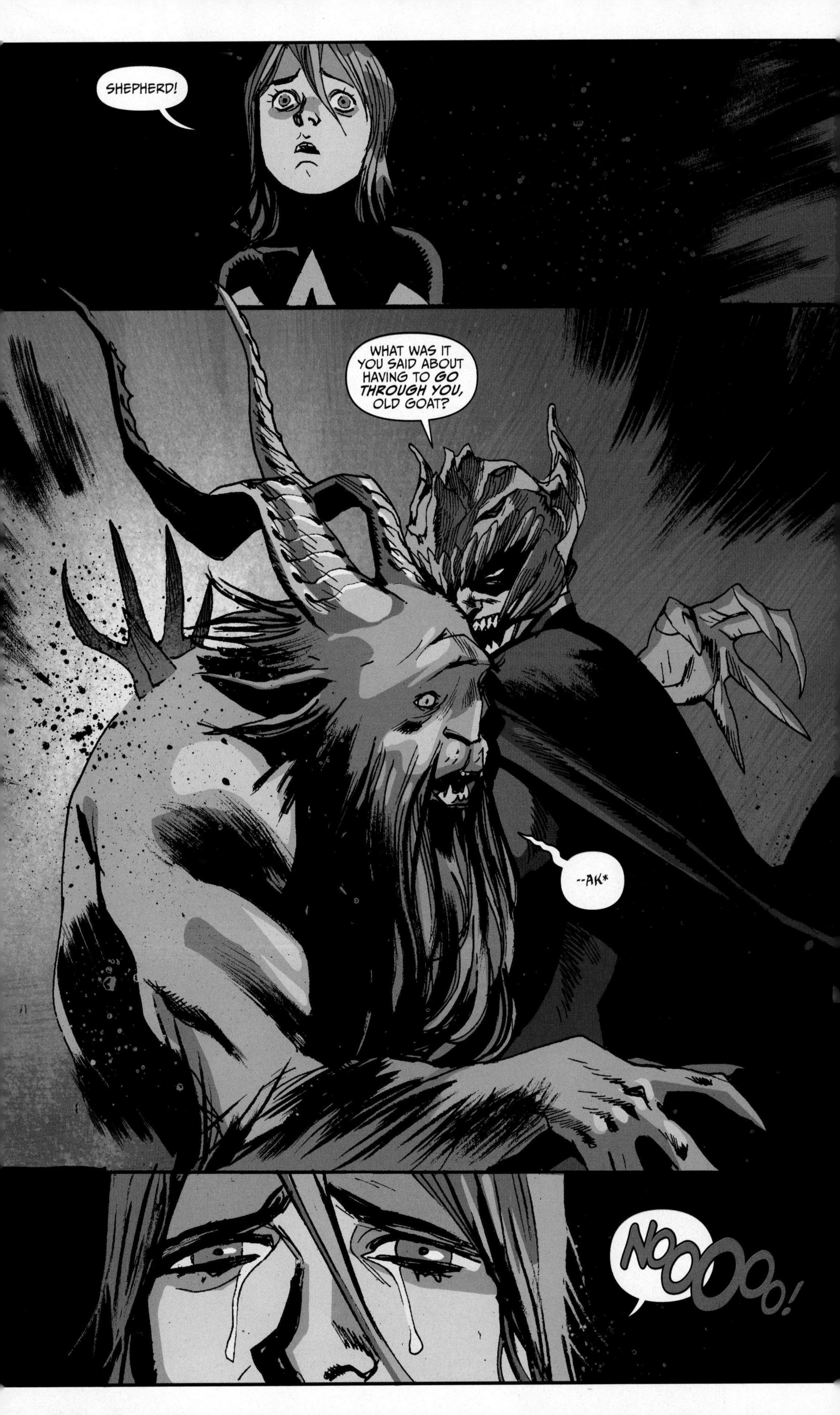
SHEPHERD!
WHAT WAS IT YOU SAID ABOUT HAVING TO GO THROUGH YOU, OLD GOAT?
--AK*
NOOOOO!

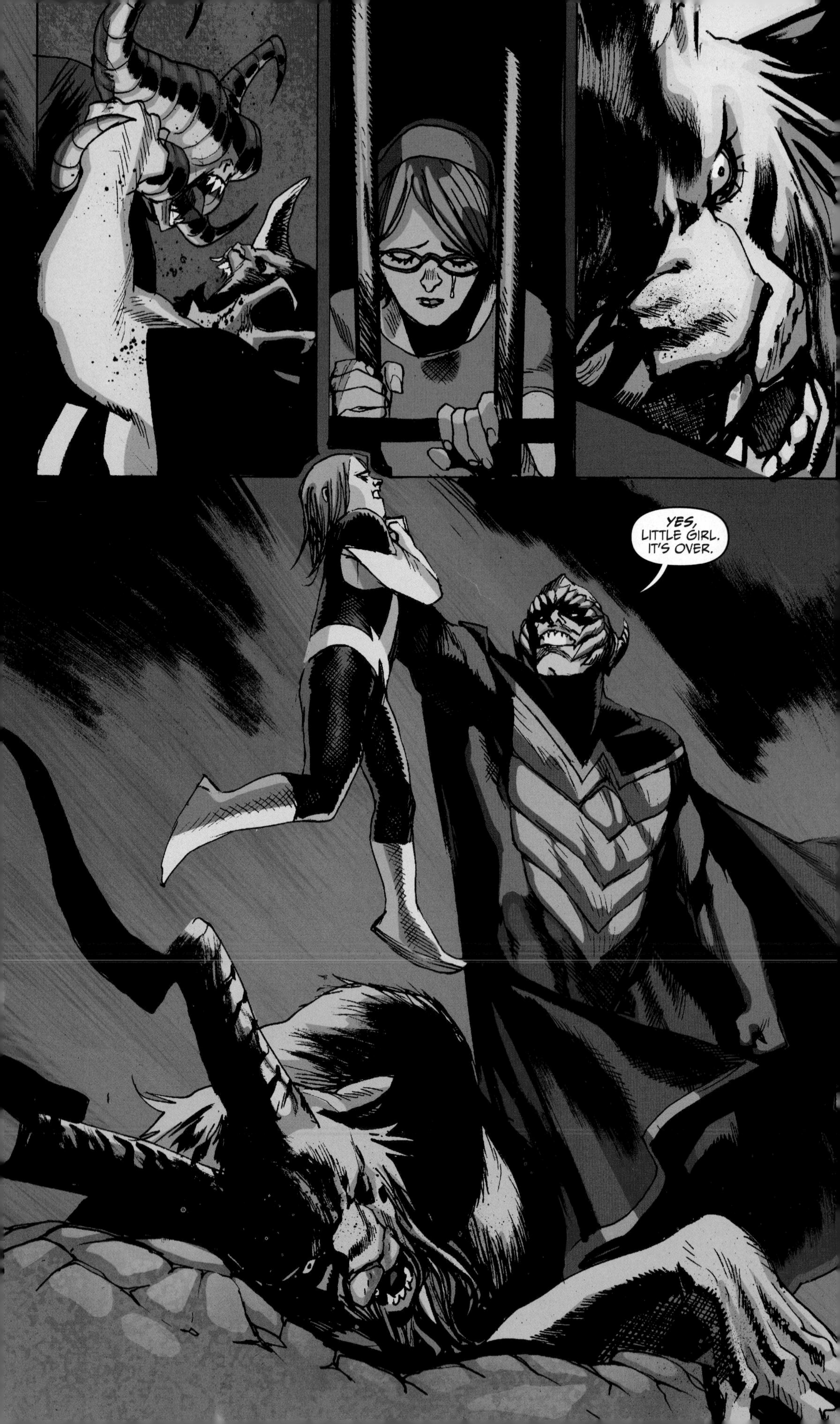
YES, LITTLE GIRL. IT'S OVER.

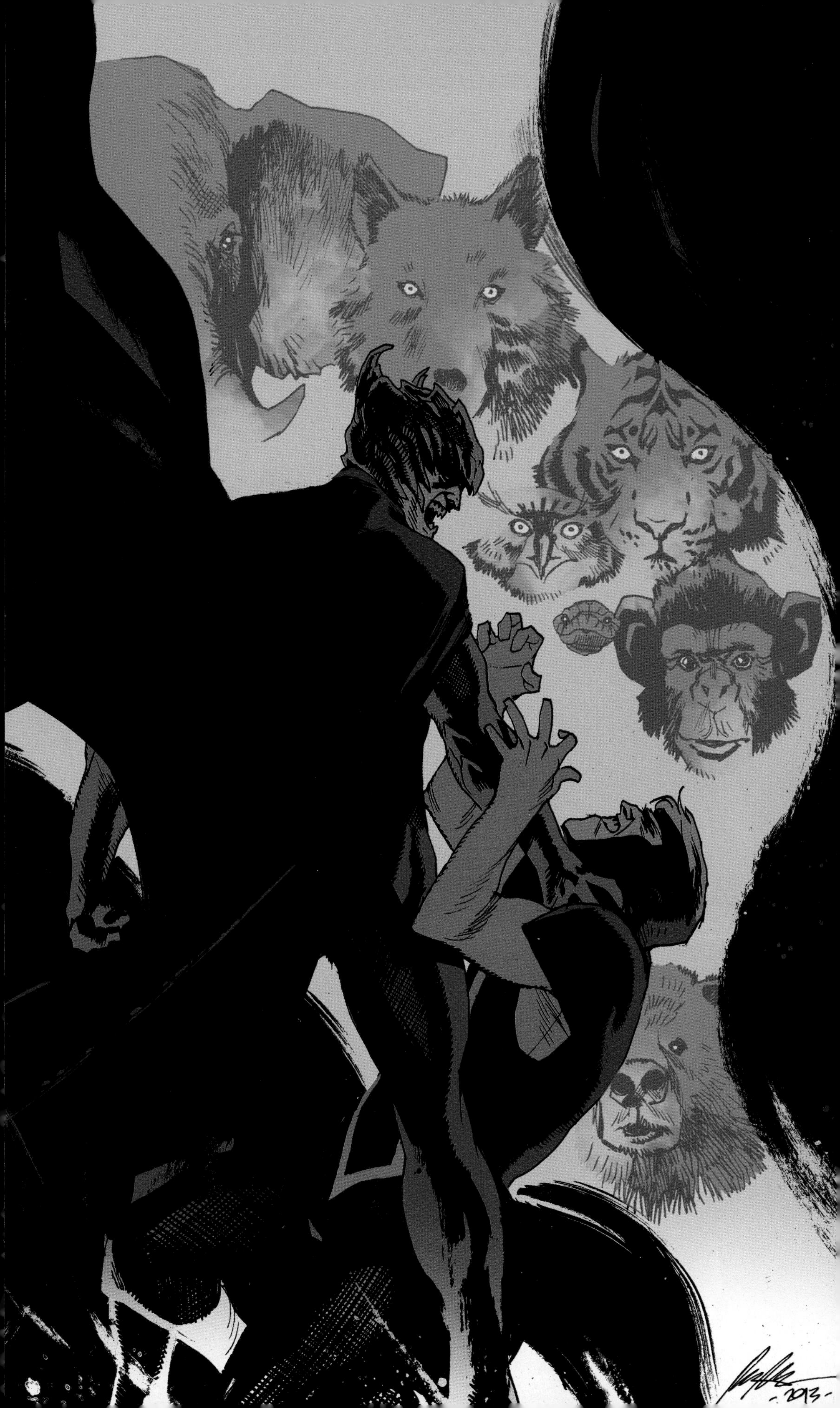

EVOLVE OR DIE PART 2

JEFF LEMIRE writer **RAFAEL ALBUQUERQUE** artist, interior and cover

DAVE McCAIG colorist **JARED K. FLETCHER** letterer

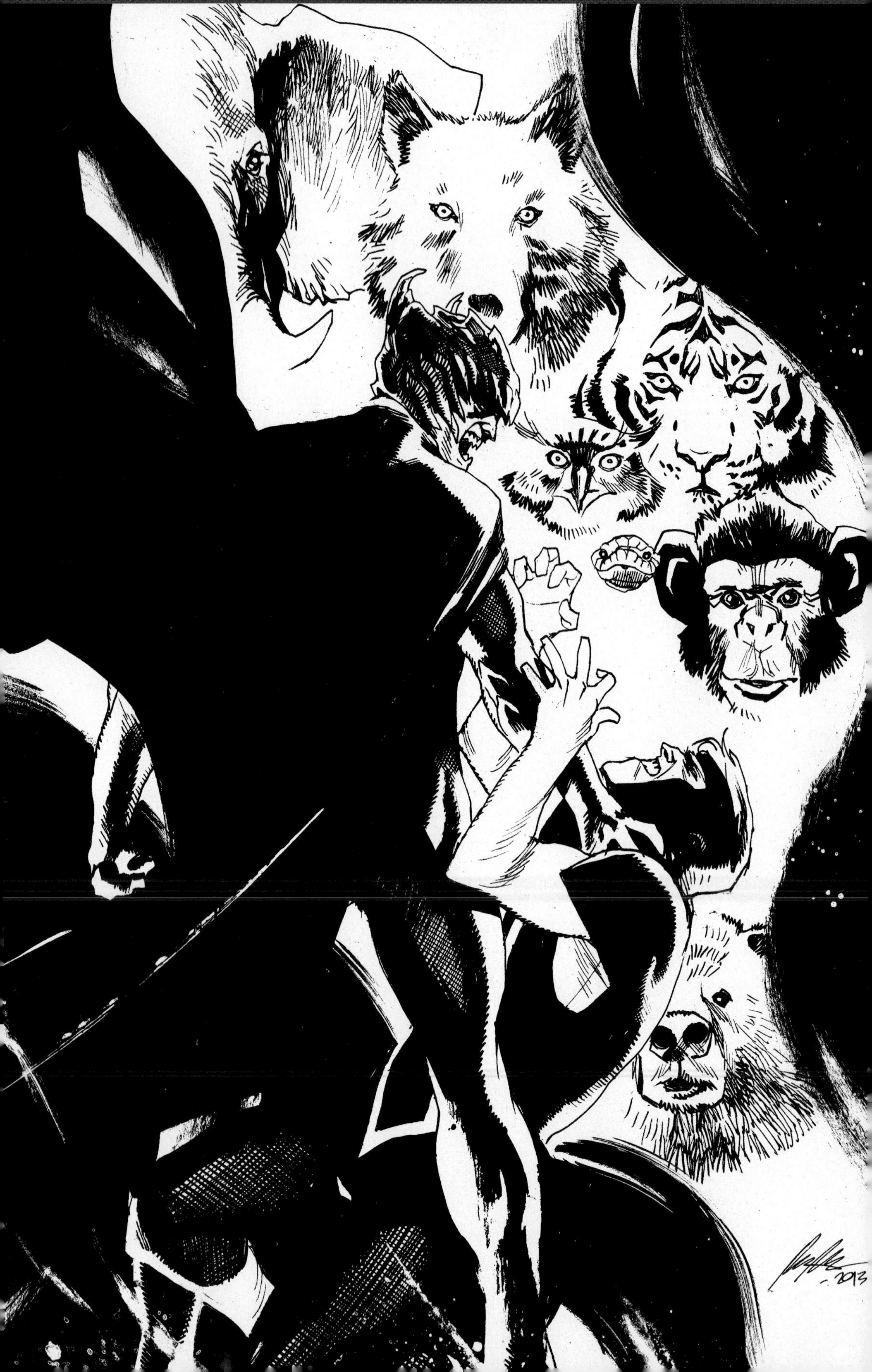

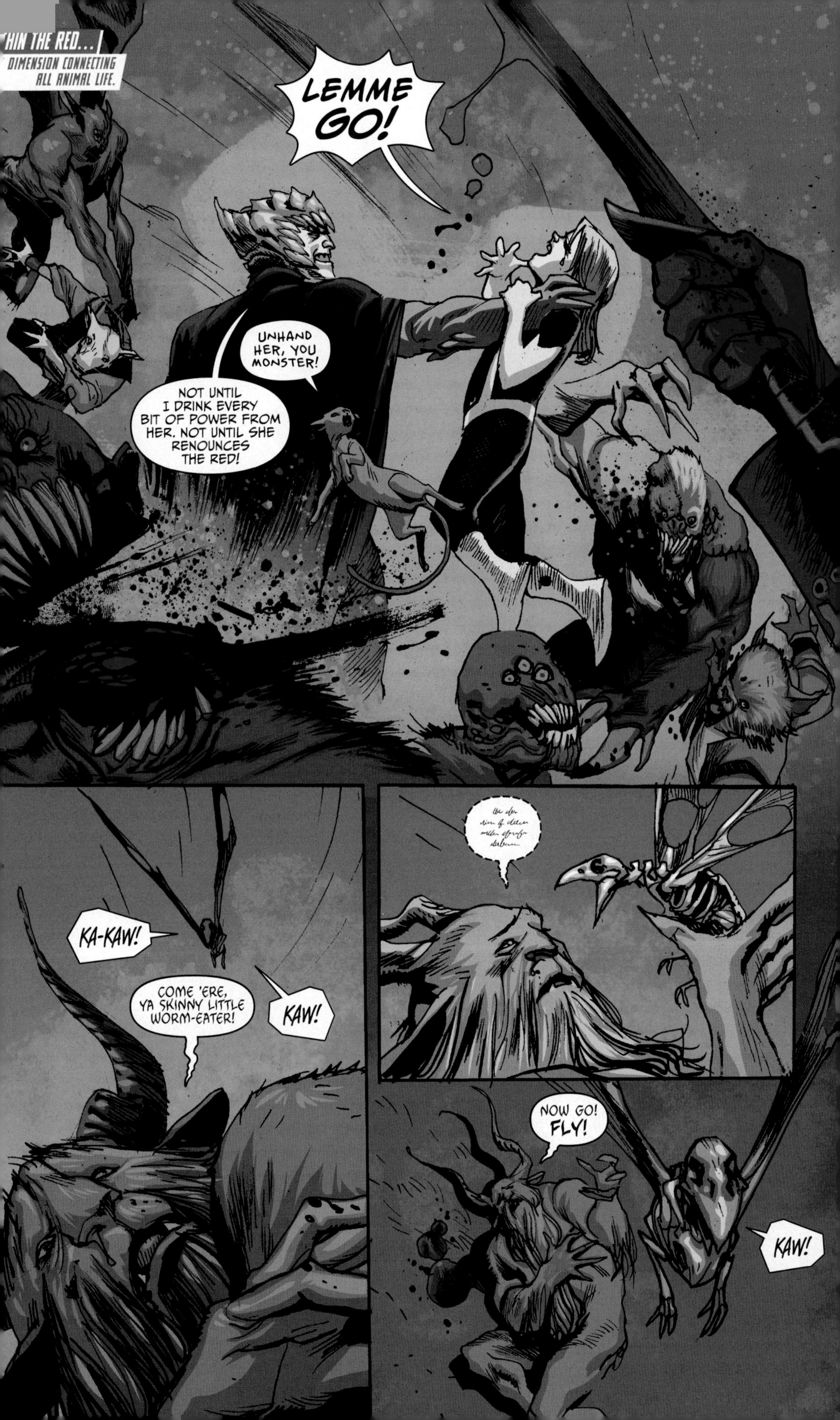
HIN THE RED...
DIMENSION CONNECTING ALL ANIMAL LIFE.
LEMME GO!
UNHAND HER, YOU MONSTER!
NOT UNTIL I DRINK EVERY BIT OF POWER FROM HER. NOT UNTIL SHE RENOUNCES THE RED!
KA-KAW!
COME 'ERE, YA SKINNY LITTLE WORM-EATER!
KAW!
NOW GO! FLY!
KAW!

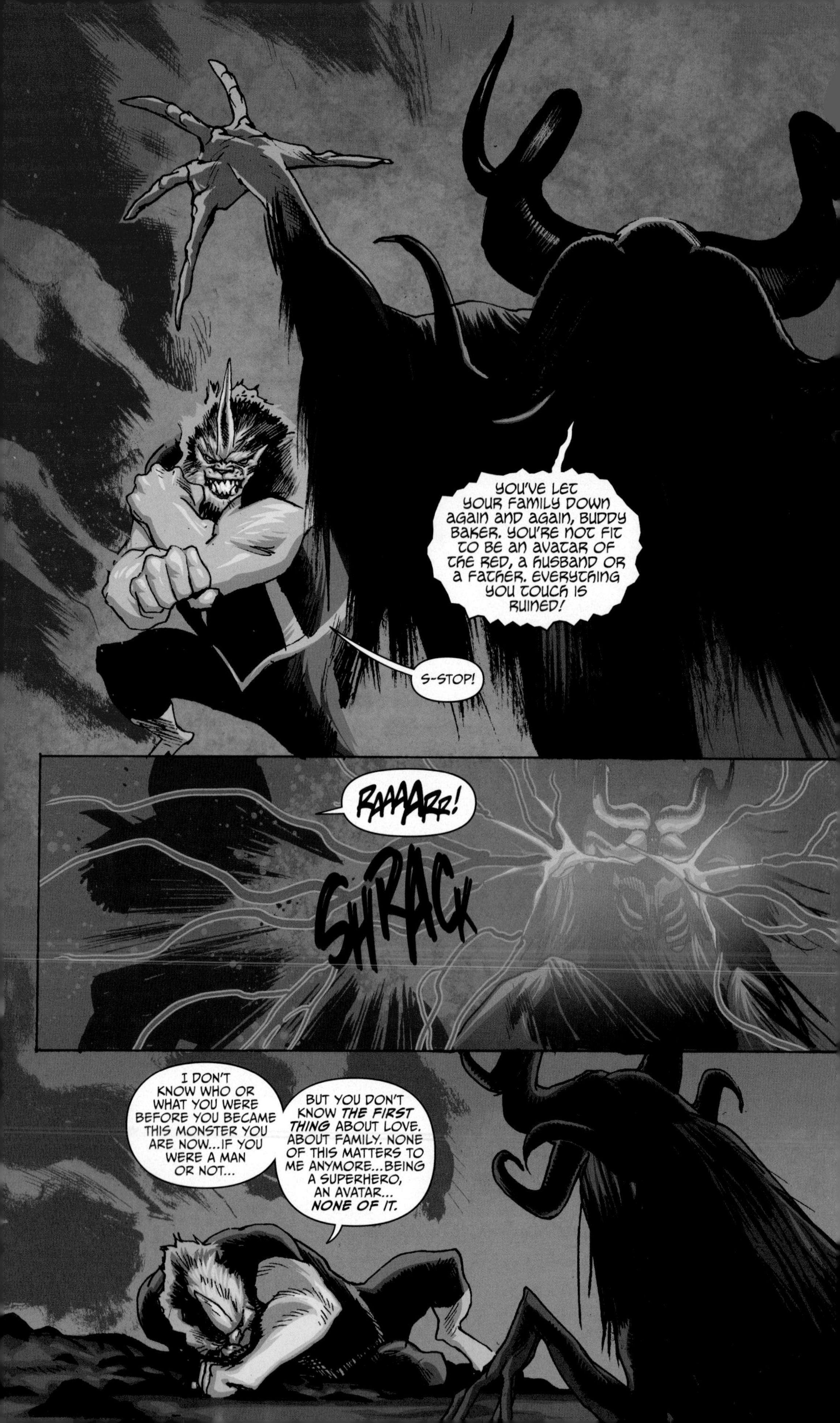
YOU'VE LET YOUR FAMILY DOWN AGAIN AND AGAIN, BUDDY BAKER. YOU'RE NOT FIT TO BE AN AVATAR OF THE RED, A HUSBAND OR A FATHER. EVERYTHING YOU TOUCH IS RUINED!
S-STOP!
RAAAARR!
SHRACK
I DON'T KNOW WHO OR WHAT YOU WERE BEFORE YOU BECAME THIS MONSTER YOU ARE NOW...IF YOU WERE A MAN OR NOT...
BUT YOU DON'T KNOW *THE FIRST THING* ABOUT LOVE. ABOUT FAMILY. NONE OF THIS MATTERS TO ME ANYMORE...BEING A SUPERHERO, AN AVATAR... *NONE OF IT.*

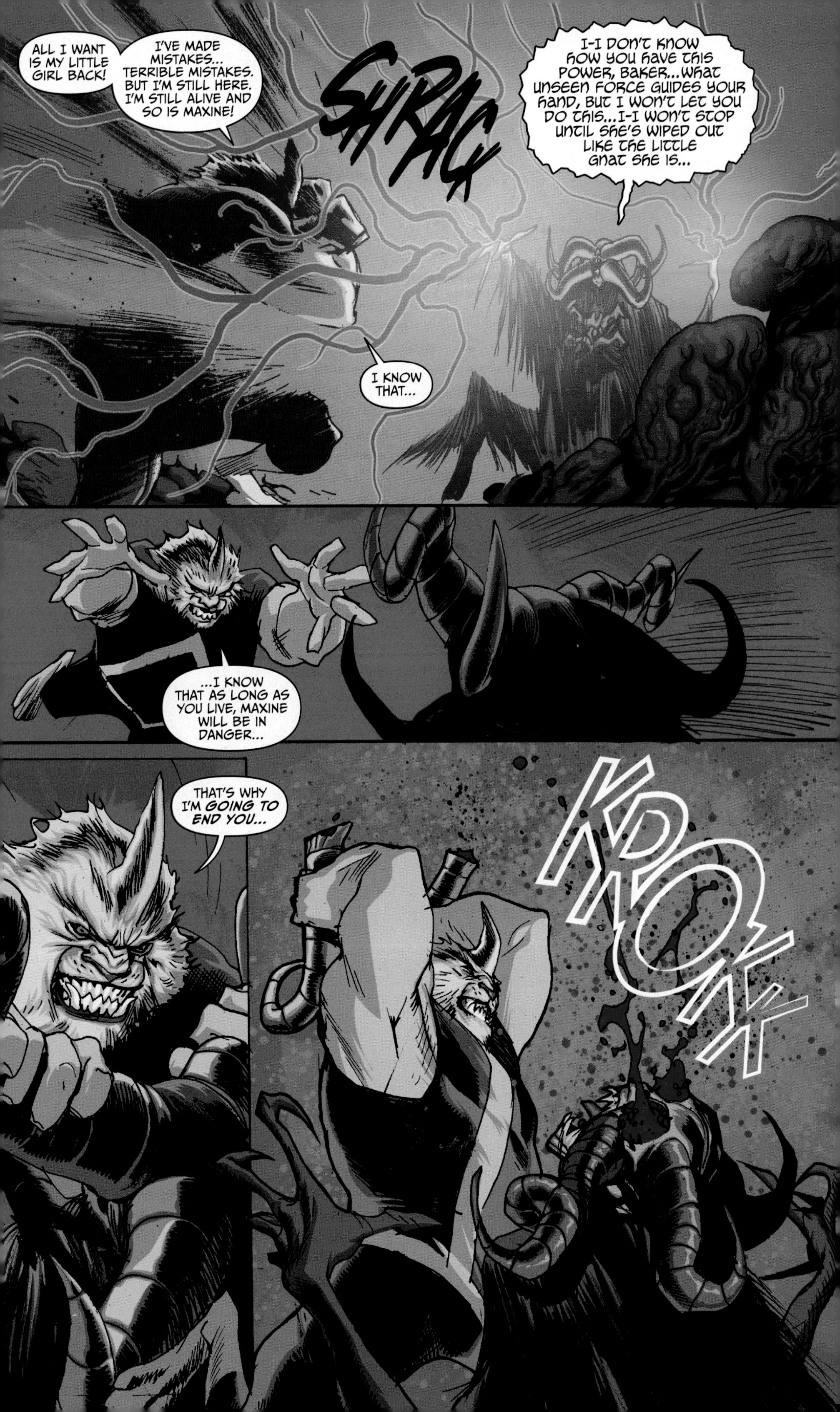
ALL I WANT IS MY LITTLE GIRL BACK!
I'VE MADE MISTAKES... TERRIBLE MISTAKES. BUT I'M STILL HERE. I'M STILL ALIVE AND SO IS MAXINE!
SHRACK
I-I DON'T KNOW HOW YOU HAVE THIS POWER, BAKER...WHAT UNSEEN FORCE GUIDES YOUR HAND, BUT I WON'T LET YOU DO THIS...I-I WON'T STOP UNTIL SHE'S WIPED OUT LIKE THE LITTLE GNAT SHE IS...
I KNOW THAT...
...I KNOW THAT AS LONG AS YOU LIVE, MAXINE WILL BE IN DANGER...
THAT'S WHY I'M GOING TO END YOU...
KROOOX

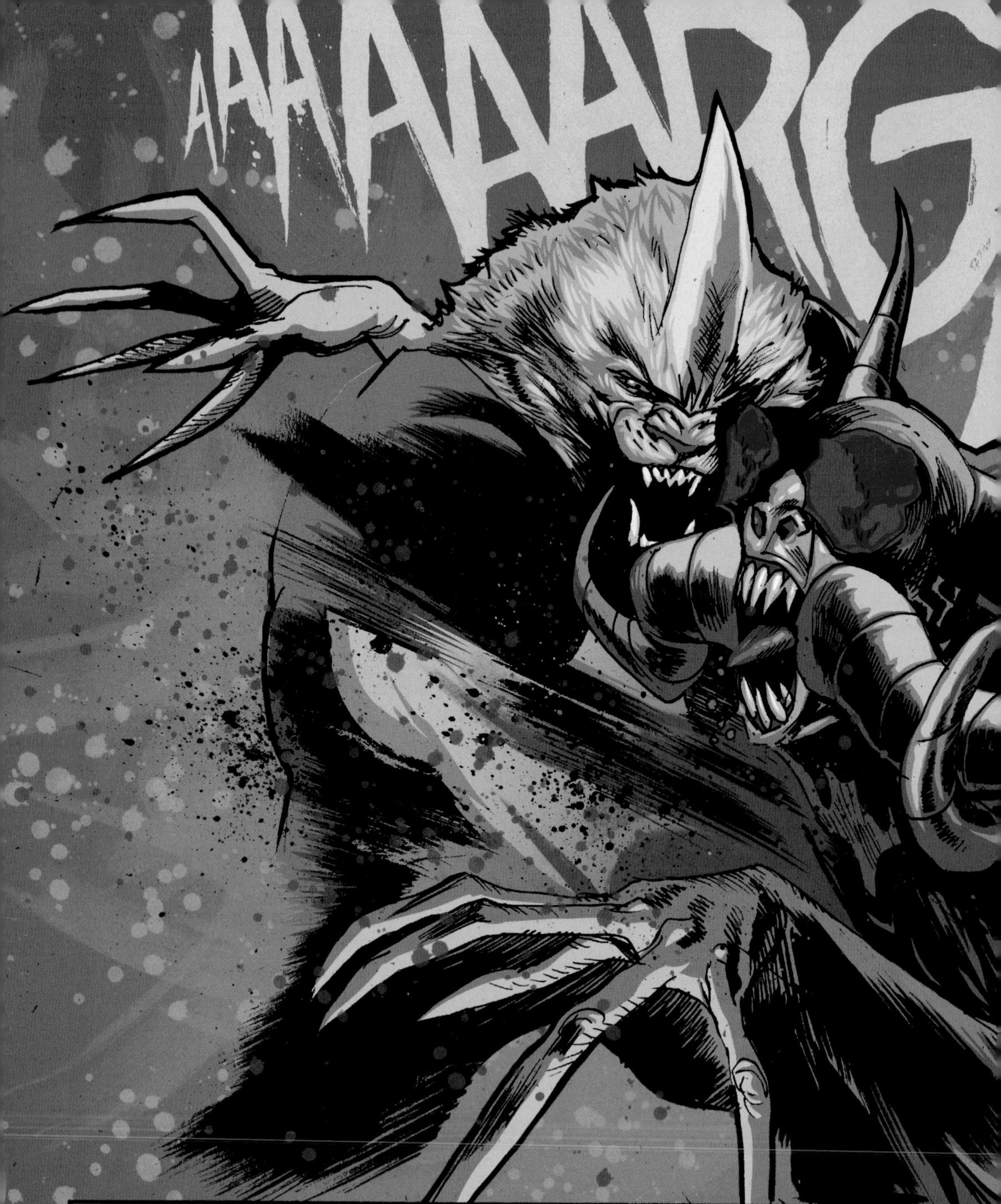
AAAAARG

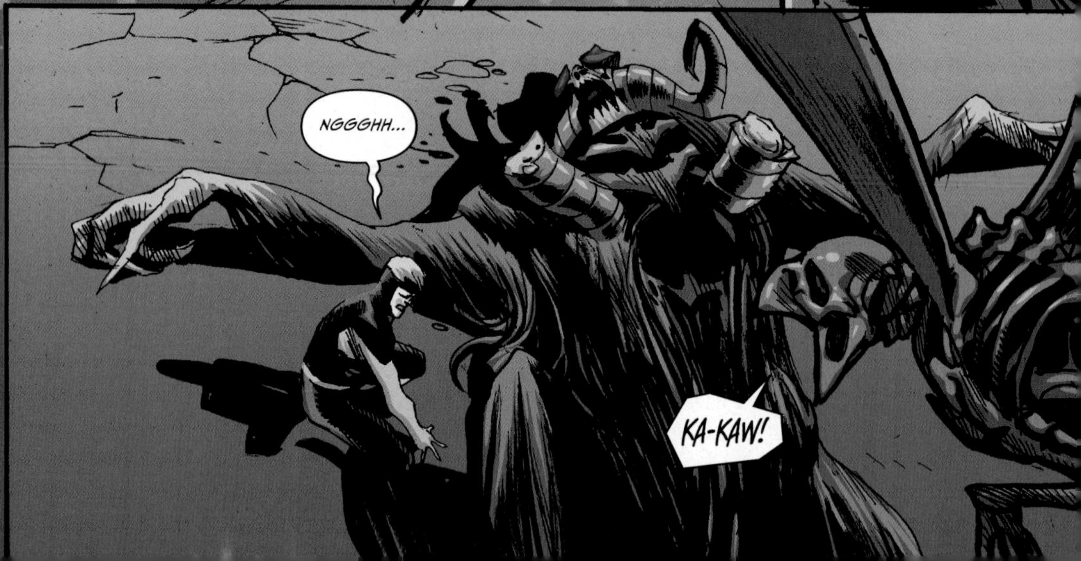
NGGGHH...
KA-KAW!

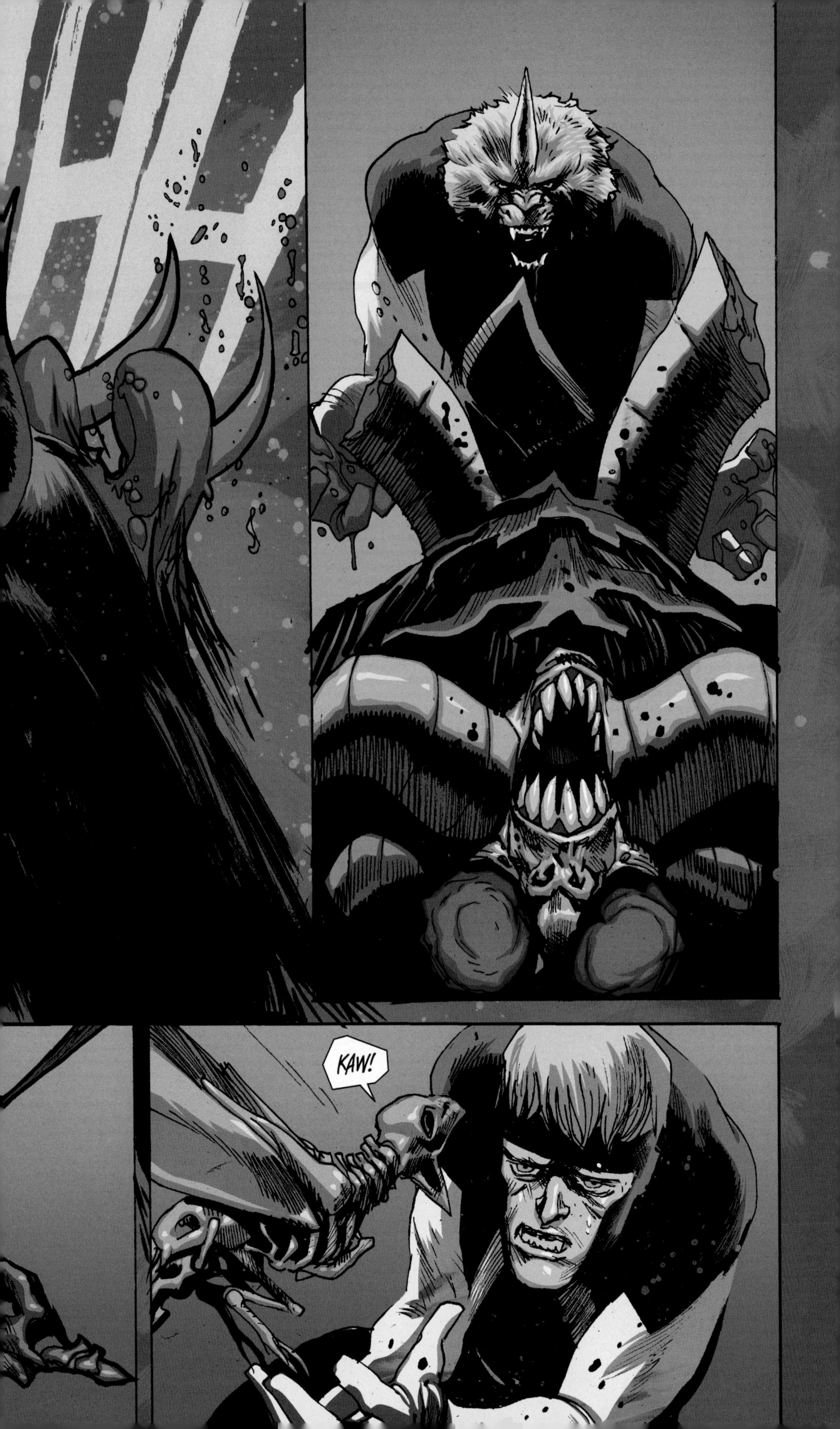
KAW!

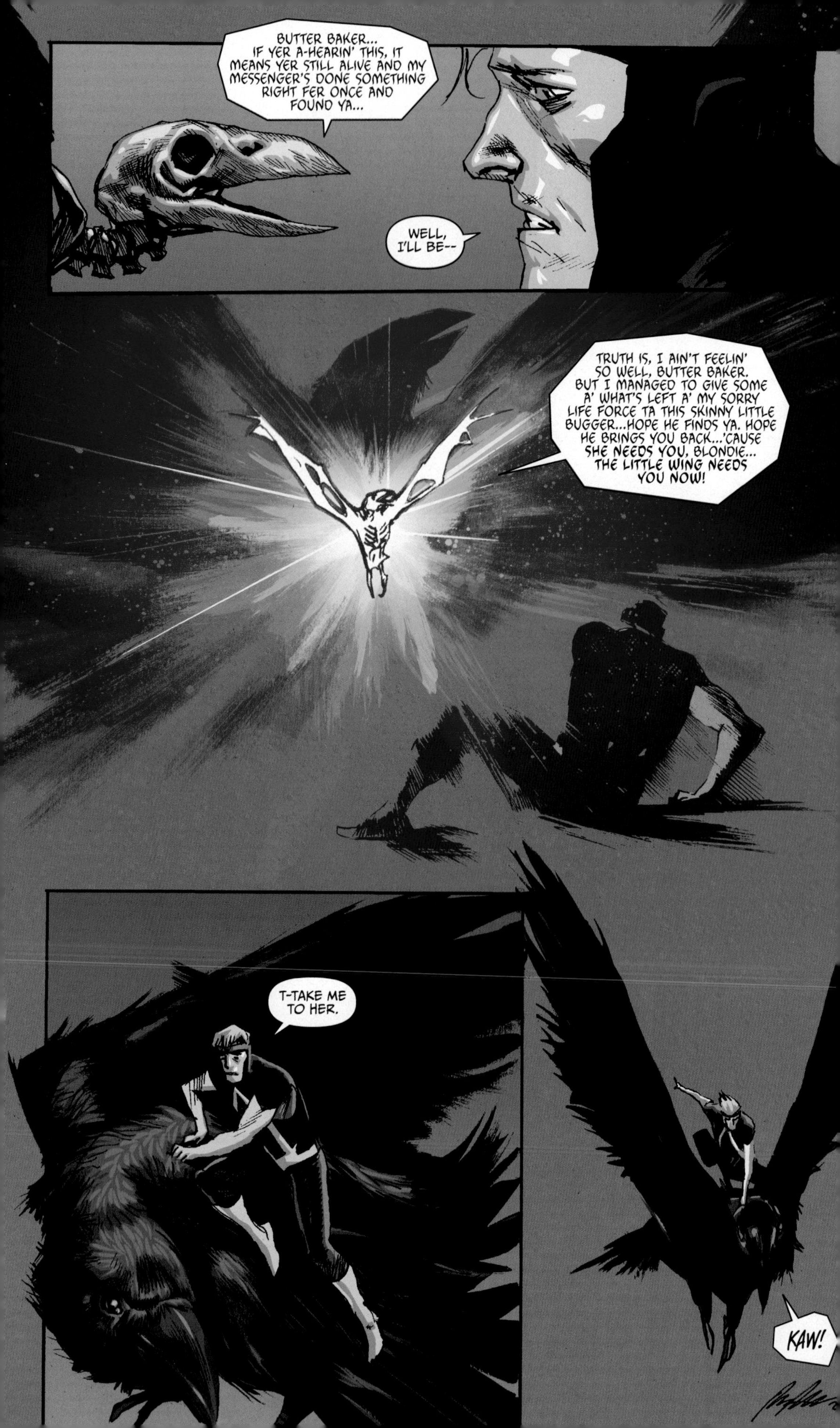
BUTTER BAKER... IF YER A-HEARIN' THIS, IT MEANS YER STILL ALIVE AND MY MESSENGER'S DONE SOMETHING RIGHT FER ONCE AND FOUND YA...
WELL, I'LL BE--
TRUTH IS, I AIN'T FEELIN' SO WELL, BUTTER BAKER. BUT I MANAGED TO GIVE SOME A' WHAT'S LEFT A' MY SORRY LIFE FORCE TA THIS SKINNY LITTLE BUGGER...HOPE HE FINDS YA. HOPE HE BRINGS YOU BACK...'CAUSE SHE NEEDS YOU, BLONDIE... THE LITTLE WING NEEDS YOU NOW!
T-TAKE ME TO HER.
KAW!

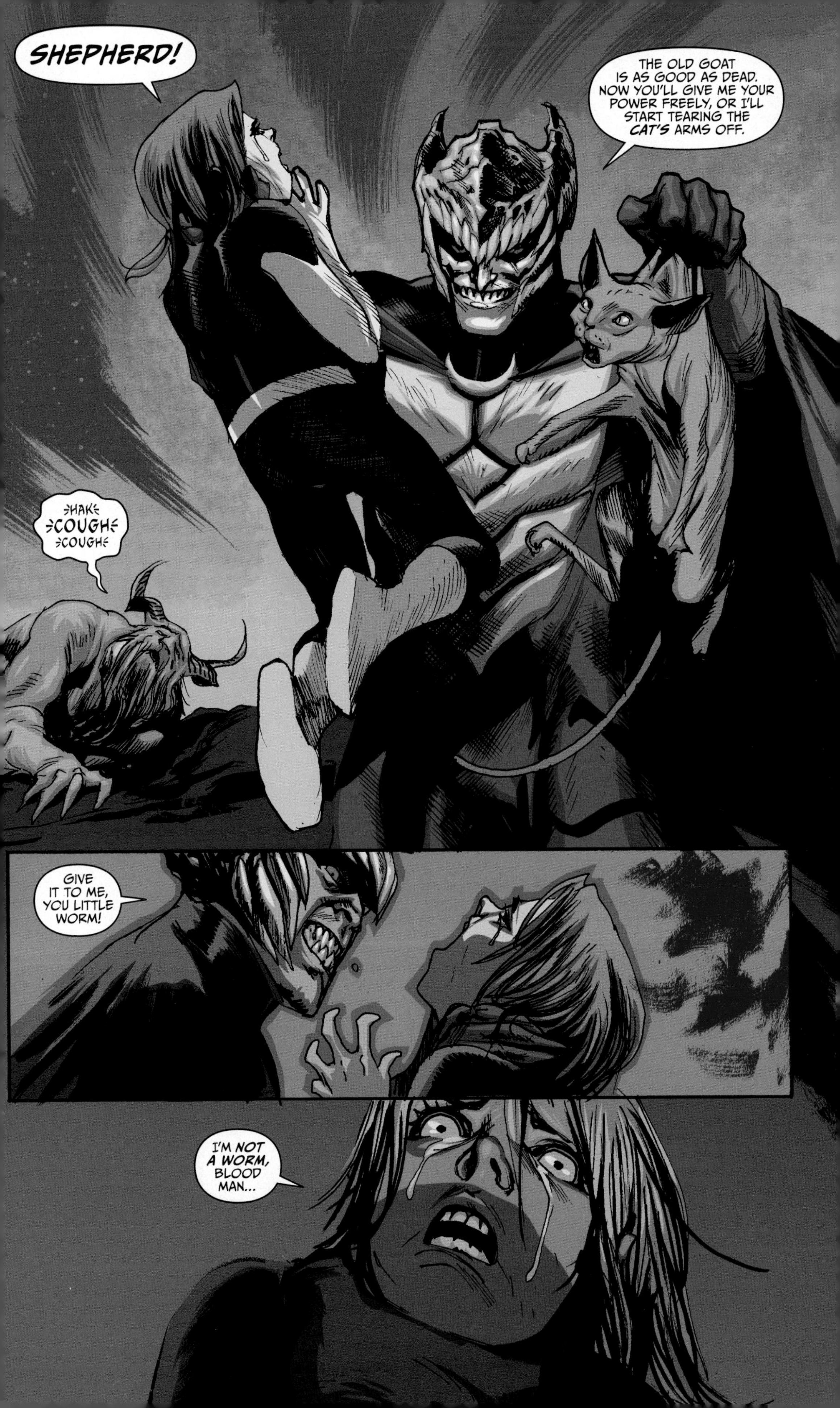
SHEPHERD!
THE OLD GOAT IS AS GOOD AS DEAD. NOW YOU'LL GIVE ME YOUR POWER FREELY, OR I'LL START TEARING THE CAT'S ARMS OFF.
HAK COUGH COUGH
GIVE IT TO ME, YOU LITTLE WORM!
I'M NOT A WORM, BLOOD MAN...

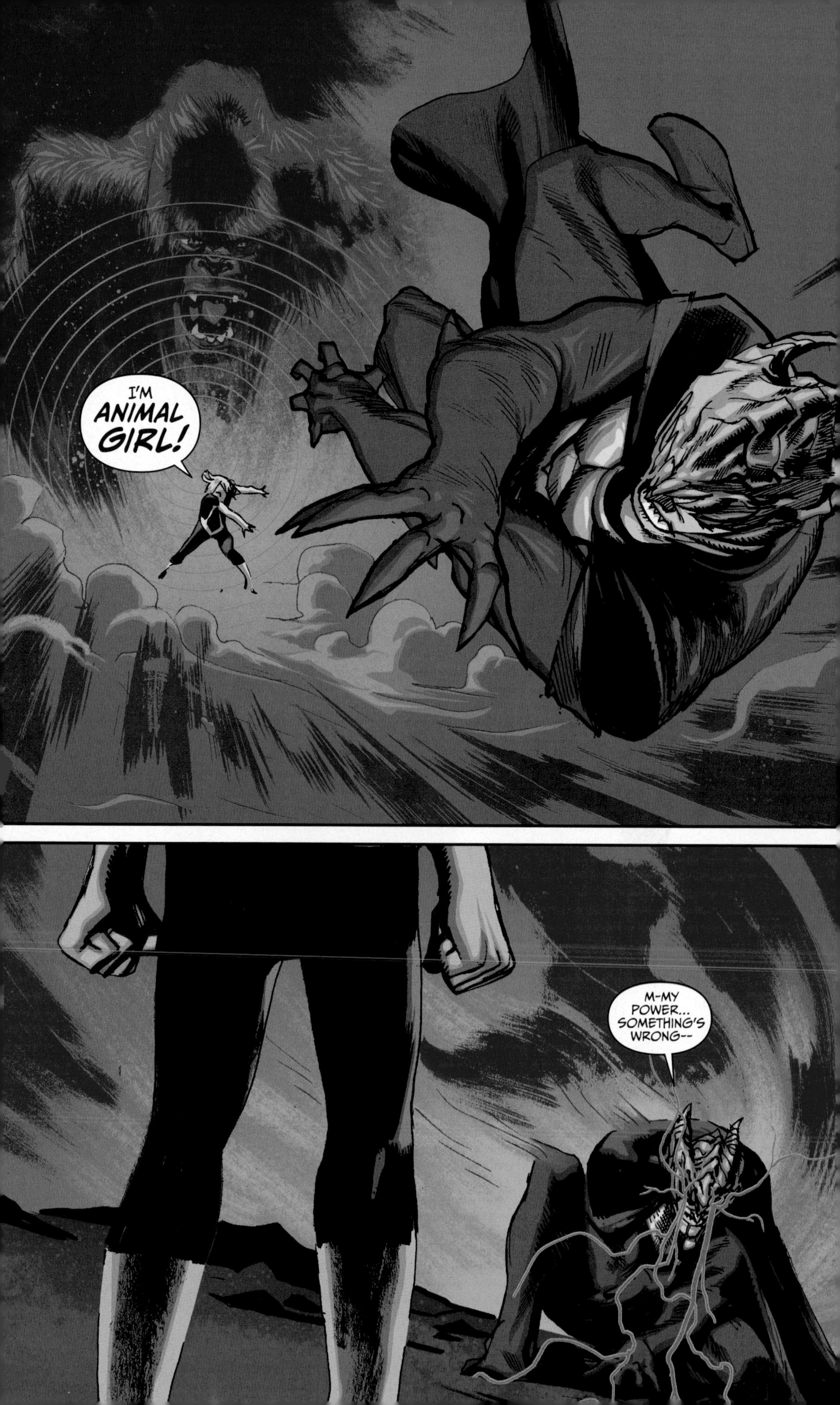
I'M ANIMAL GIRL!
M-MY POWER... SOMETHING'S WRONG--

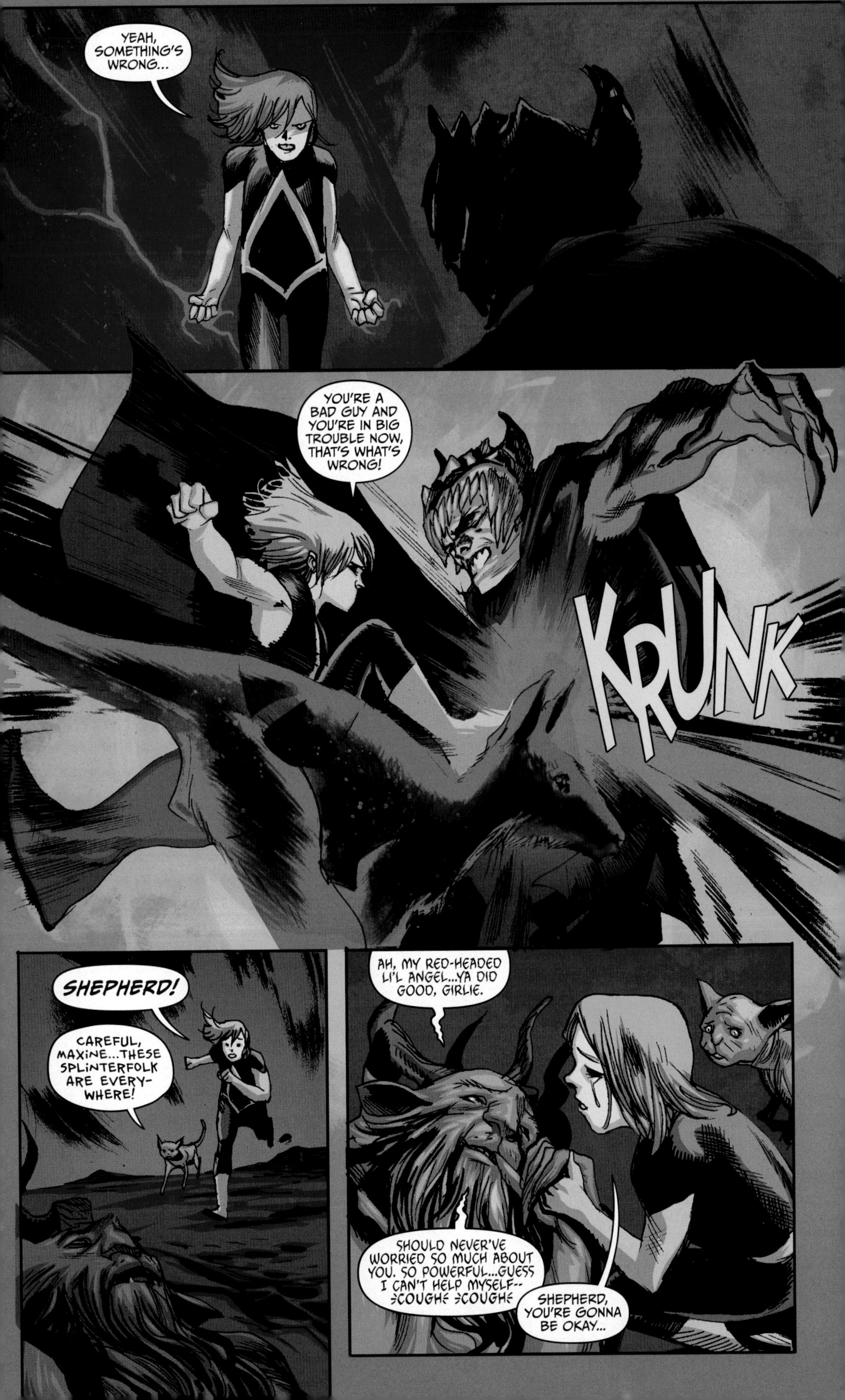
YEAH, SOMETHING'S WRONG...
YOU'RE A BAD GUY AND YOU'RE IN BIG TROUBLE NOW, THAT'S WHAT'S WRONG!
KRUNK
SHEPHERD!
CAREFUL, MAXINE...THESE SPLINTERFOLK ARE EVERY-WHERE!
AH, MY RED-HEADED LI'L ANGEL...YA DID GOOD, GIRLIE.
SHOULD NEVER'VE WORRIED SO MUCH ABOUT YOU. SO POWERFUL...GUESS I CAN'T HELP MYSELF-- ≯COUGH≮ ≯COUGH≮
SHEPHERD, YOU'RE GONNA BE OKAY...

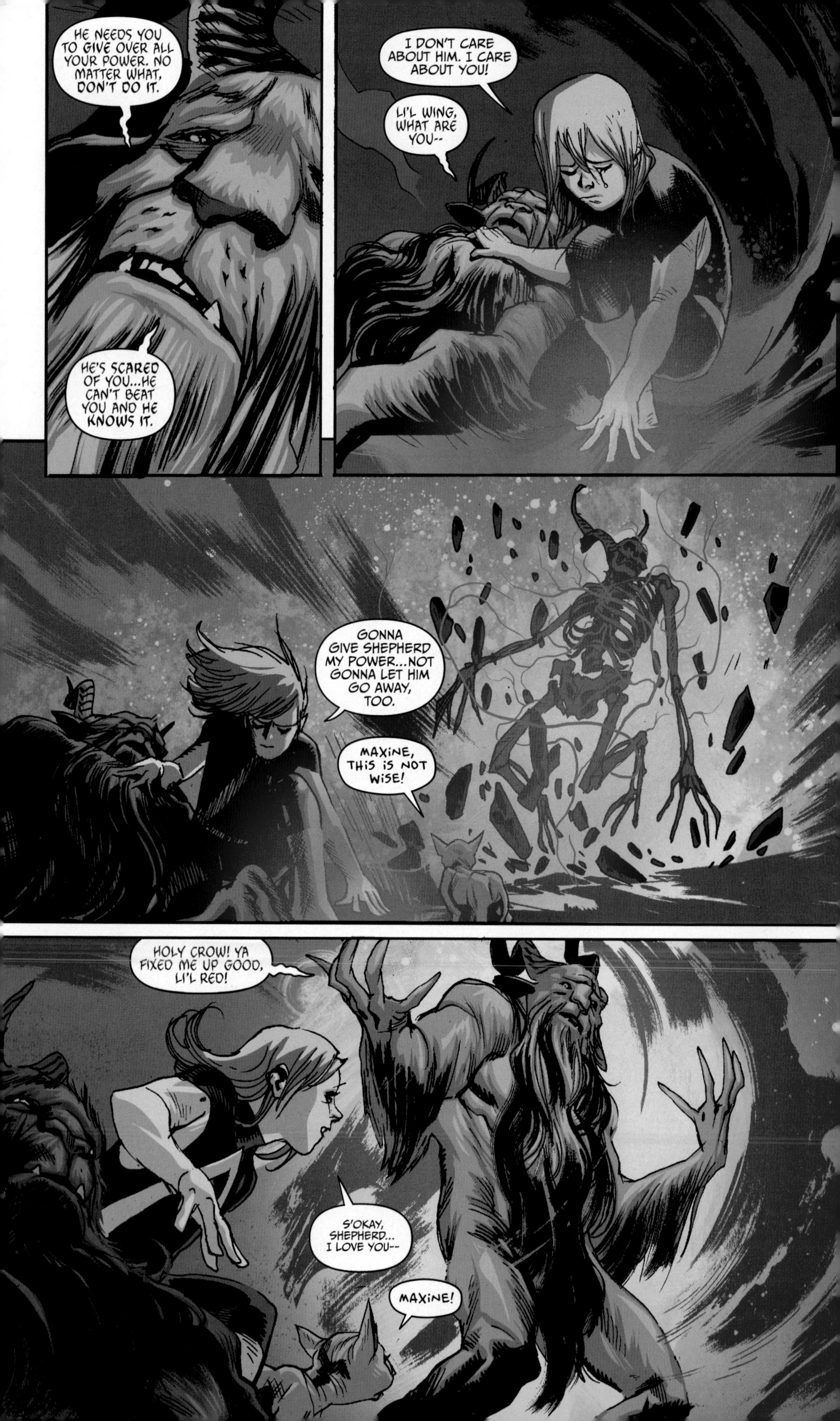
HE NEEDS YOU TO GIVE OVER ALL YOUR POWER. NO MATTER WHAT, DON'T DO IT.
HE'S SCARED OF YOU...HE CAN'T BEAT YOU AND HE KNOWS IT.
I DON'T CARE ABOUT HIM. I CARE ABOUT YOU!
LI'L WING, WHAT ARE YOU--
GONNA GIVE SHEPHERD MY POWER...NOT GONNA LET HIM GO AWAY, TOO.
MAXINE, THIS IS NOT WISE!
HOLY CROW! YA FIXED ME UP GOOD, LI'L RED!
S'OKAY, SHEPHERD... I LOVE YOU--
MAXINE!

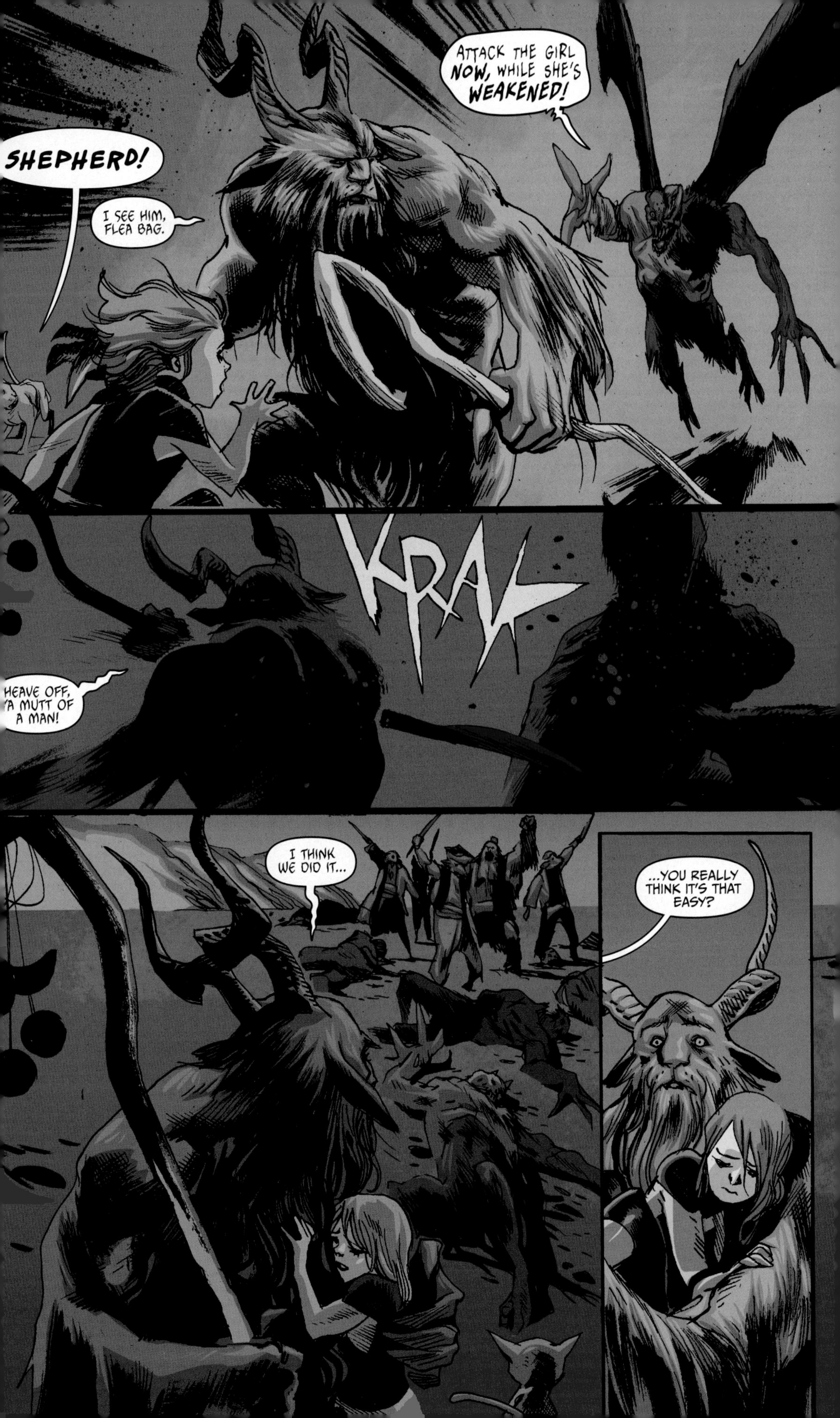
SHEPHERD!
I SEE HIM, FLEA BAG.
ATTACK THE GIRL NOW, WHILE SHE'S WEAKENED!
KRAK
HEAVE OFF, YA MUTT OF A MAN!
I THINK WE DID IT...
...YOU REALLY THINK IT'S THAT EASY?

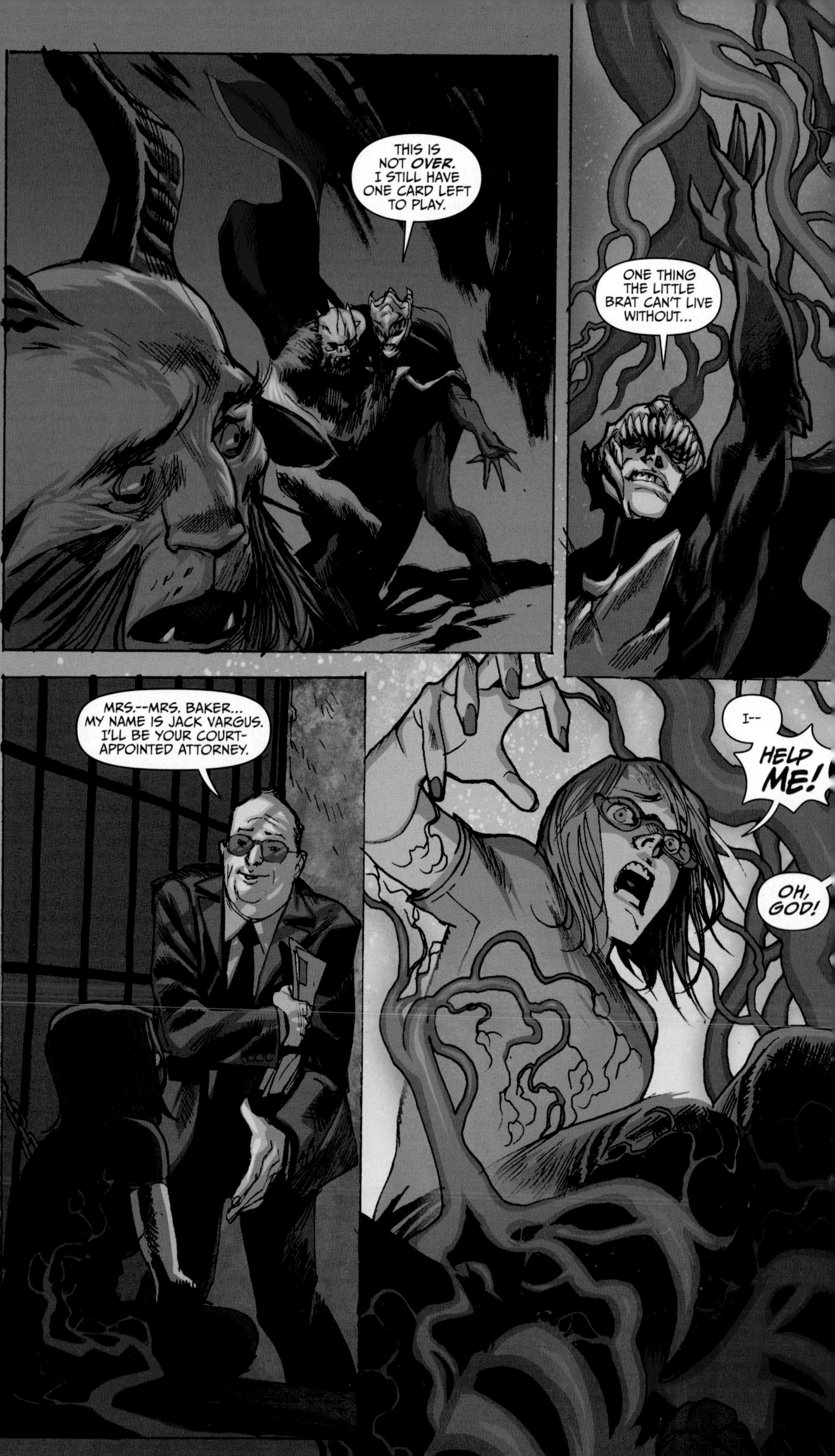
THIS IS NOT *OVER.* I STILL HAVE ONE CARD LEFT TO PLAY.
ONE THING THE LITTLE BRAT CAN'T LIVE WITHOUT...
MRS.--MRS. BAKER... MY NAME IS JACK VARGUS. I'LL BE YOUR COURT-APPOINTED ATTORNEY.
I--
HELP ME!
OH, GOD!

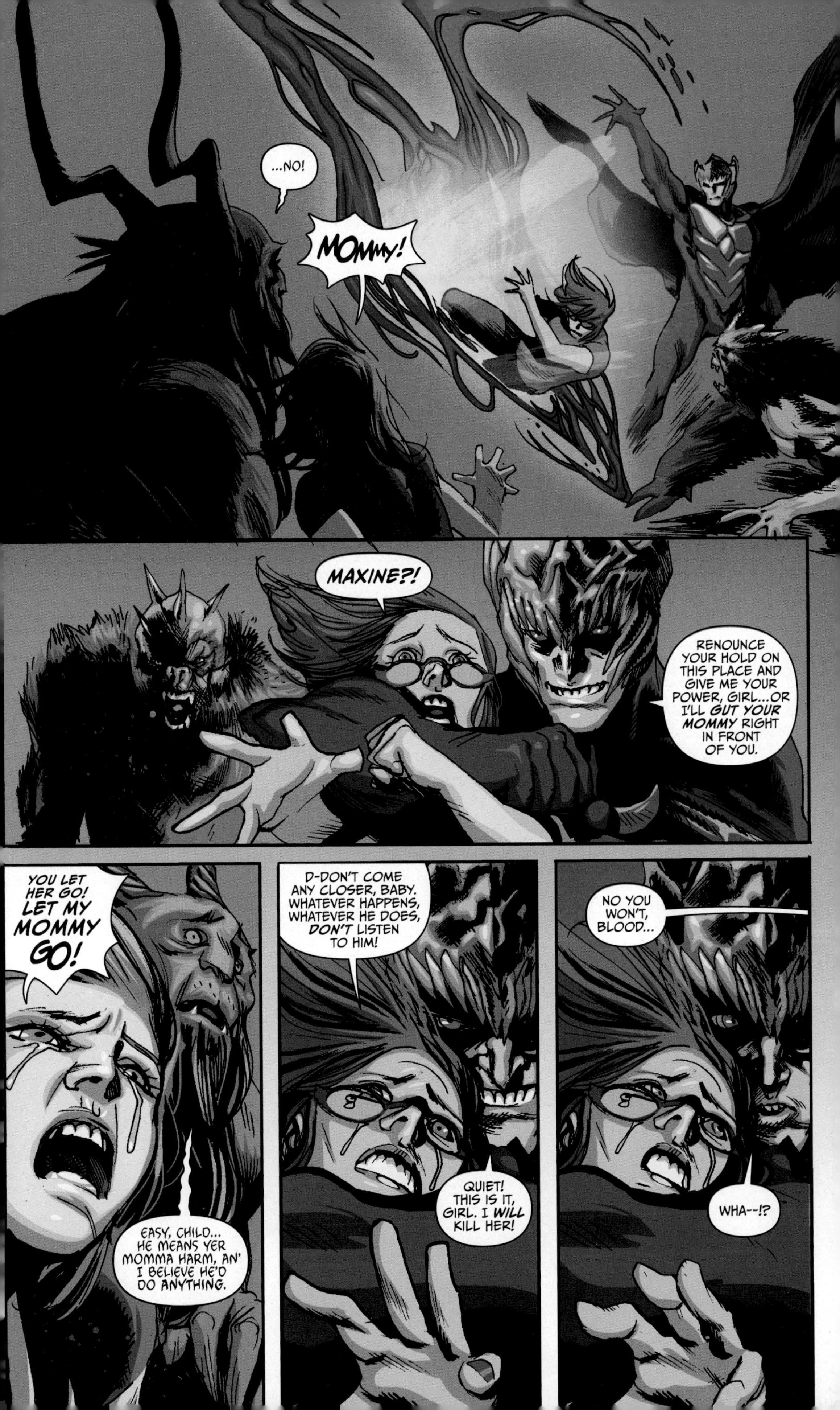
...NO!
MOMMY!
MAXINE?!
RENOUNCE YOUR HOLD ON THIS PLACE AND GIVE ME YOUR POWER, GIRL...OR I'LL GUT YOUR MOMMY RIGHT IN FRONT OF YOU.
YOU LET HER GO! LET MY MOMMY GO!
EASY, CHILD... HE MEANS YER MOMMA HARM, AN' I BELIEVE HE'D DO ANYTHING.
D-DON'T COME ANY CLOSER, BABY. WHATEVER HAPPENS, WHATEVER HE DOES, DON'T LISTEN TO HIM!
QUIET! THIS IS IT, GIRL. I WILL KILL HER!
NO YOU WON'T, BLOOD...
WHA--!?

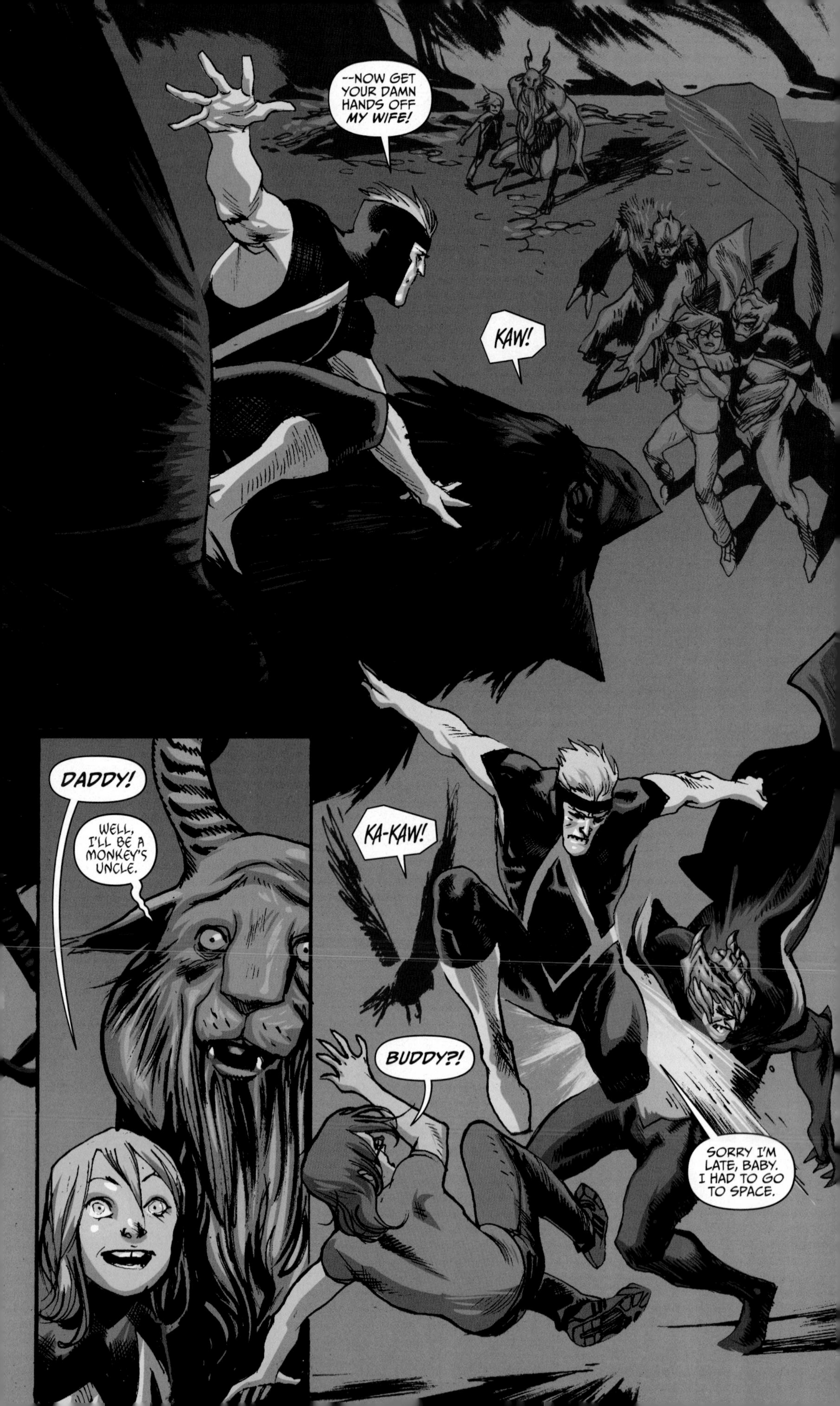
--NOW GET YOUR DAMN HANDS OFF MY WIFE!
KAW!
DADDY!
WELL, I'LL BE A MONKEY'S UNCLE.
KA-KAW!
BUDDY?!
SORRY I'M LATE, BABY. I HAD TO GO TO SPACE.

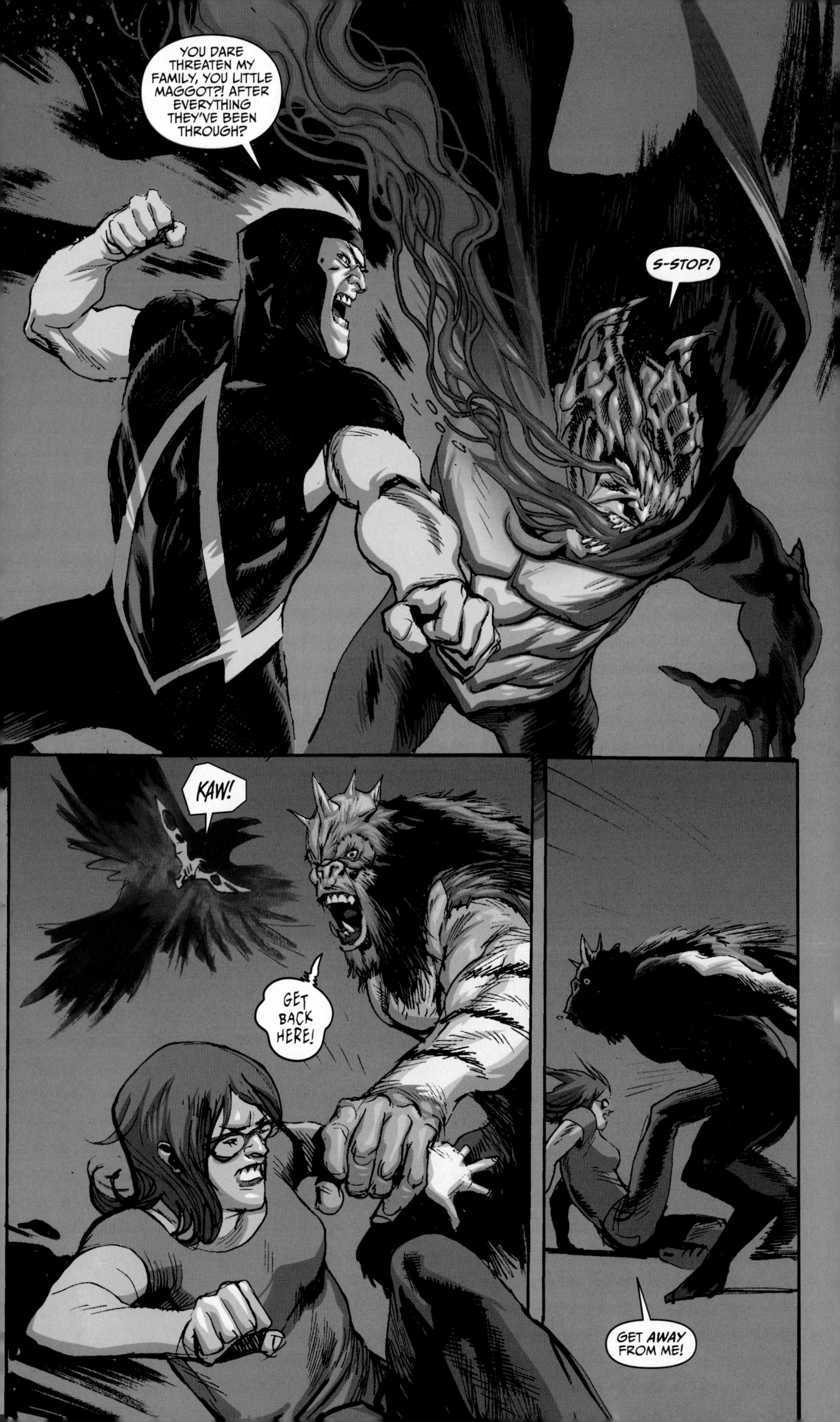
YOU DARE THREATEN MY FAMILY, YOU LITTLE MAGGOT?! AFTER EVERYTHING THEY'VE BEEN THROUGH?
S-STOP!
KAW!
GET BACK HERE!
GET AWAY FROM ME!

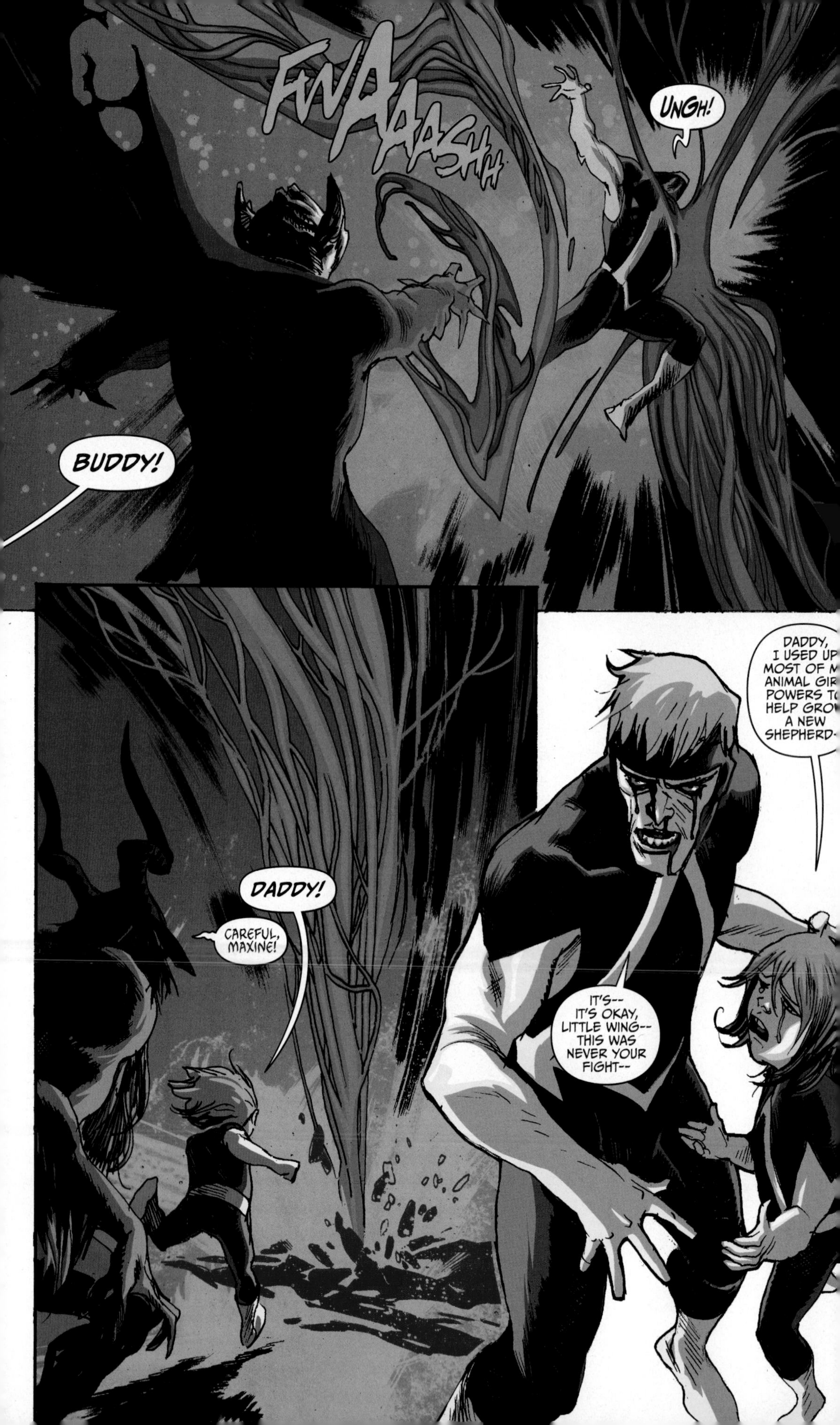
FWAAASHH
UNGH!
BUDDY!
DADDY, I USED UP MOST OF M ANIMAL GIR POWERS T HELP GRO A NEW SHEPHERD-
DADDY!
CAREFUL, MAXINE!
IT'S-- IT'S OKAY, LITTLE WING-- THIS WAS NEVER YOUR FIGHT--

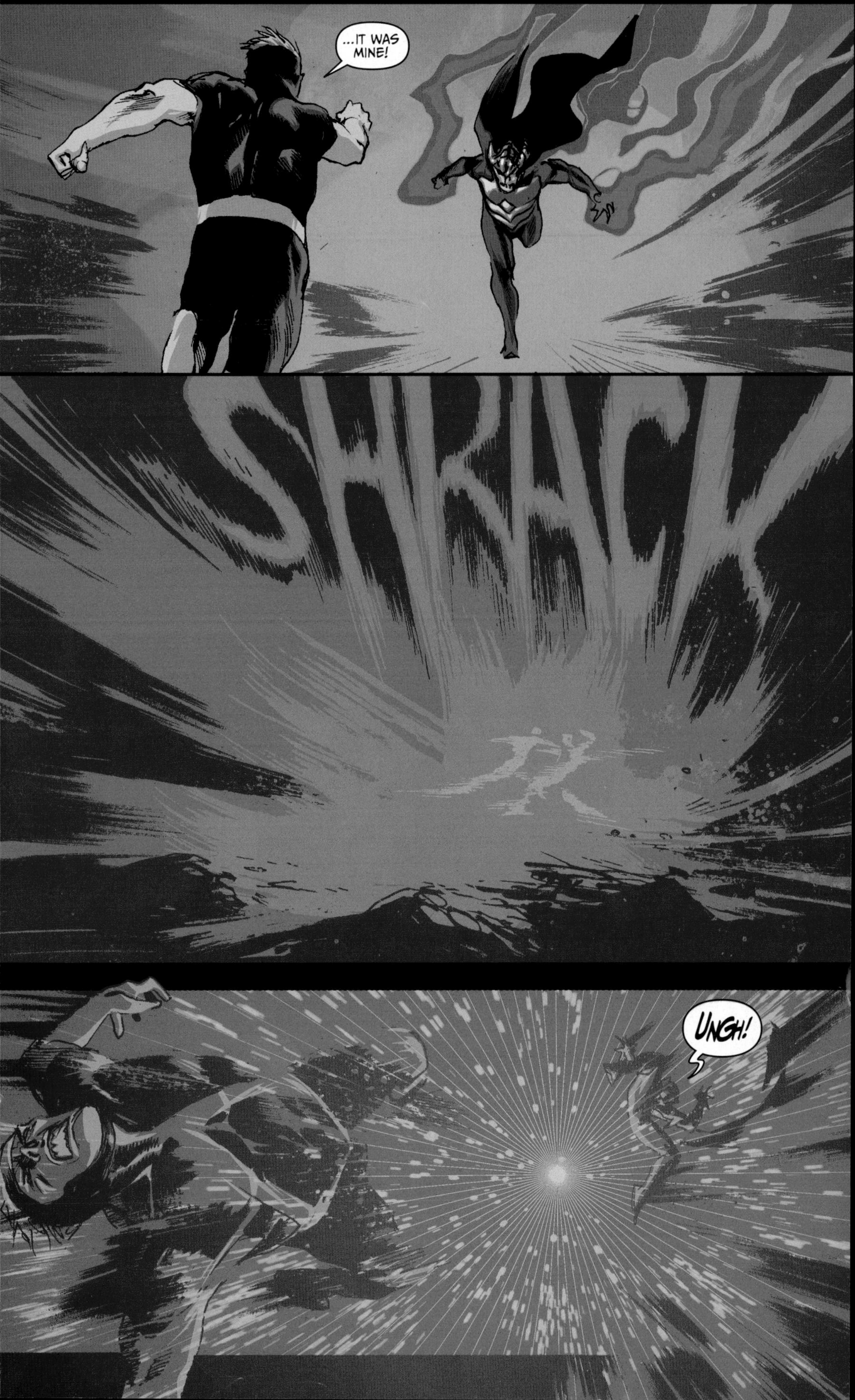
...IT WAS MINE!
SHRACK
UNGH!

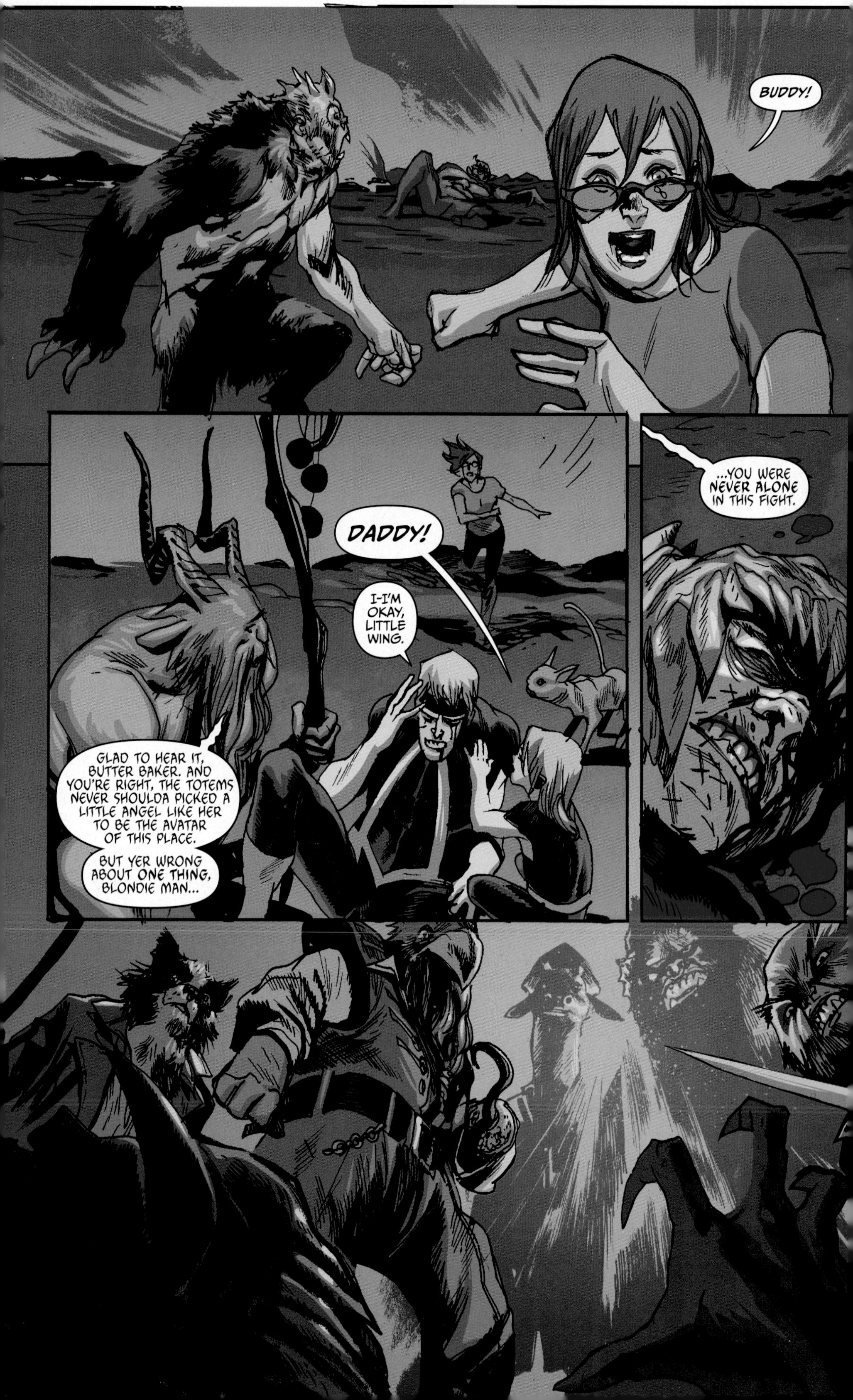
BUDDY!
DADDY!
I-I'M OKAY, LITTLE WING.
GLAD TO HEAR IT, BUTTER BAKER. AND YOU'RE RIGHT, THE TOTEMS NEVER SHOULDA PICKED A LITTLE ANGEL LIKE HER TO BE THE AVATAR OF THIS PLACE.
BUT YER WRONG ABOUT ONE THING, BLONDIE MAN...
...YOU WERE NEVER ALONE IN THIS FIGHT.

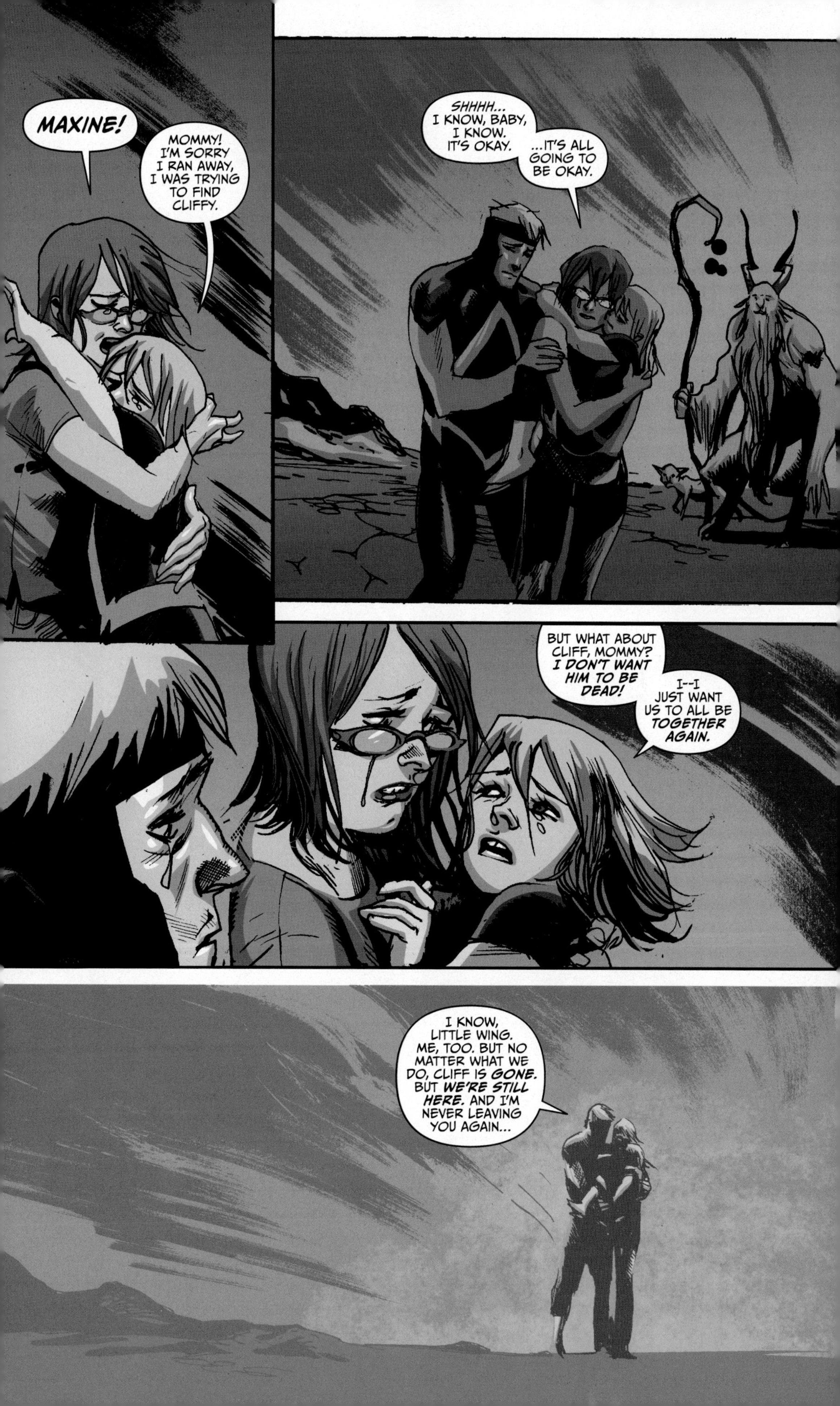
MAXINE!
MOMMY! I'M SORRY I RAN AWAY, I WAS TRYING TO FIND CLIFFY.
SHHHH... I KNOW, BABY, I KNOW. IT'S OKAY.
...IT'S ALL GOING TO BE OKAY.
BUT WHAT ABOUT CLIFF, MOMMY? I DON'T WANT HIM TO BE DEAD!
I--I JUST WANT US TO ALL BE TOGETHER AGAIN.
I KNOW, LITTLE WING. ME, TOO. BUT NO MATTER WHAT WE DO, CLIFF IS GONE. BUT WE'RE STILL HERE. AND I'M NEVER LEAVING YOU AGAIN...

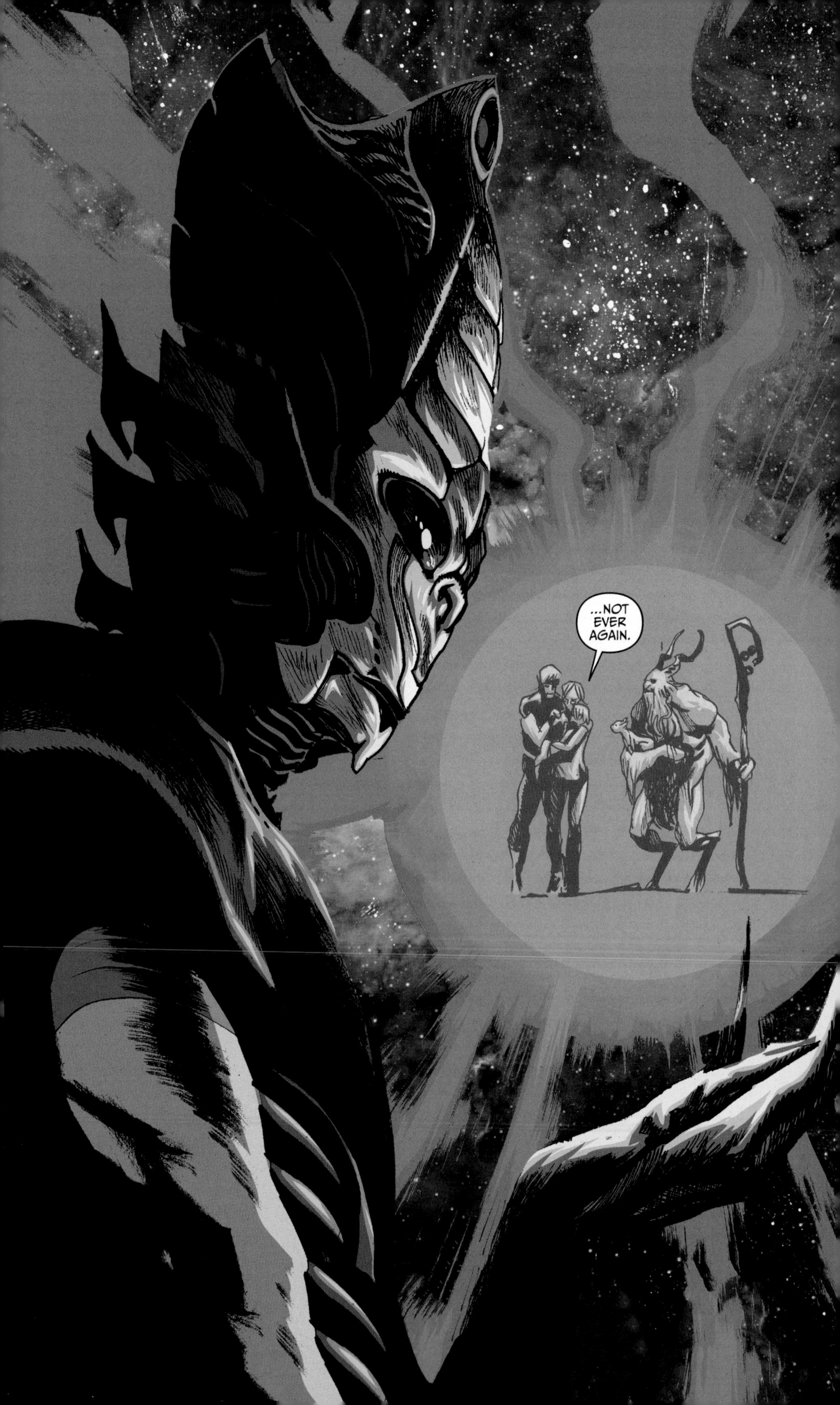
...NOT EVER AGAIN.

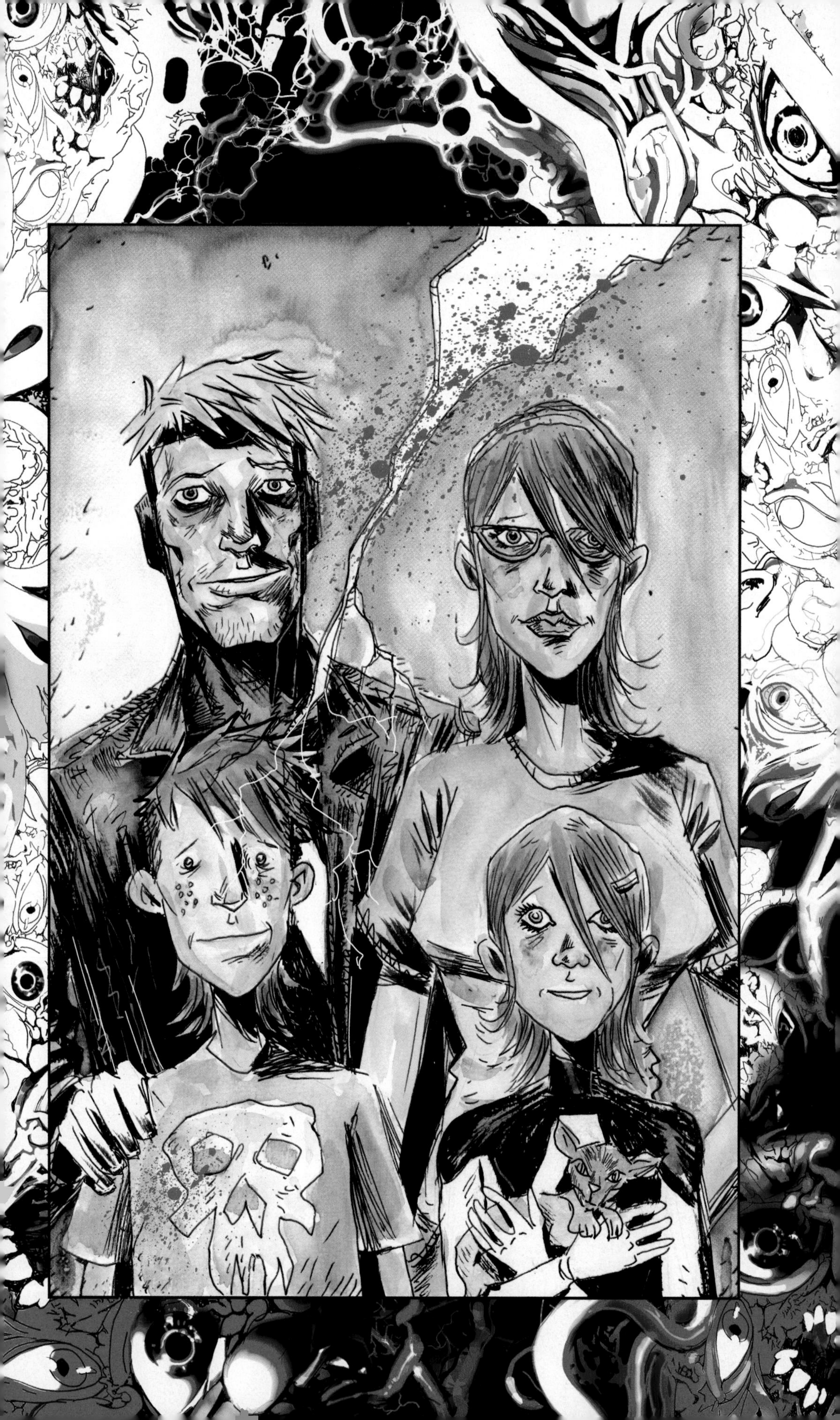

JEFF LEMIRE writer JEFF LEMIRE artist (pages 123-133) TRAVEL FOREM[illegible] artist (pages 117-122, 134-136)
JOSE VILLARRUBIA colorist (pages 123-133) LOVERN KINDZIERSKI colorist (pages 117-122, 134-136)
JARED K. FLETCHER letterer JEFF LEMIRE and TRAVEL FOREMAN cover art JEFF LEMIRE cover color

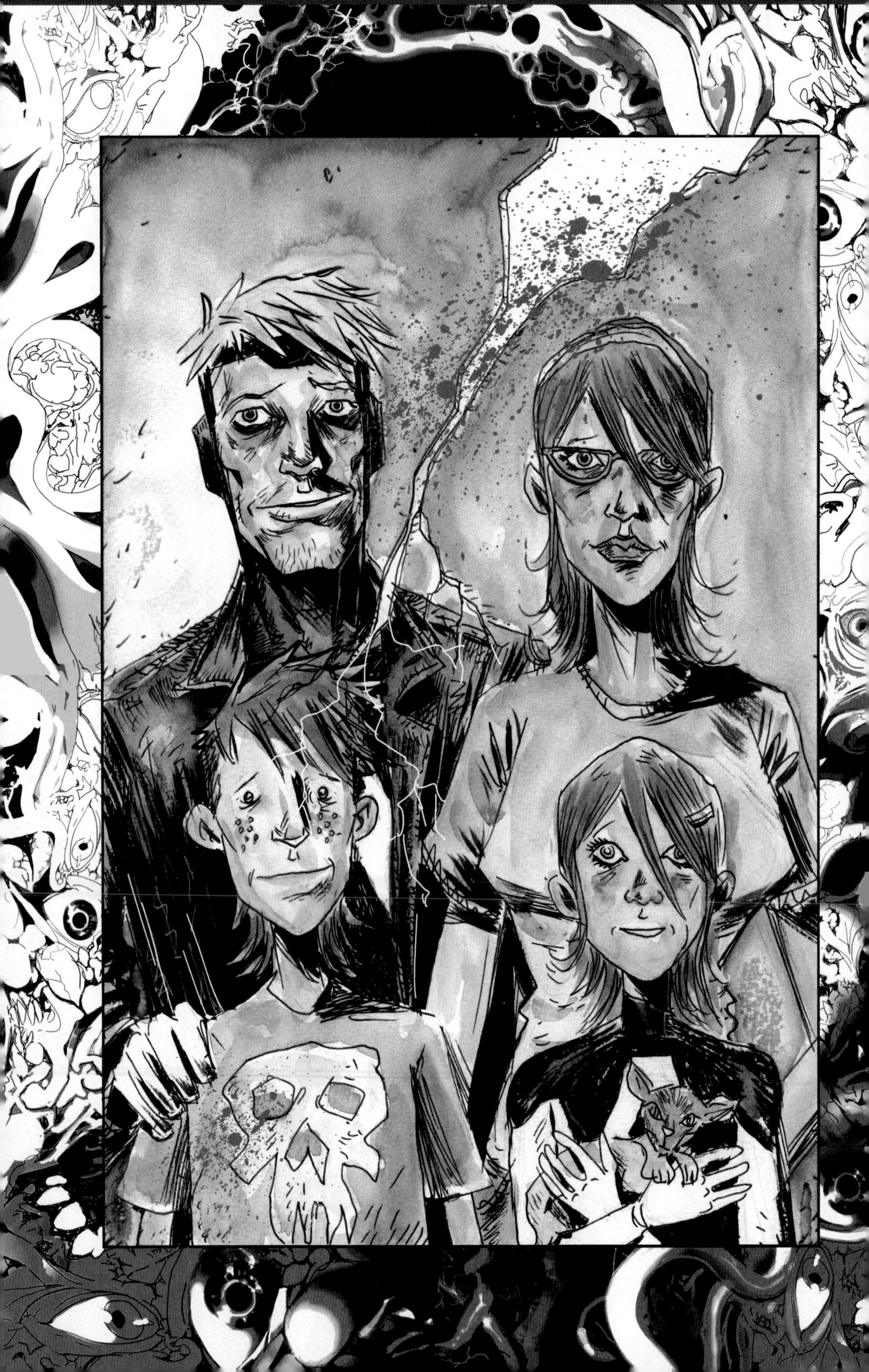

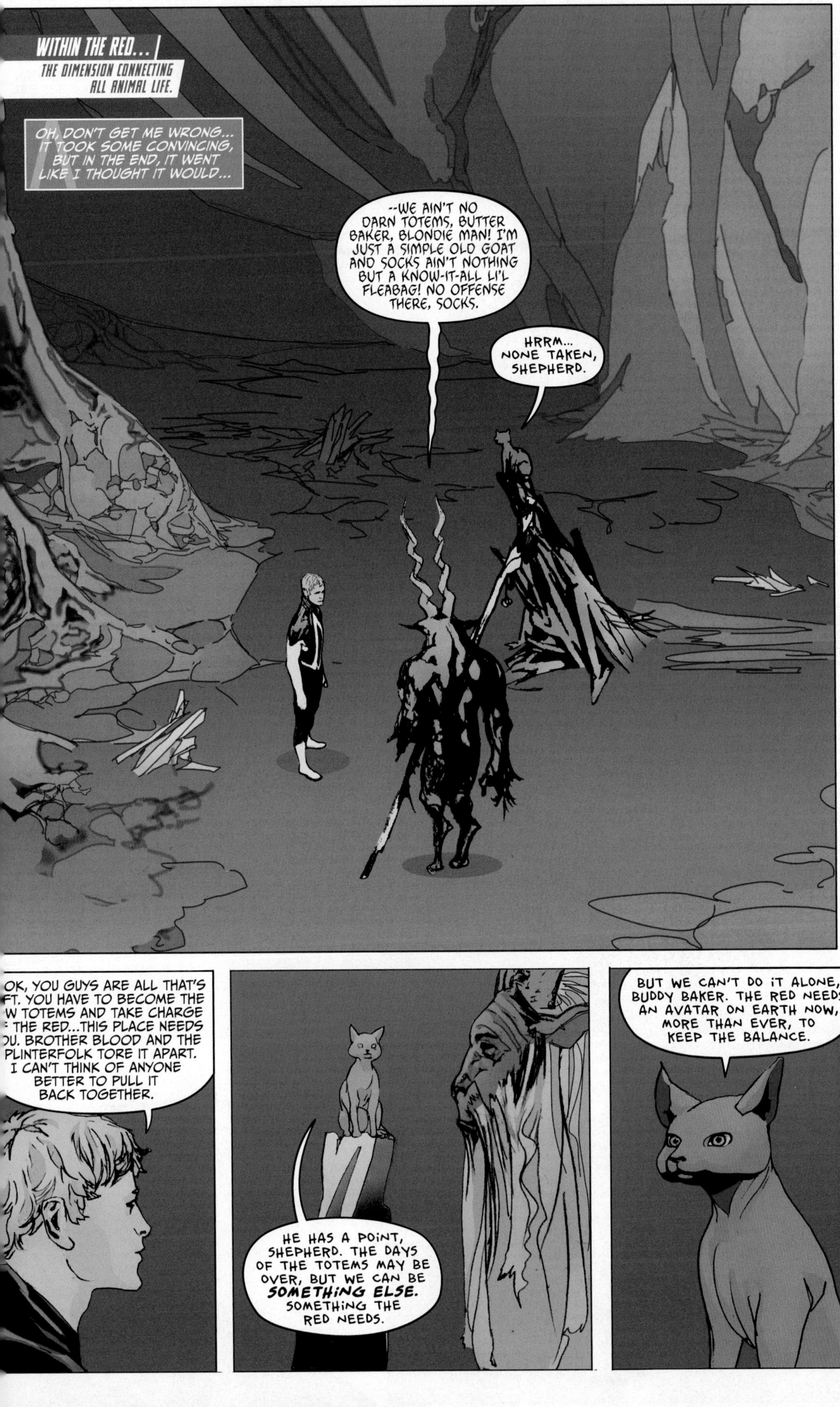

WITHIN THE RED...
THE DIMENSION CONNECTING ALL ANIMAL LIFE.
OH, DON'T GET ME WRONG... IT TOOK SOME CONVINCING, BUT IN THE END, IT WENT LIKE I THOUGHT IT WOULD...
--WE AIN'T NO DARN TOTEMS, BUTTER BAKER, BLONDIE MAN! I'M JUST A SIMPLE OLD GOAT AND SOCKS AIN'T NOTHING BUT A KNOW-IT-ALL LI'L FLEABAG! NO OFFENSE THERE, SOCKS.
HRRM... NONE TAKEN, SHEPHERD.
OK, YOU GUYS ARE ALL THAT'S FT. YOU HAVE TO BECOME THE W TOTEMS AND TAKE CHARGE THE RED...THIS PLACE NEEDS OU. BROTHER BLOOD AND THE PLINTERFOLK TORE IT APART. I CAN'T THINK OF ANYONE BETTER TO PULL IT BACK TOGETHER.
HE HAS A POINT, SHEPHERD. THE DAYS OF THE TOTEMS MAY BE OVER, BUT WE CAN BE SOMETHING ELSE. SOMETHING THE RED NEEDS.
BUT WE CAN'T DO IT ALONE, BUDDY BAKER. THE RED NEEDS AN AVATAR ON EARTH NOW, MORE THAN EVER, TO KEEP THE BALANCE.

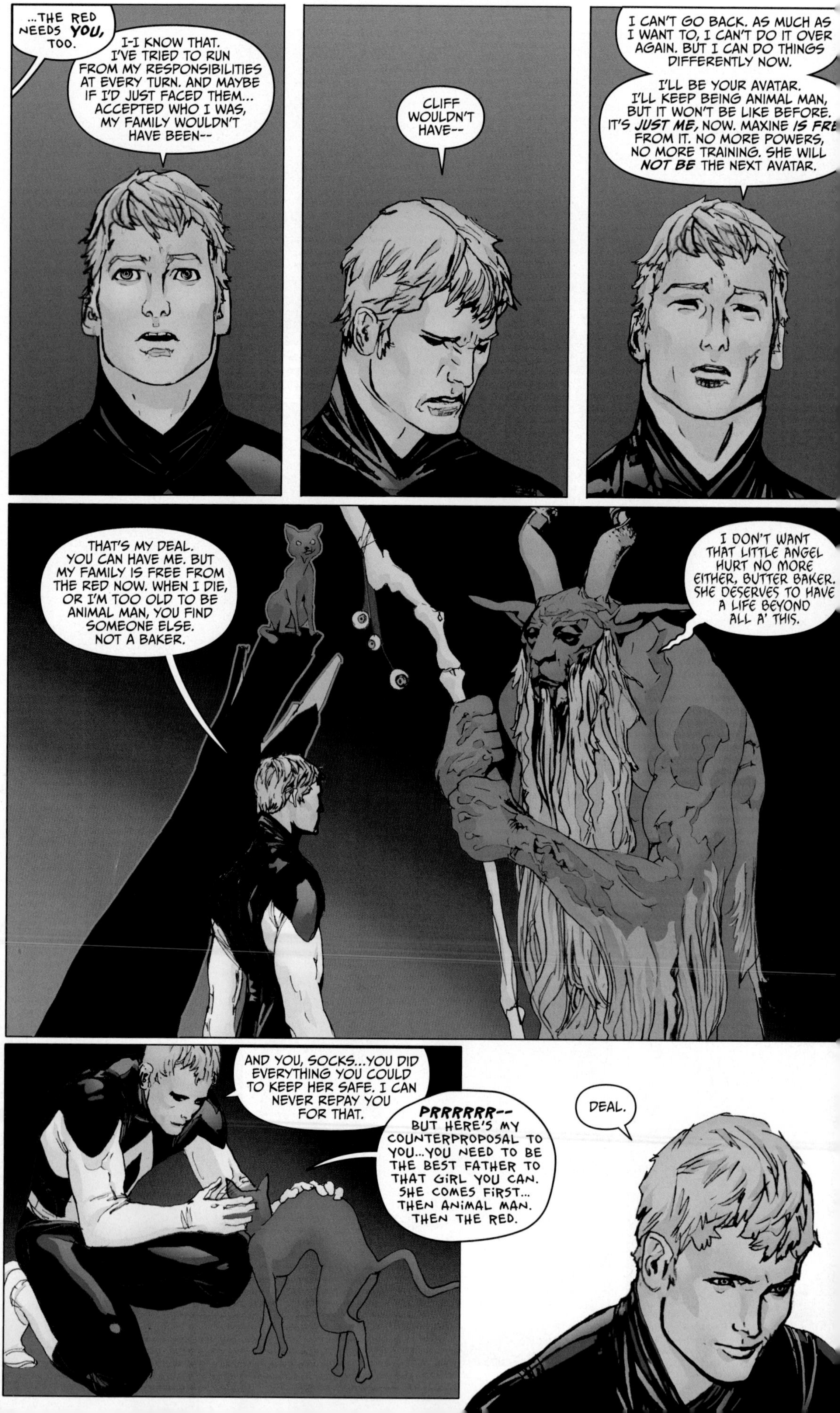

...THE RED NEEDS YOU, TOO.
I-I KNOW THAT. I'VE TRIED TO RUN FROM MY RESPONSIBILITIES AT EVERY TURN. AND MAYBE IF I'D JUST FACED THEM... ACCEPTED WHO I WAS, MY FAMILY WOULDN'T HAVE BEEN--
CLIFF WOULDN'T HAVE--
I CAN'T GO BACK. AS MUCH AS I WANT TO, I CAN'T DO IT OVER AGAIN. BUT I CAN DO THINGS DIFFERENTLY NOW.
I'LL BE YOUR AVATAR. I'LL KEEP BEING ANIMAL MAN, BUT IT WON'T BE LIKE BEFORE. IT'S JUST ME, NOW. MAXINE IS FREE FROM IT. NO MORE POWERS, NO MORE TRAINING. SHE WILL NOT BE THE NEXT AVATAR.
THAT'S MY DEAL. YOU CAN HAVE ME. BUT MY FAMILY IS FREE FROM THE RED NOW. WHEN I DIE, OR I'M TOO OLD TO BE ANIMAL MAN, YOU FIND SOMEONE ELSE. NOT A BAKER.
I DON'T WANT THAT LITTLE ANGEL HURT NO MORE EITHER, BUTTER BAKER. SHE DESERVES TO HAVE A LIFE BEYOND ALL A' THIS.
AND YOU, SOCKS...YOU DID EVERYTHING YOU COULD TO KEEP HER SAFE. I CAN NEVER REPAY YOU FOR THAT.
PRRRRRR-- BUT HERE'S MY COUNTERPROPOSAL TO YOU...YOU NEED TO BE THE BEST FATHER TO THAT GIRL YOU CAN. SHE COMES FIRST... THEN ANIMAL MAN. THEN THE RED.
DEAL.

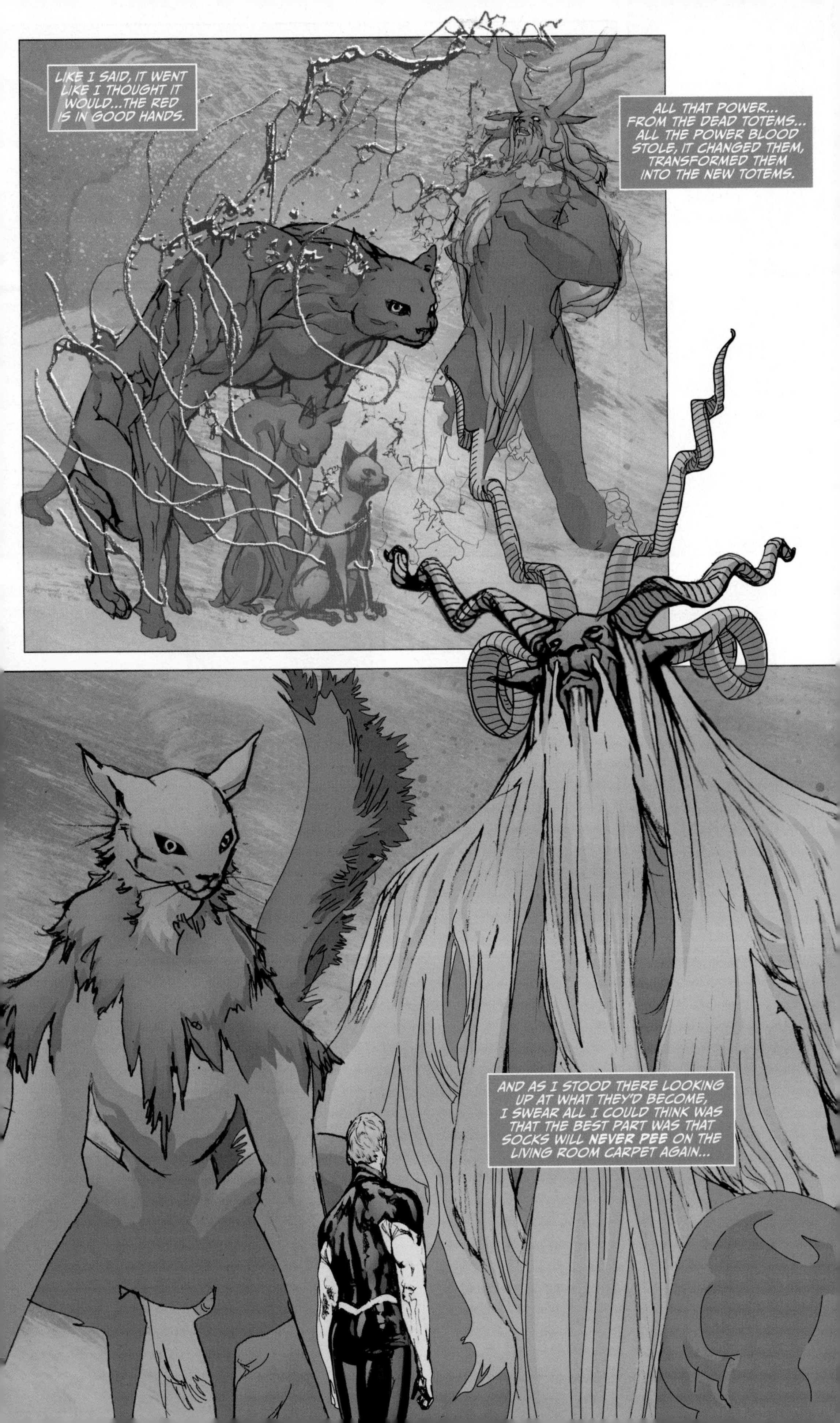
LIKE I SAID, IT WENT LIKE I THOUGHT IT WOULD...THE RED IS IN GOOD HANDS.
ALL THAT POWER... FROM THE DEAD TOTEMS... ALL THE POWER BLOOD STOLE, IT CHANGED THEM, TRANSFORMED THEM INTO THE NEW TOTEMS.
AND AS I STOOD THERE LOOKING UP AT WHAT THEY'D BECOME, I SWEAR ALL I COULD THINK WAS THAT THE BEST PART WAS THAT SOCKS WILL **NEVER PEE** ON THE LIVING ROOM CARPET AGAIN...

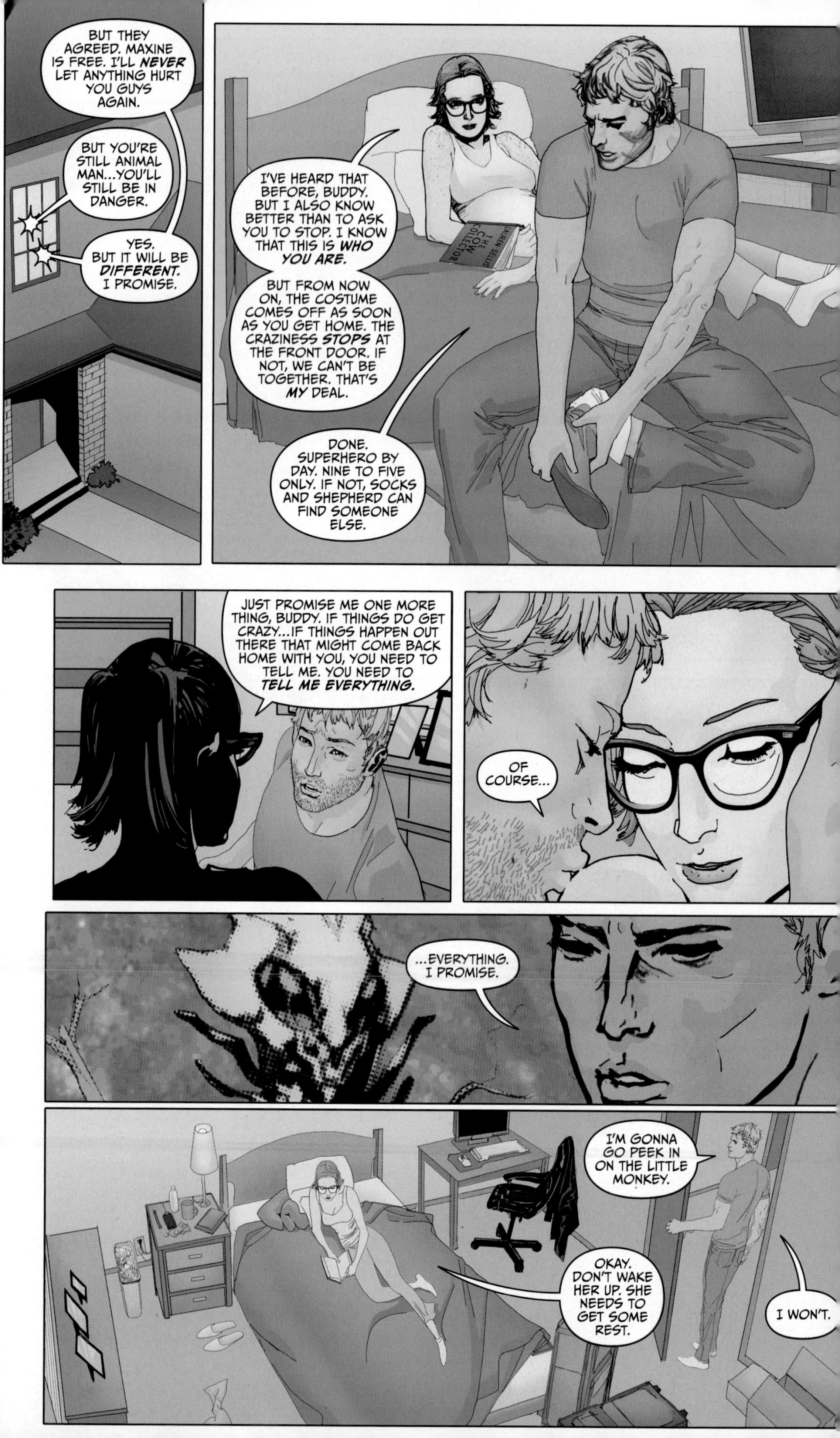
BUT THEY AGREED. MAXINE IS FREE. I'LL NEVER LET ANYTHING HURT YOU GUYS AGAIN.
BUT YOU'RE STILL ANIMAL MAN...YOU'LL STILL BE IN DANGER.
YES. BUT IT WILL BE DIFFERENT. I PROMISE.
I'VE HEARD THAT BEFORE, BUDDY. BUT I ALSO KNOW BETTER THAN TO ASK YOU TO STOP. I KNOW THAT THIS IS WHO YOU ARE.
LAUREN SELLIS THE COW COLLECTOR
BUT FROM NOW ON, THE COSTUME COMES OFF AS SOON AS YOU GET HOME. THE CRAZINESS STOPS AT THE FRONT DOOR. IF NOT, WE CAN'T BE TOGETHER. THAT'S MY DEAL.
DONE. SUPERHERO BY DAY. NINE TO FIVE ONLY. IF NOT, SOCKS AND SHEPHERD CAN FIND SOMEONE ELSE.
JUST PROMISE ME ONE MORE THING, BUDDY. IF THINGS DO GET CRAZY...IF THINGS HAPPEN OUT THERE THAT MIGHT COME BACK HOME WITH YOU, YOU NEED TO TELL ME. YOU NEED TO TELL ME EVERYTHING.
OF COURSE...
...EVERYTHING. I PROMISE.
I'M GONNA GO PEEK IN ON THE LITTLE MONKEY.
OKAY. DON'T WAKE HER UP. SHE NEEDS TO GET SOME REST.
I WON'T.

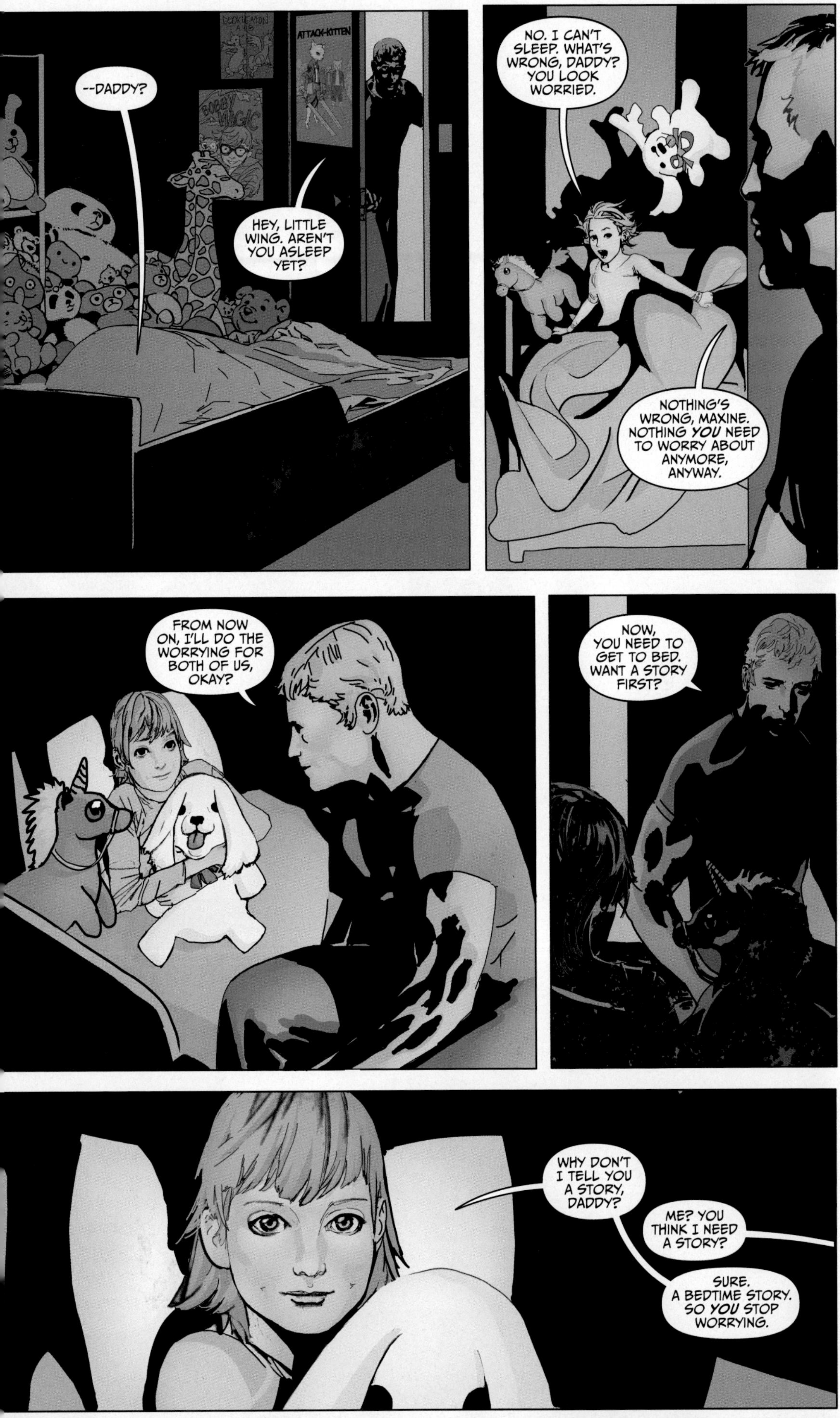
--DADDY?
ATTACK-KITTEN
HEY, LITTLE WING. AREN'T YOU ASLEEP YET?
NO. I CAN'T SLEEP. WHAT'S WRONG, DADDY? YOU LOOK WORRIED.
NOTHING'S WRONG, MAXINE. NOTHING *YOU* NEED TO WORRY ABOUT ANYMORE, ANYWAY.
FROM NOW ON, I'LL DO THE WORRYING FOR BOTH OF US, OKAY?
NOW, YOU NEED TO GET TO BED. WANT A STORY FIRST?
WHY DON'T I TELL YOU A STORY, DADDY?
ME? YOU THINK I NEED A STORY?
SURE. A BEDTIME STORY. SO *YOU* STOP WORRYING.

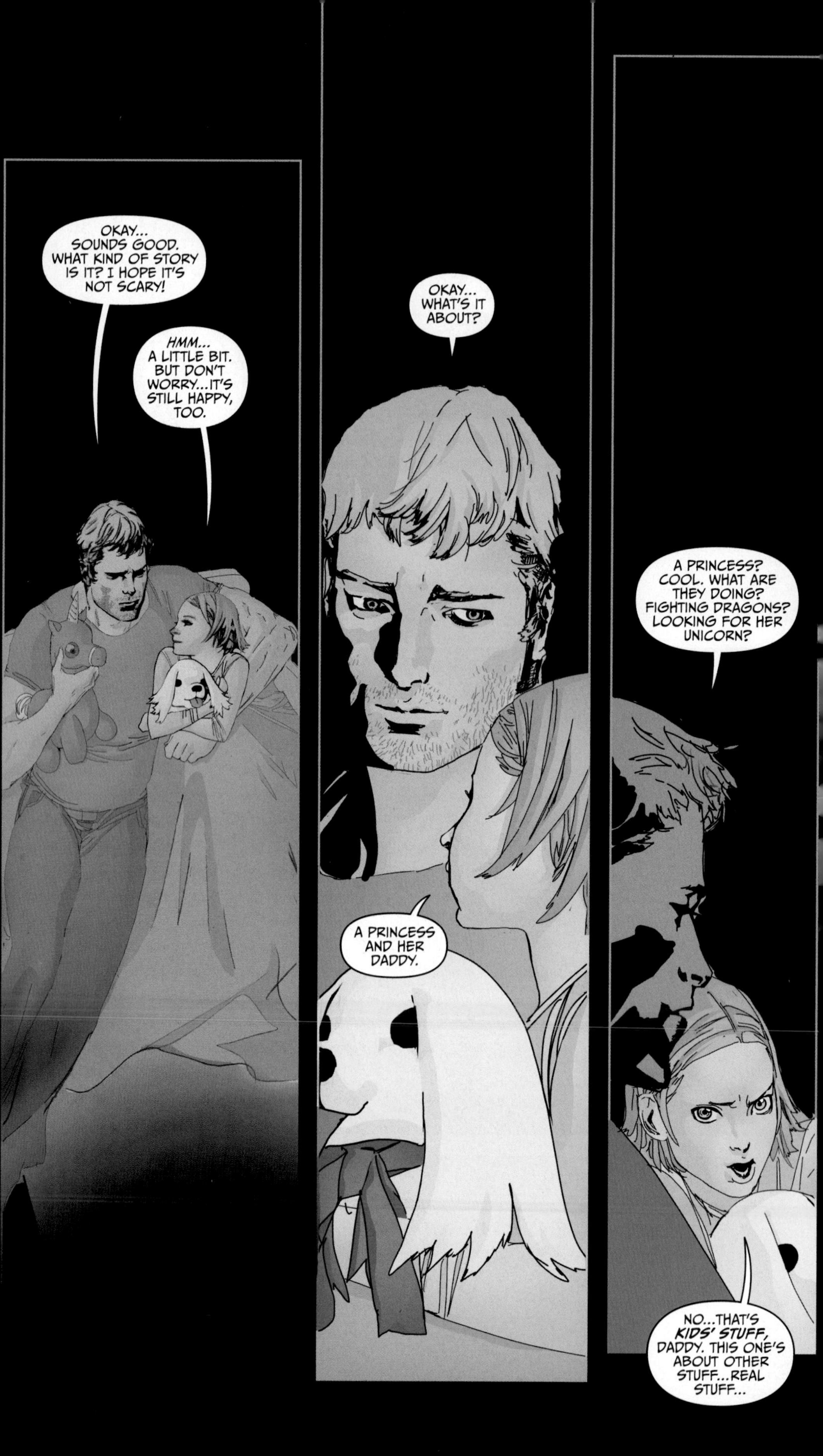
OKAY... SOUNDS GOOD. WHAT KIND OF STORY IS IT? I HOPE IT'S NOT SCARY!
HMM... A LITTLE BIT. BUT DON'T WORRY...IT'S STILL HAPPY, TOO.
OKAY... WHAT'S IT ABOUT?
A PRINCESS AND HER DADDY.
A PRINCESS? COOL. WHAT ARE THEY DOING? FIGHTING DRAGONS? LOOKING FOR HER UNICORN?
NO...THAT'S *KIDS' STUFF*, DADDY. THIS ONE'S ABOUT OTHER STUFF...REAL STUFF...

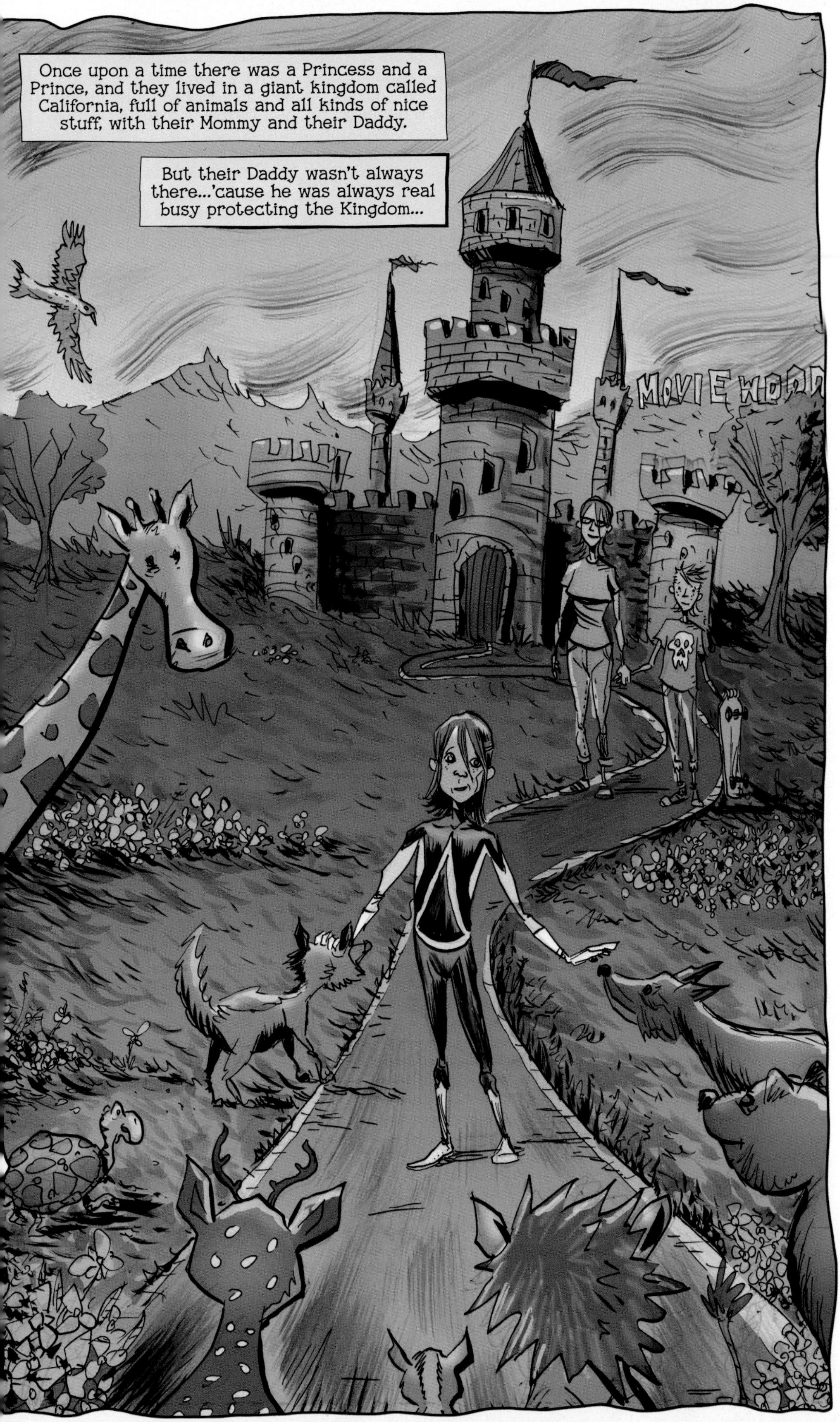
Once upon a time there was a Princess and a Prince, and they lived in a giant kingdom called California, full of animals and all kinds of nice stuff, with their Mommy and their Daddy.
But their Daddy wasn't always there...'cause he was always real busy protecting the Kingdom...
MOVIEWOOD

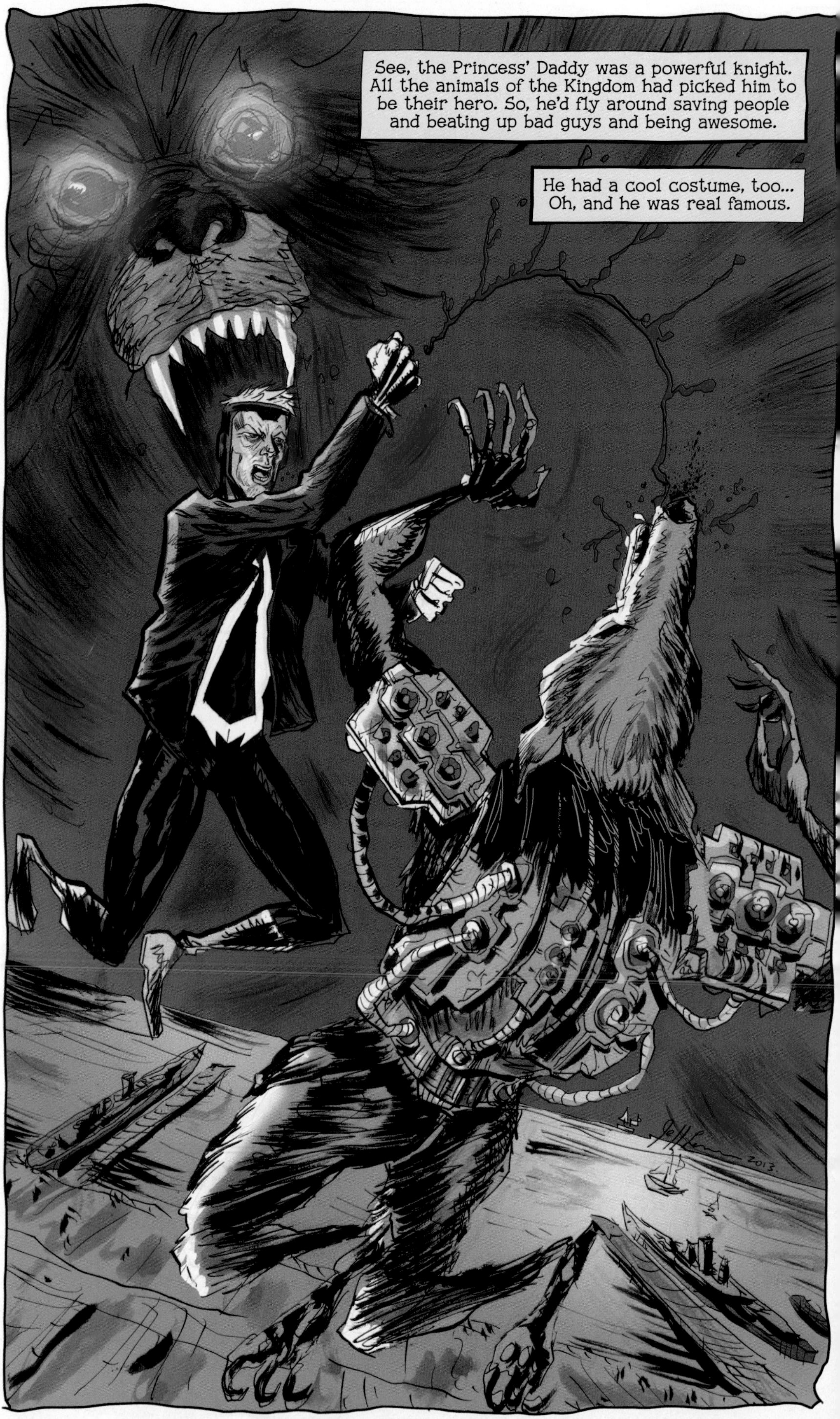
See, the Princess' Daddy was a powerful knight. All the animals of the Kingdom had picked him to be their hero. So, he'd fly around saving people and beating up bad guys and being awesome.
He had a cool costume, too... Oh, and he was real famous.

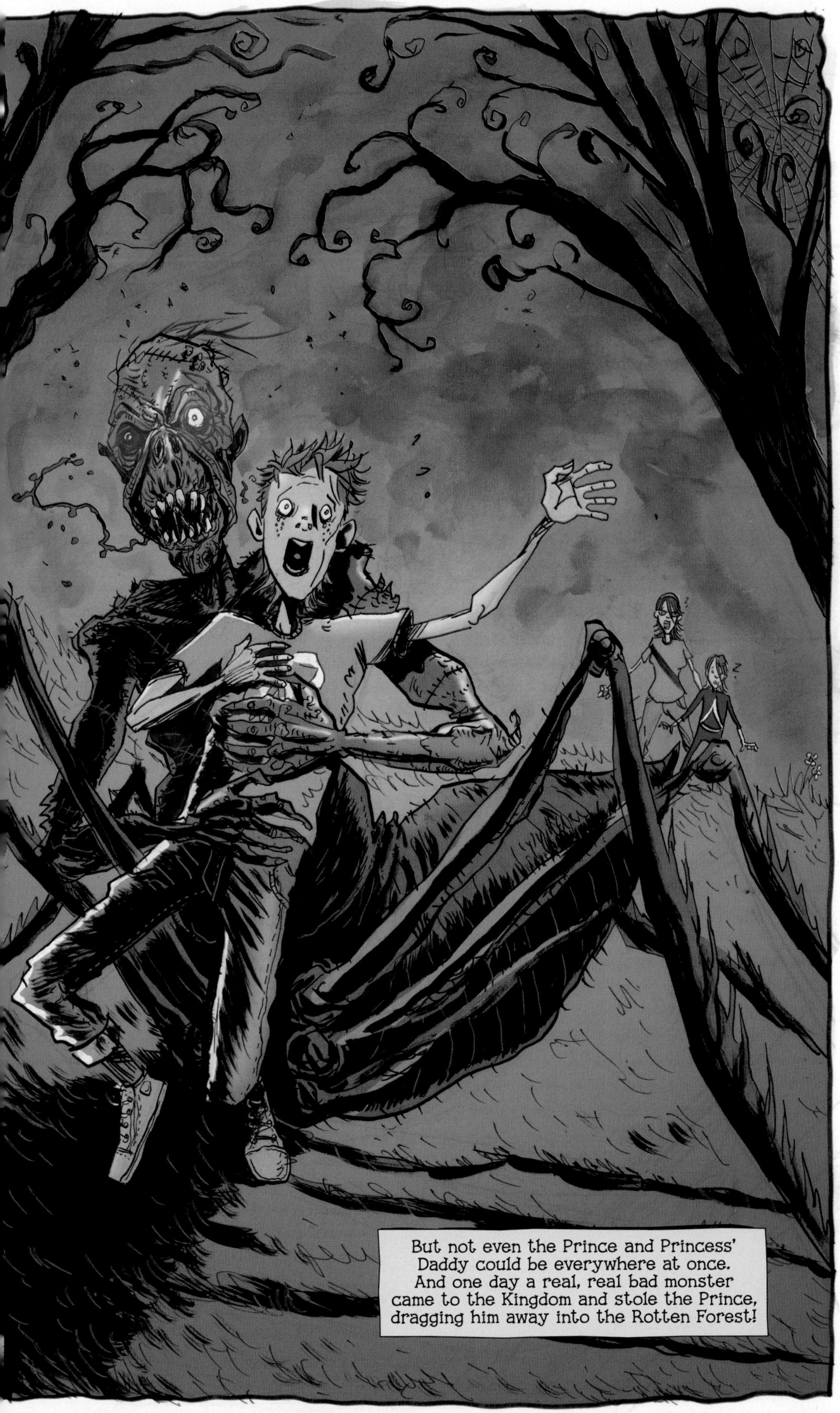
But not even the Prince and Princess' Daddy could be everywhere at once. And one day a real, real bad monster came to the Kingdom and stole the Prince, dragging him away into the Rotten Forest!

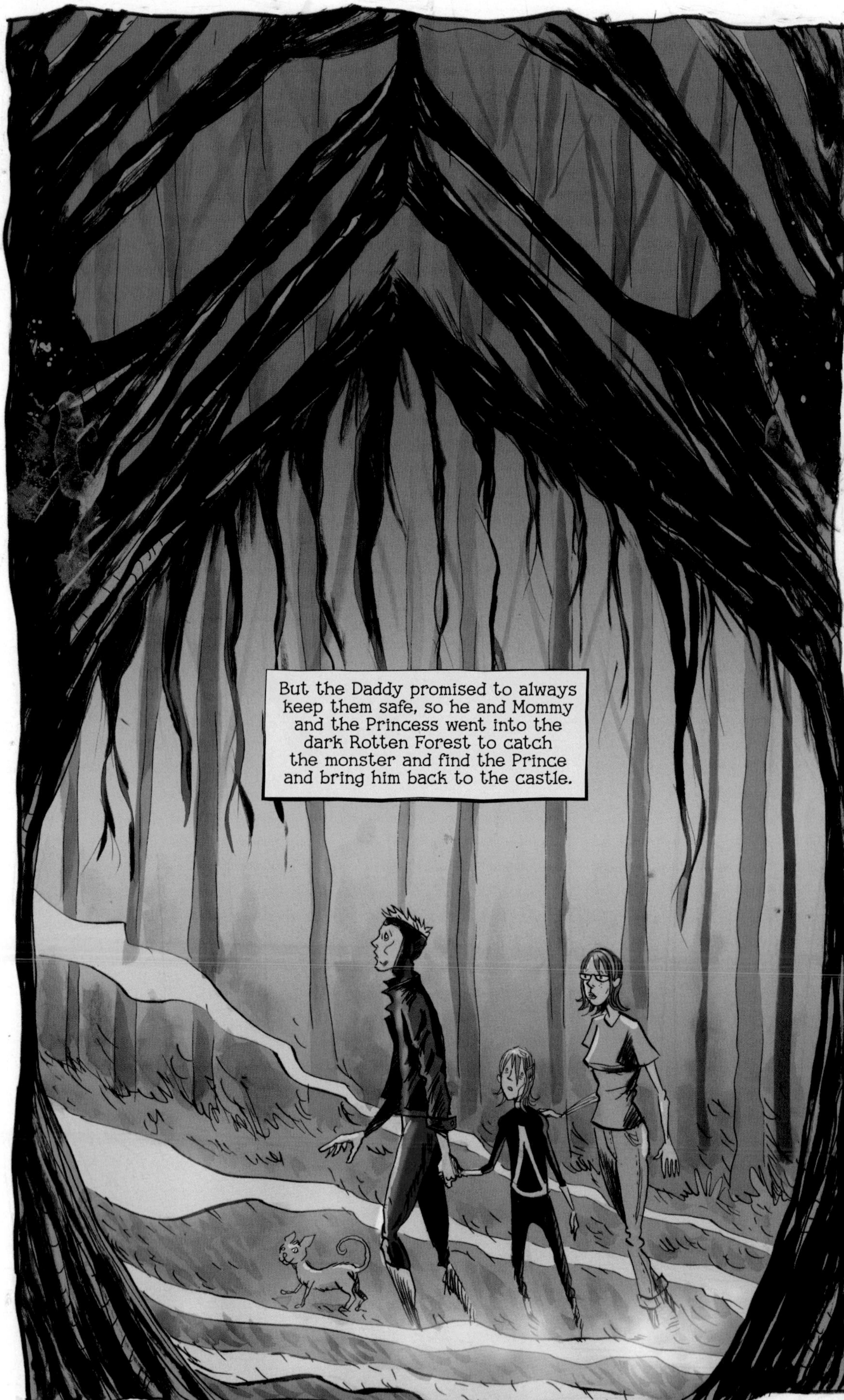
But the Daddy promised to always keep them safe, so he and Mommy and the Princess went into the dark Rotten Forest to catch the monster and find the Prince and bring him back to the castle.

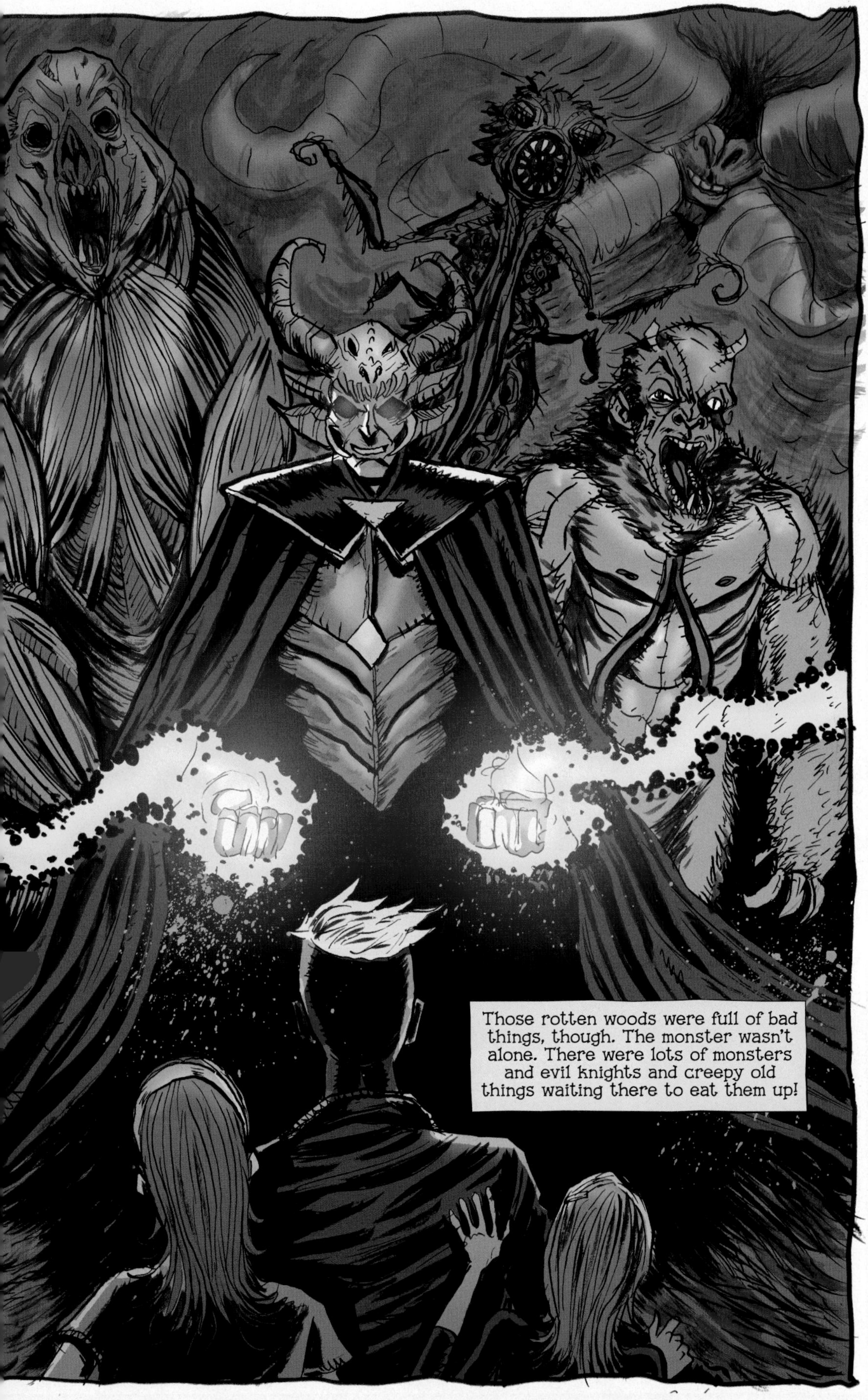
Those rotten woods were full of bad things, though. The monster wasn't alone. There were lots of monsters and evil knights and creepy old things waiting there to eat them up!

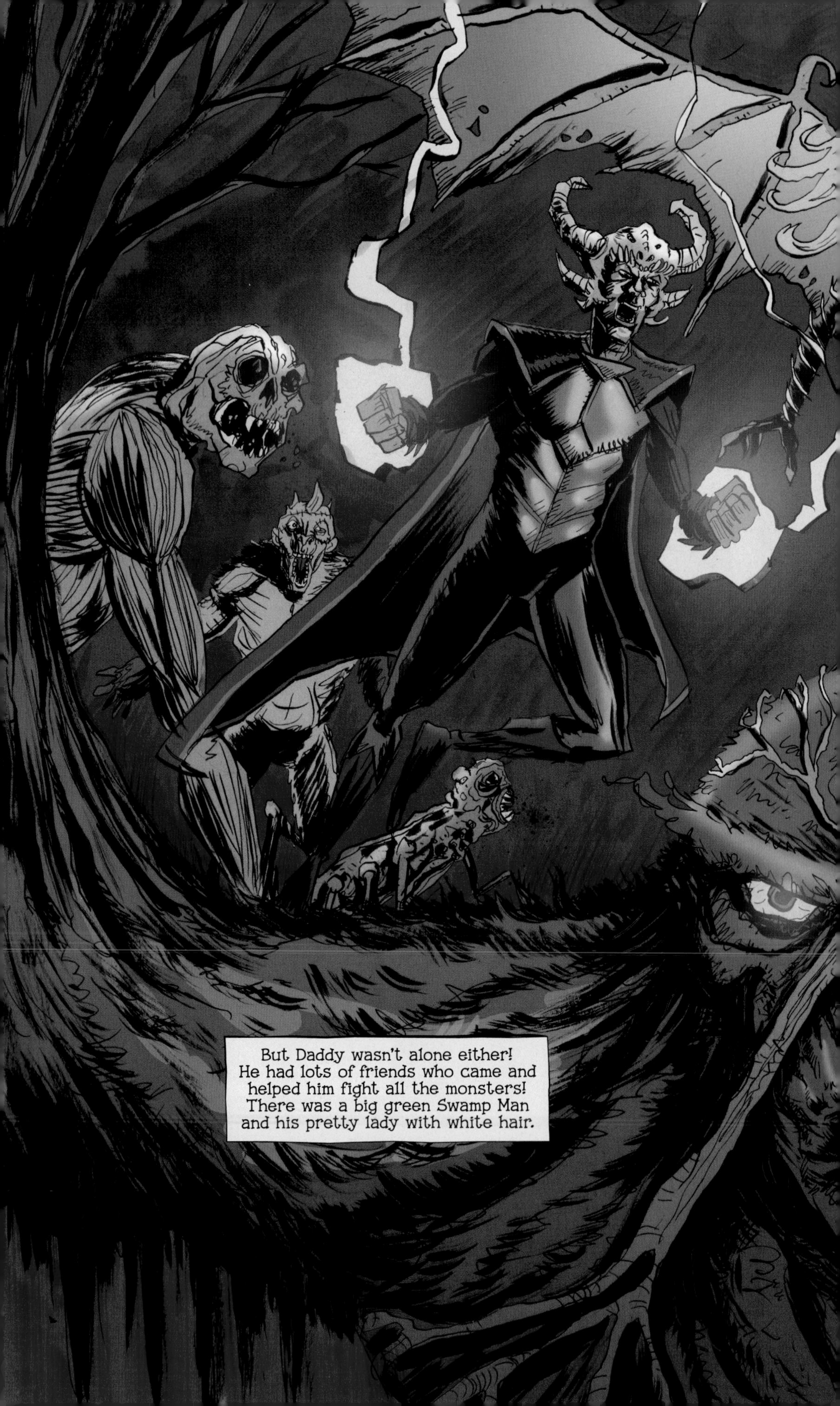
But Daddy wasn't alone either! He had lots of friends who came and helped him fight all the monsters! There was a big green Swamp Man and his pretty lady with white hair.

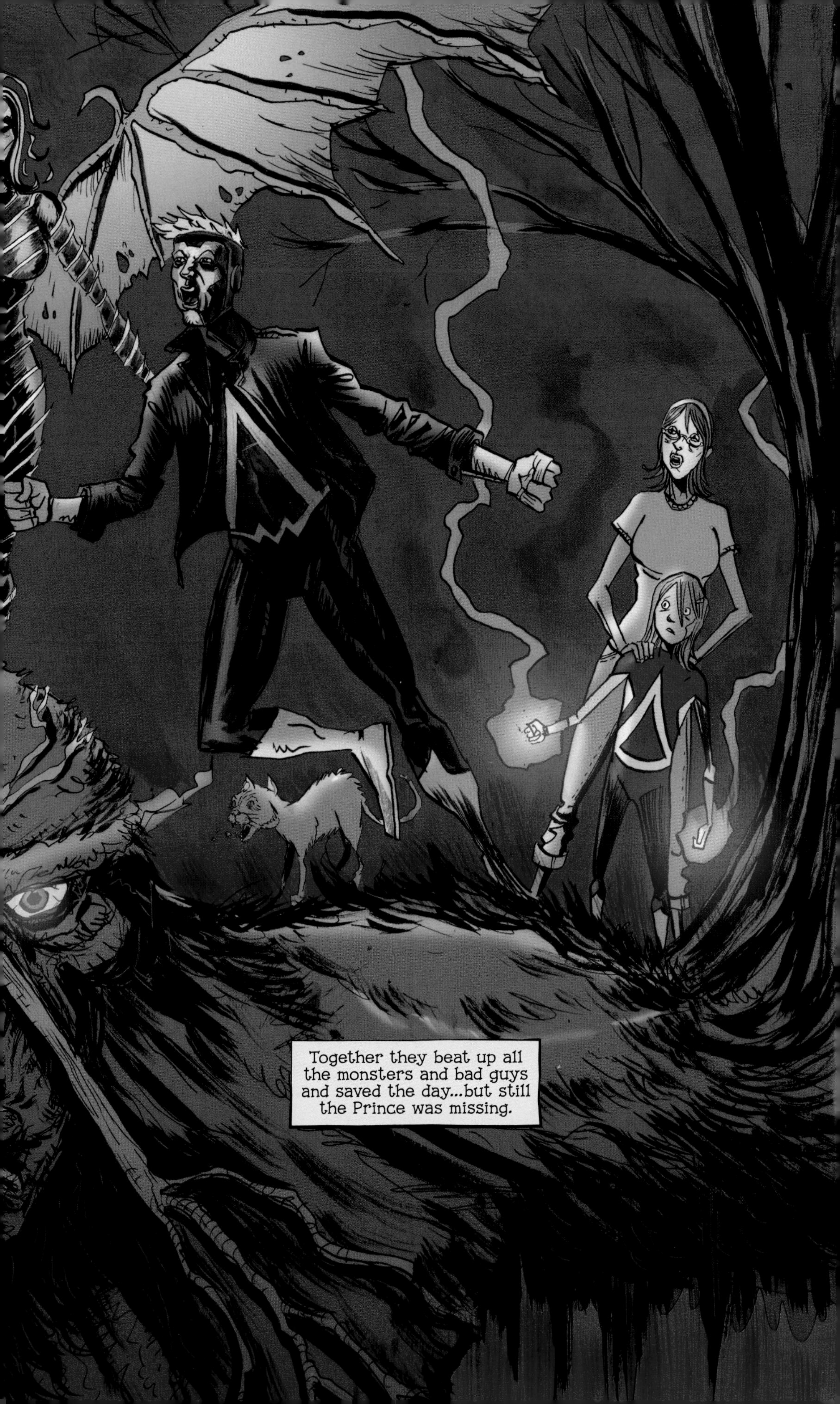
Together they beat up all the monsters and bad guys and saved the day...but still the Prince was missing.

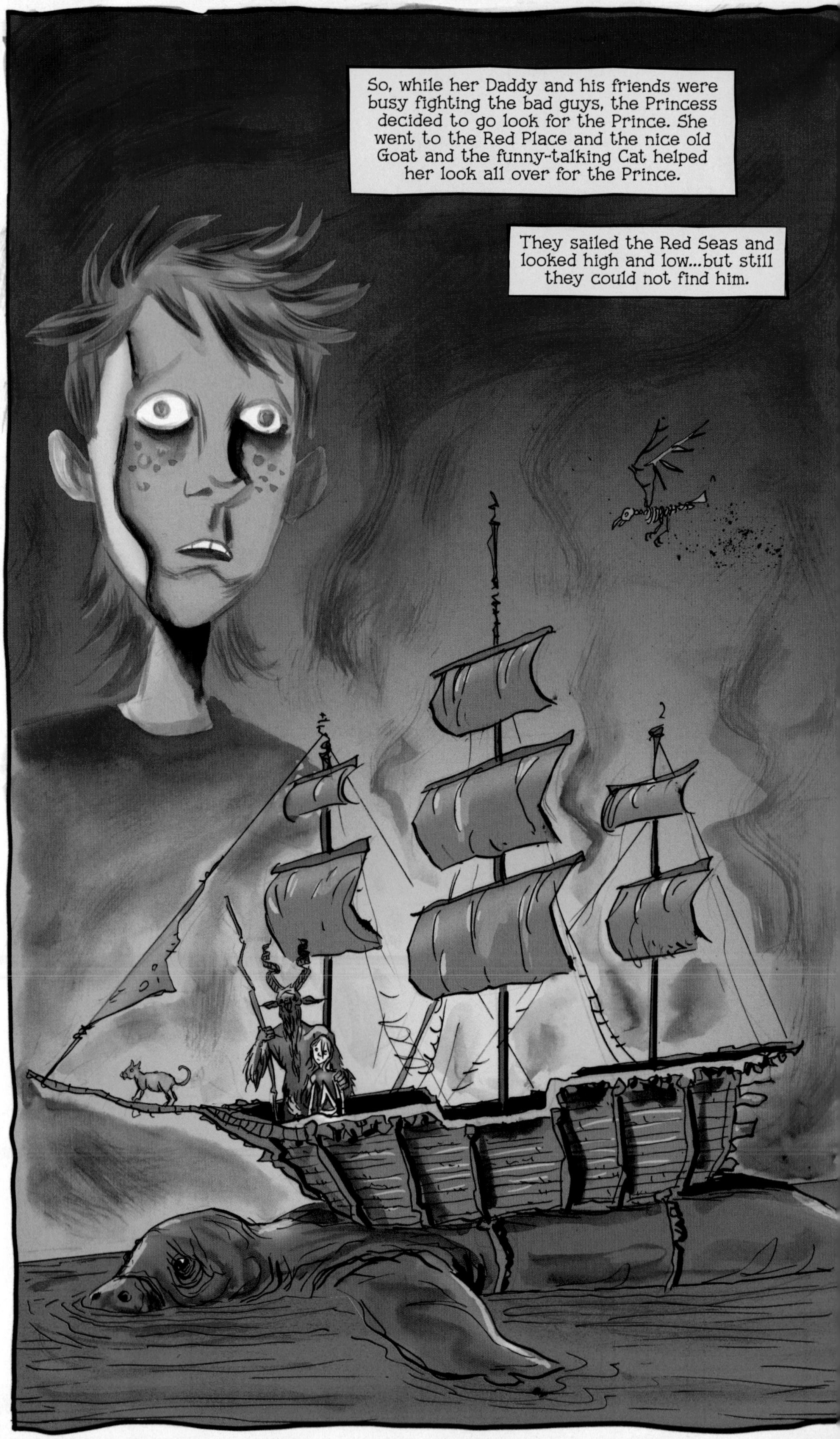
So, while her Daddy and his friends were busy fighting the bad guys, the Princess decided to go look for the Prince. She went to the Red Place and the nice old Goat and the funny-talking Cat helped her look all over for the Prince.
They sailed the Red Seas and looked high and low...but still they could not find him.

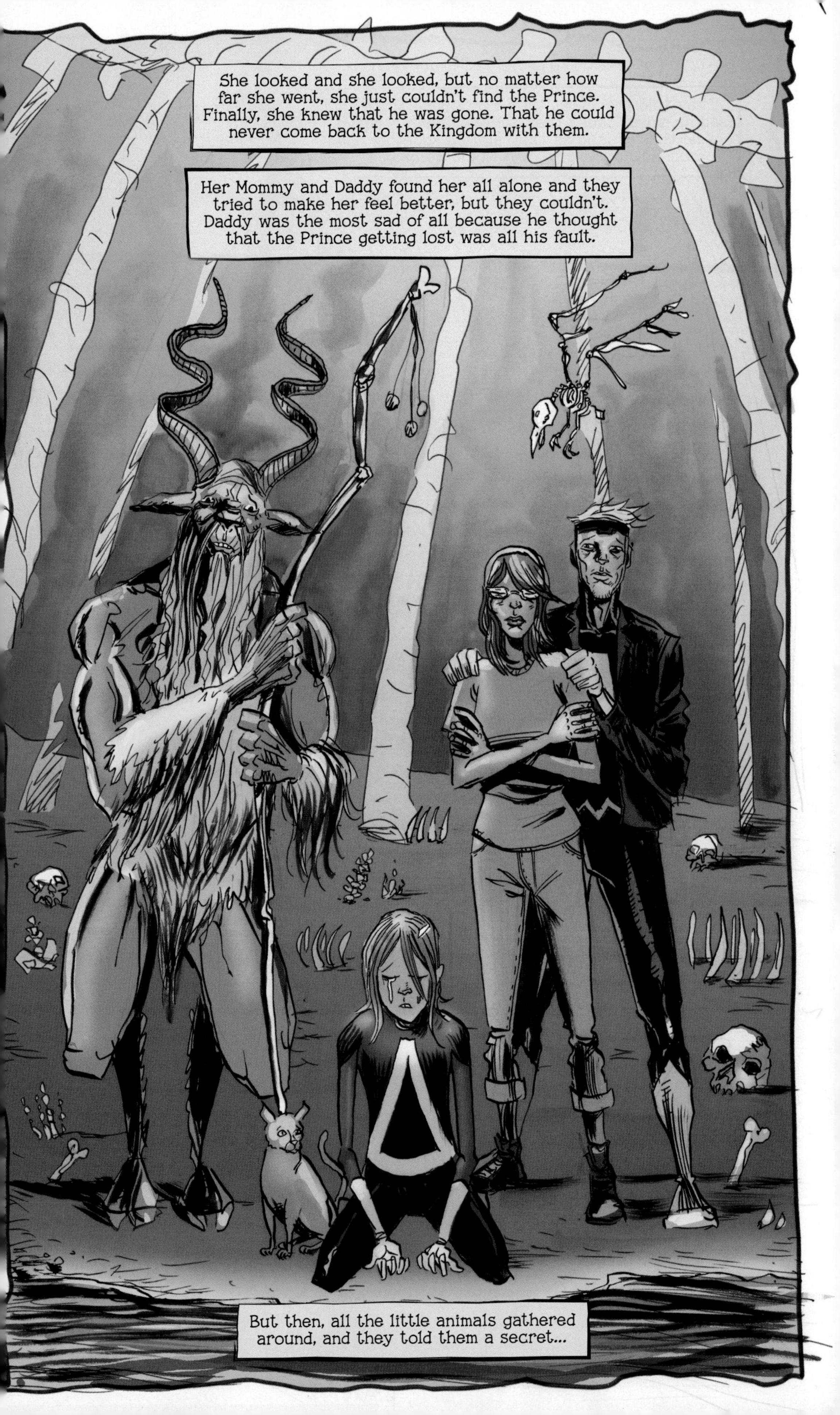
She looked and she looked, but no matter how far she went, she just couldn't find the Prince. Finally, she knew that he was gone. That he could never come back to the Kingdom with them.
Her Mommy and Daddy found her all alone and they tried to make her feel better, but they couldn't. Daddy was the most sad of all because he thought that the Prince getting lost was all his fault.
But then, all the little animals gathered around, and they told them a secret...

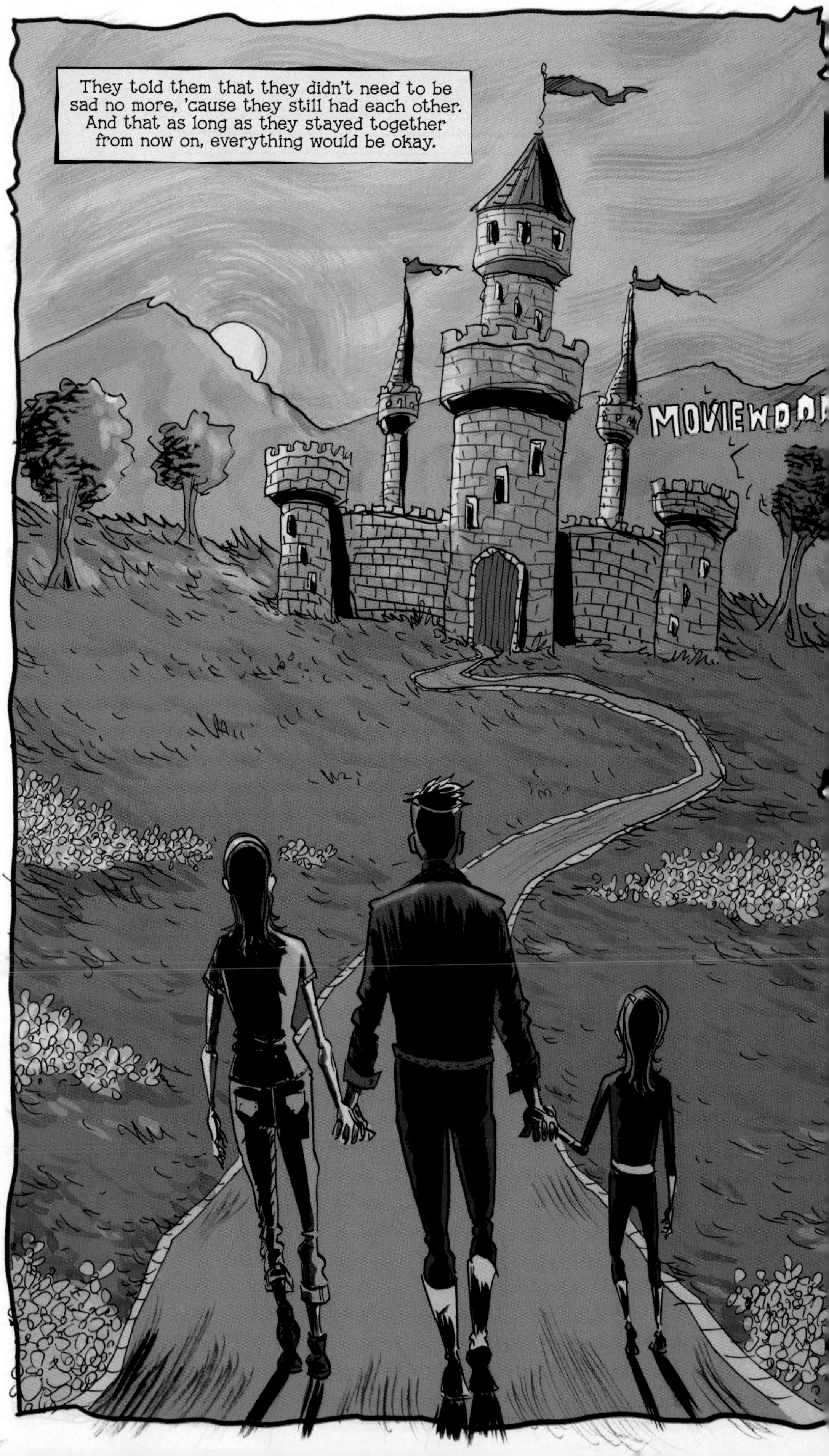
They told them that they didn't need to be sad no more, 'cause they still had each other. And that as long as they stayed together from now on, everything would be okay.

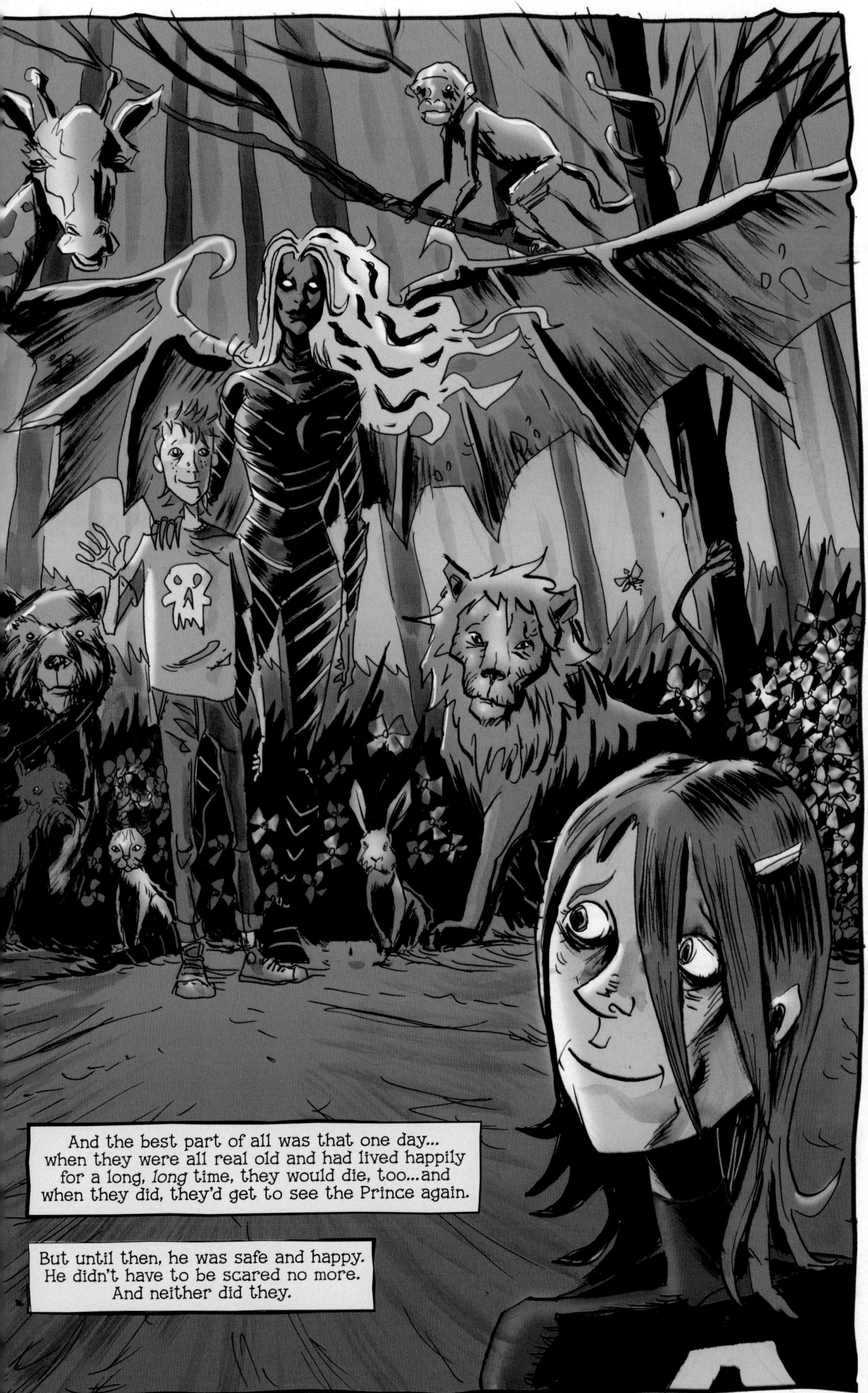

And the best part of all was that one day... when they were all real old and had lived happily for a long, *long* time, they would die, too...and when they did, they'd get to see the Prince again.
But until then, he was safe and happy. He didn't have to be scared no more. And neither did they.

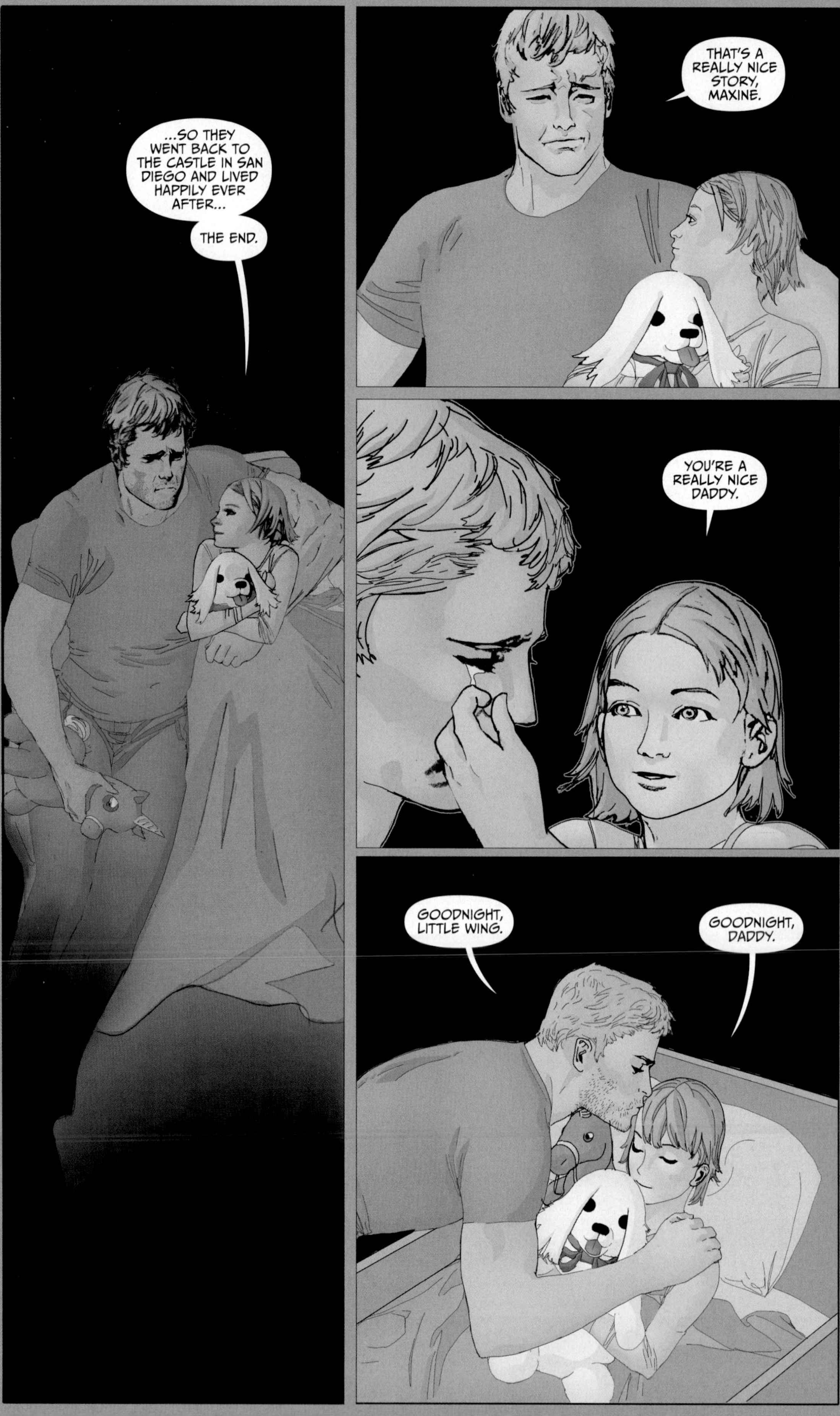
...SO THEY WENT BACK TO THE CASTLE IN SAN DIEGO AND LIVED HAPPILY EVER AFTER...
THE END.
THAT'S A REALLY NICE STORY, MAXINE.
YOU'RE A REALLY NICE DADDY.
GOODNIGHT, LITTLE WING.
GOODNIGHT, DADDY.

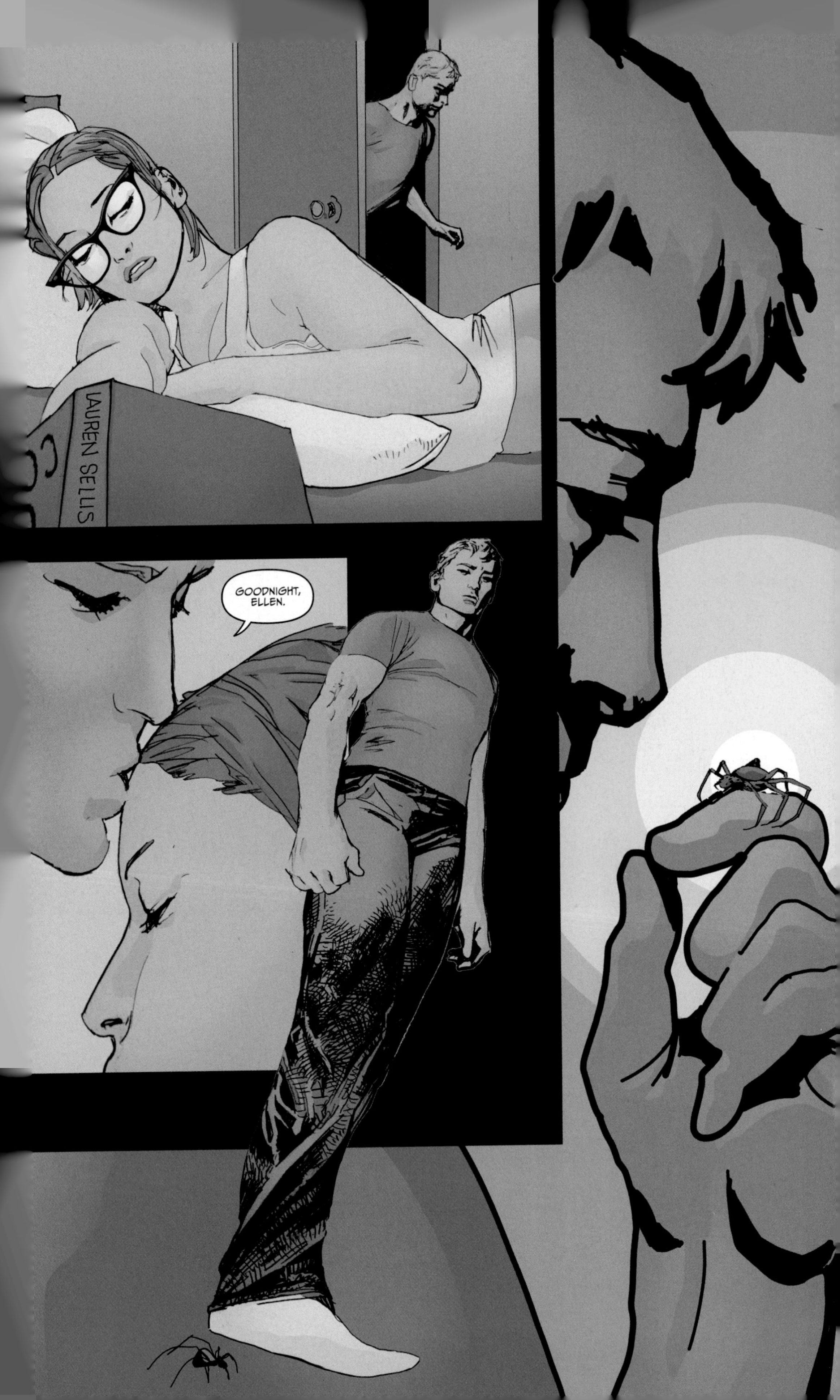
LAUREN SELLIS
GOODNIGHT, ELLEN.

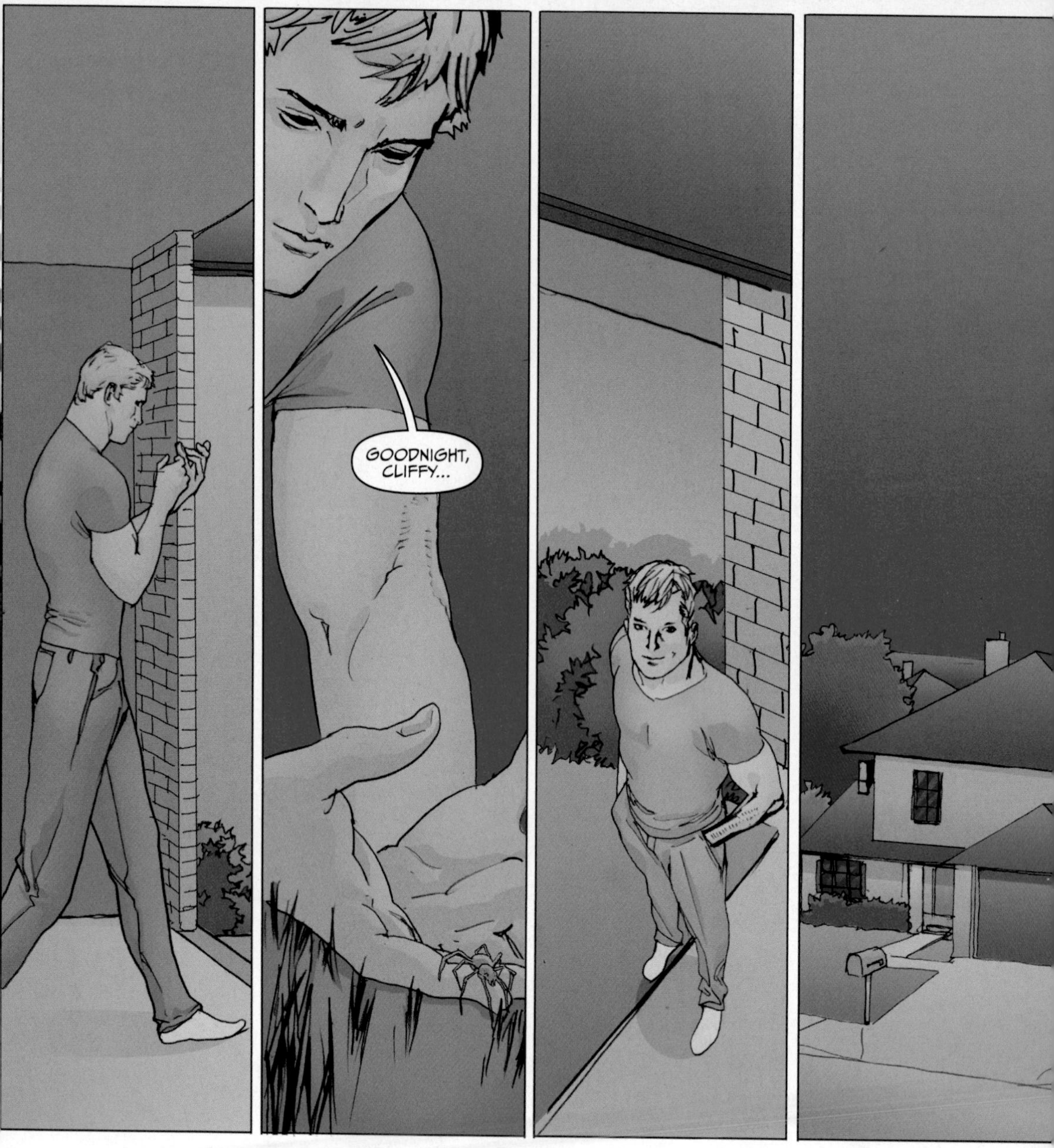
GOODNIGHT, CLIFFY...

...GOODNIGHT,

Animal Man

ANIMAL MAN
PAGES BY RAFAEL ALBUQUERQUE

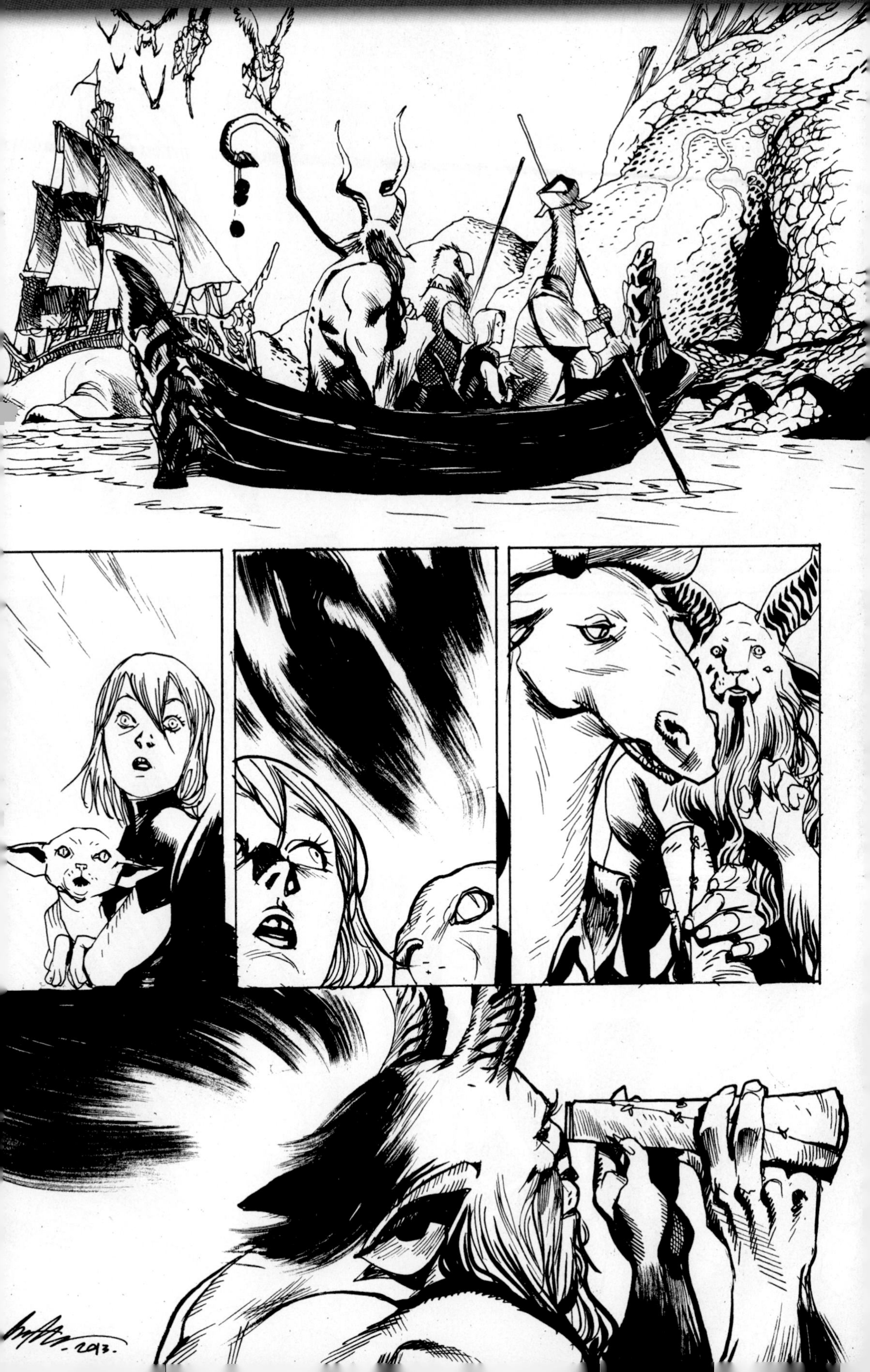

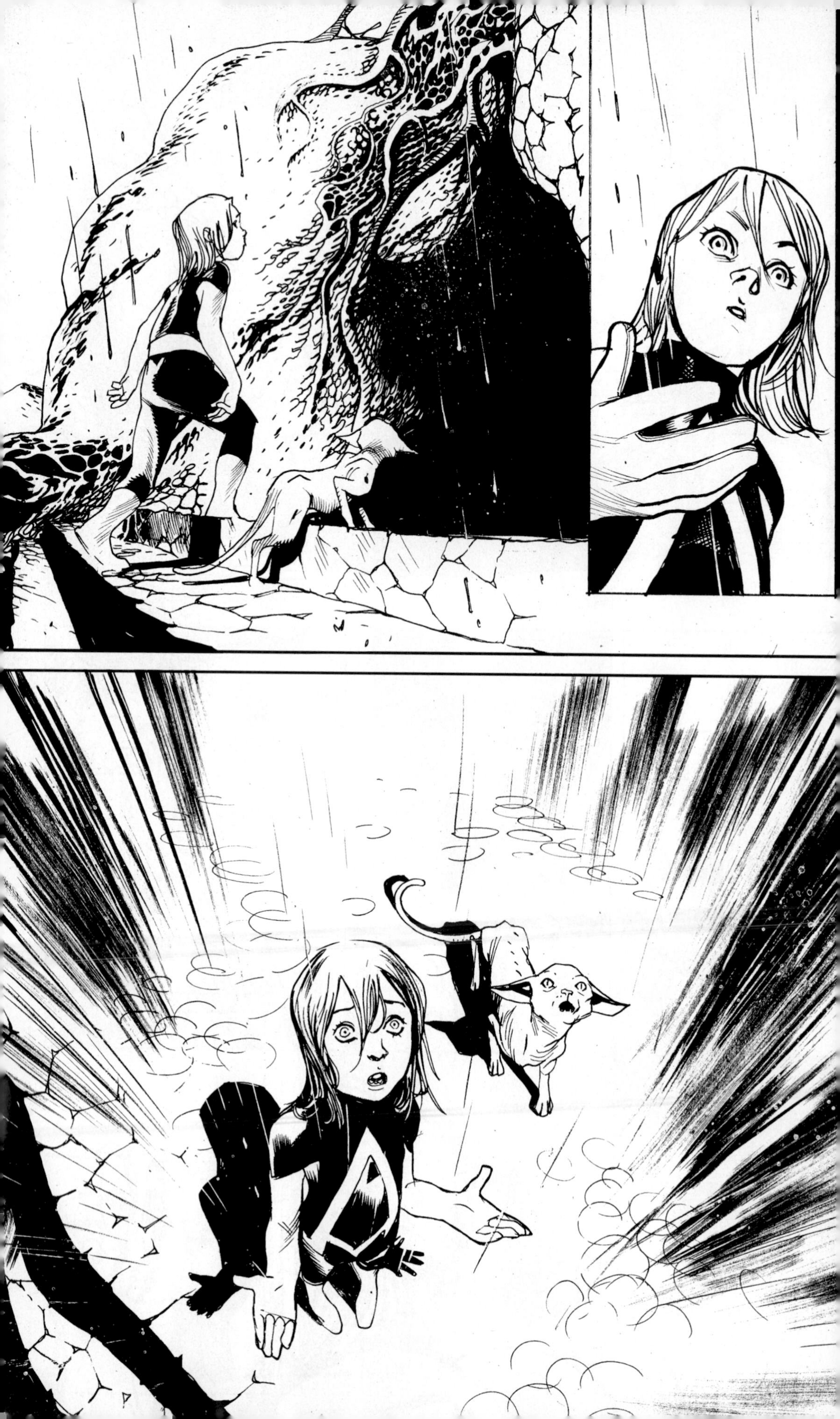

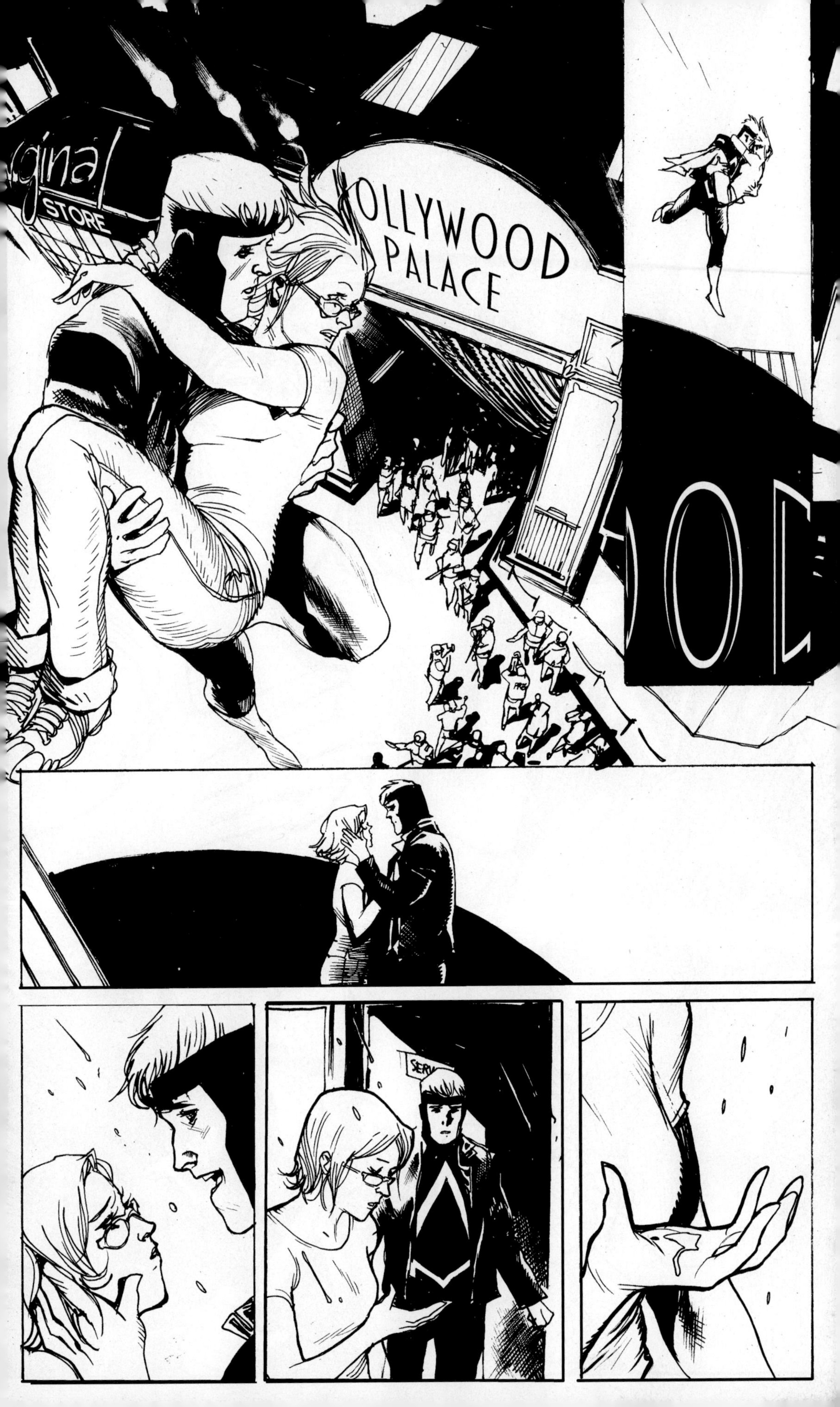
STORE
OLLYWOOD
PALACE

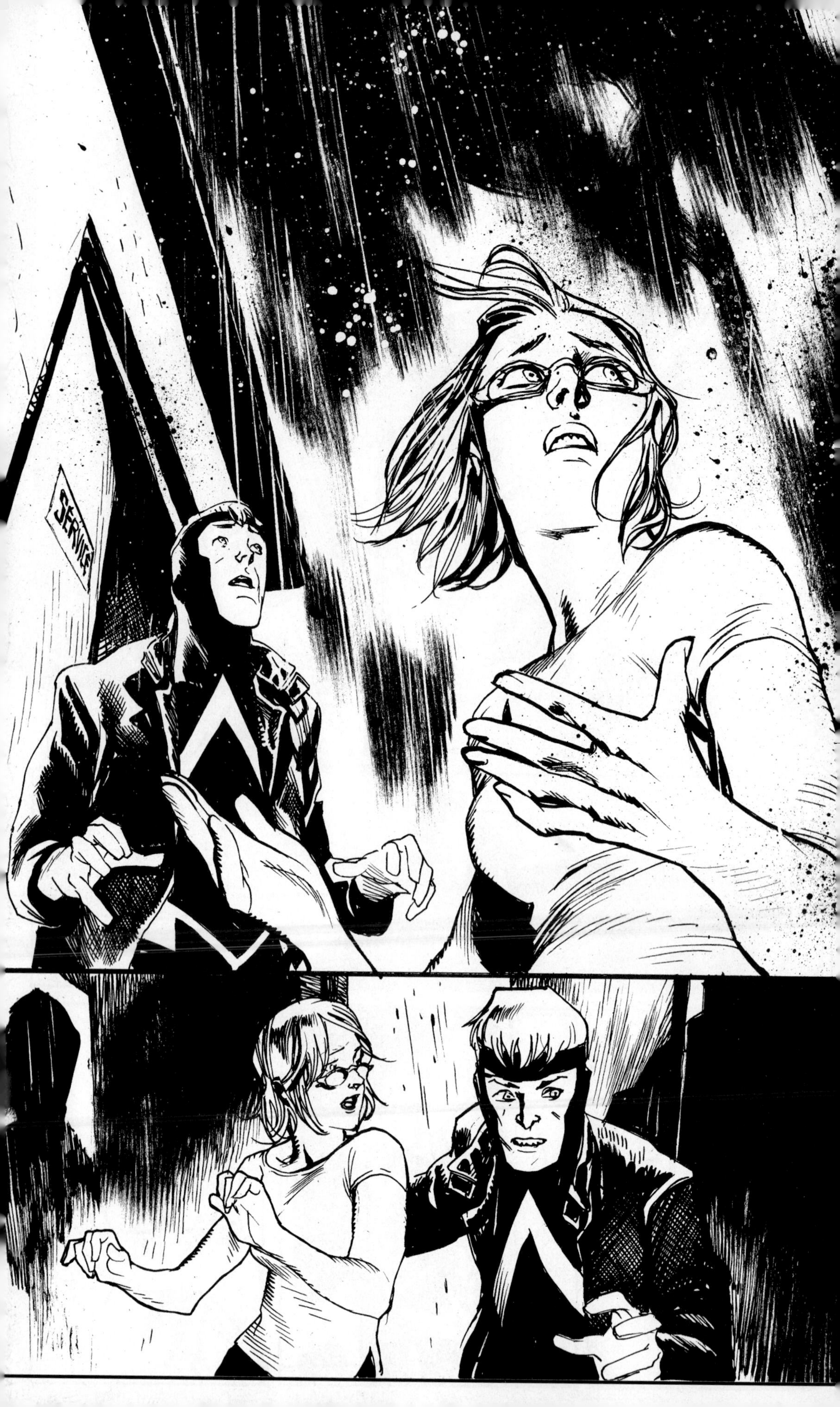
SERVICE

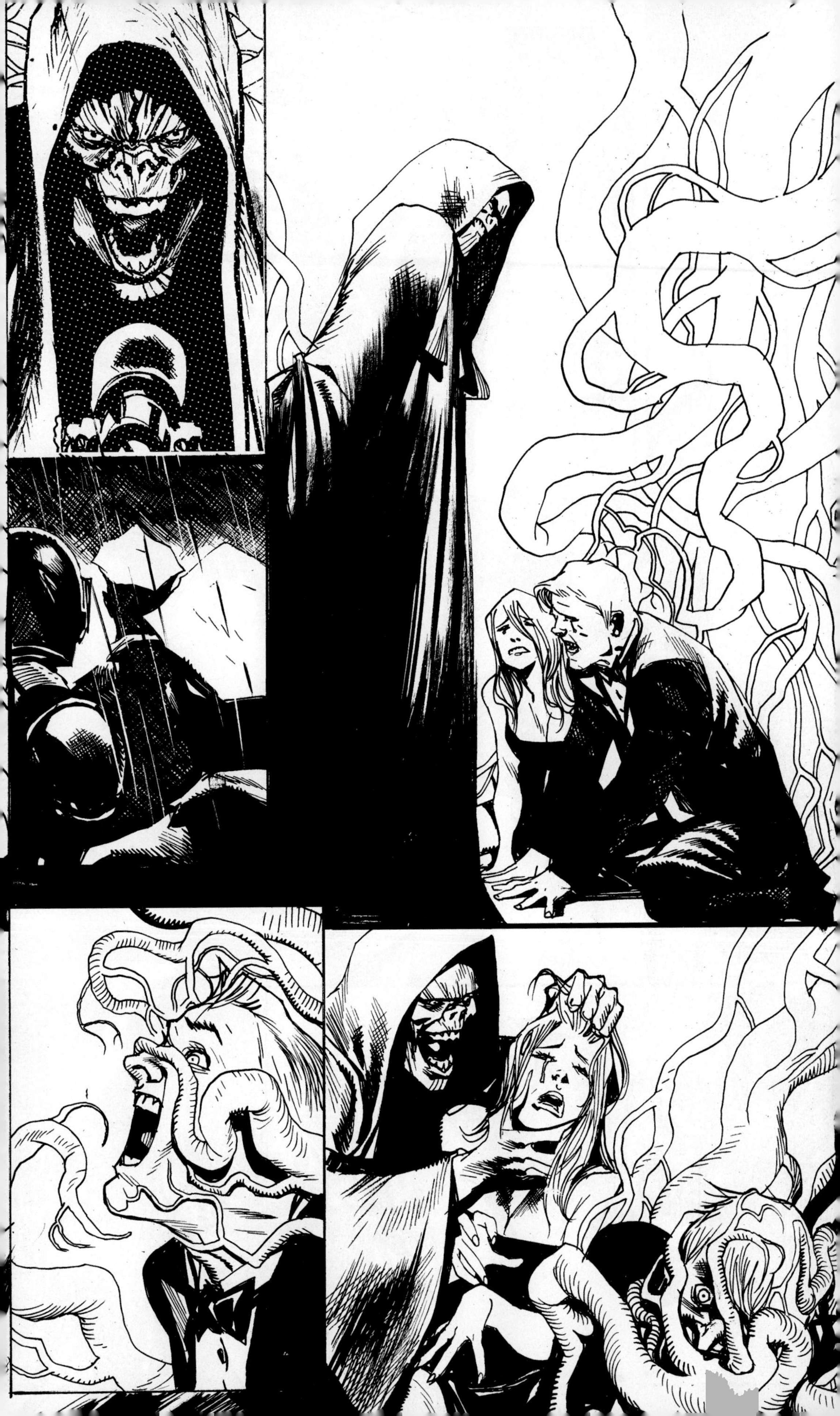

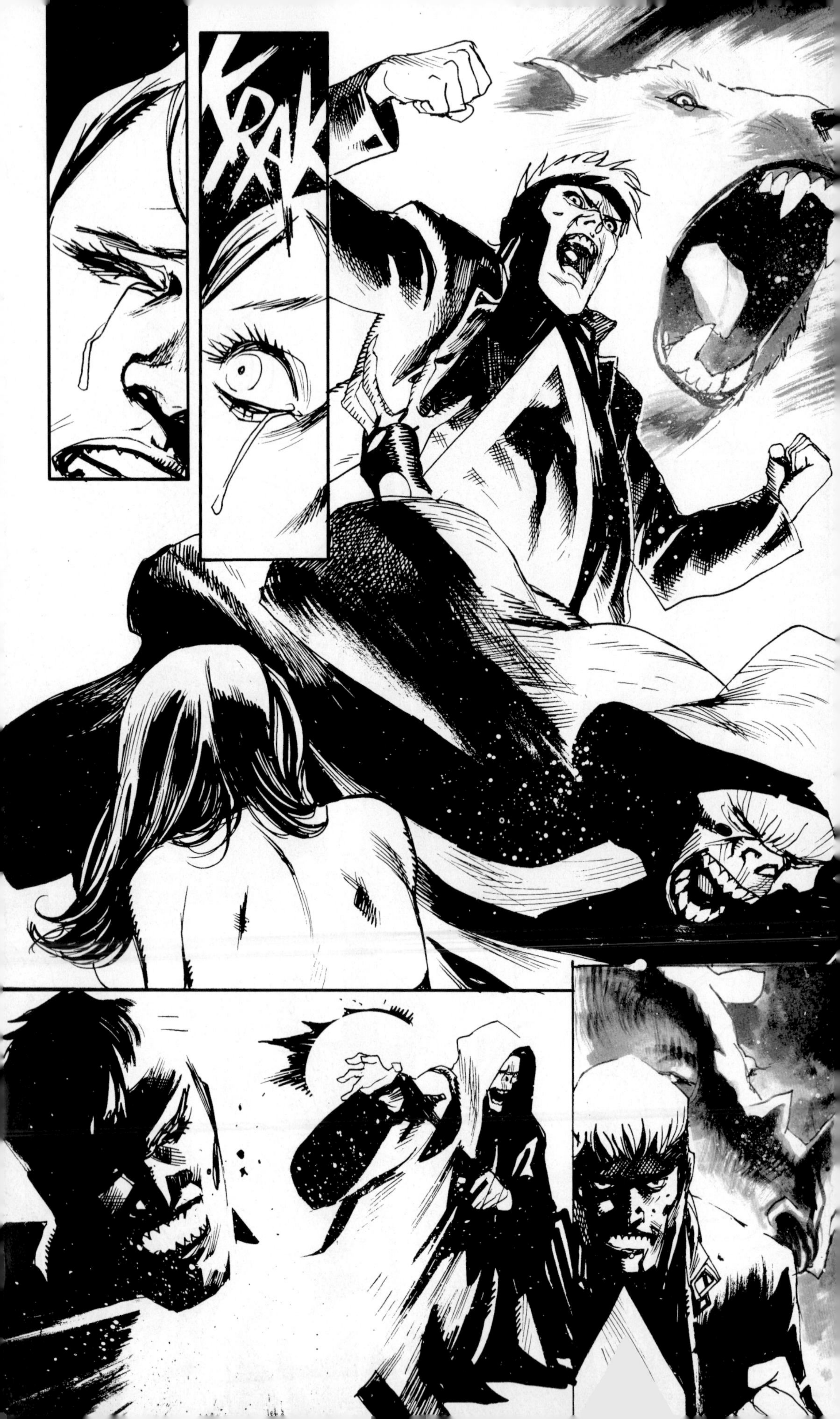
KRAK

"If you don't love it from the very first page, you're not human."
—MTV GEEK

"ANIMAL MAN has the sensational Jeff Lemire at the helm."
—ENTERTAINMENT WEEKLY

START AT THE BEGINNING!

ANIMAL MAN
VOLUME 1: THE HUNT

ANIMAL MAN VOL. 2:
ANIMAL VS. MAN

ANIMAL MAN VOL. 3:
ROTWORLD: THE RED
KINGDOM

ANIMAL MAN VOL. 4:
SPLINTER SPECIES

VOLUME 1
THE HUNT

"TRAVEL FOREMAN'S ART
IS INNOVATIVE AND
EXCELLENTLY CREEPY...
AS LEMIRE'S EVERYMAN
HERO MAKES HIS MARK IN
THE NEW DC UNIVERSE."

— USA TODAY

JEFF **LEMIRE** TRAVEL **FOREMAN**

© 2012 DC Comics. All Rights Reserved.

DC COMICS™

"SWAMP THING is a series that you need to be reading, no questions asked."—IGN

"A thoughtful, well-executed new take on a great character."—PUBLISHERS WEEKLY

START AT THE BEGINNING!

SWAMP THING
VOLUME 1: RAISE THEM BONES

SWAMP THING
VOL. 2: FAMILY TREE

with SCOTT SNYDER
and YANICK PAQUETTE

SWAMP THING
VOL. 3: ROTWORLD:
THE GREEN KINGDOM

with SCOTT SNYDER,
JEFF LEMIRE, and
YANICK PAQUETTE

ANIMAL MAN
VOL. 3: ROTWORLD:
THE RED KINGDOM

with JEFF LEMIRE,
SCOTT SNYDER, and
STEVE PUGH